Durable Ideas in Software Engineering: Concepts, Methods and Approaches from My Virtual Toolbox

James J. Cusick

New York, NY
USA

CONTENTS

Author Biography

James Cusick is a software and systems professional with 25 years of diverse applied experience in software development, testing, technical education, process engineering, project management, and systems design and operation. James spent his early career at AT&T Bell Laboratories where he programmed in C/C++ on semi-realtime UNIX telecommunications applications and learned what it meant to build large scale systems and what best practices were for all kinds of software areas. Later, as part of AT&T Labs James worked on projects throughout the company developing standards, reviewing and designing processes, and running technical seminars. James continued this work at Lucent's Bell Laboratories before joining Bluecurrent to run major infrastructure projects for Dell Professional Services in the financial industry. Today James is Director of IT Service Management at Wolters Kluwer in New York. With Wolters Kluwer James initially led B2B legal software development projects, contributed to process engineering work, managed software maintenance, and today is responsible for systems and database engineering as well as IT Service Management.

James focused on the incorporation of methods for reliability engineering, performance engineering, and other software engineering practices into his projects. From early in his career he began publishing the results of these efforts. Today James is the author of more than 50 papers and talks on Software Reliability, Object Technology, and Software Engineering Technology (see http://www.mendeley.com/profiles/james-cusick/). James' experience and his publications led him to share his knowledge as a teacher. He has held positions as an Adjunct Assistant Professor at Columbia University's Department of Computer Science and as an Instructor in Columbia's Computer Technology and Applications Program where he taught Software Engineering. This eBook is in part based on these courses.

James is a graduate of both the University of California at Santa Barbara and of Columbia University in New York City. James is a member of the IEEE and a current PMP (Project Management Professional).

FOREWORD

As any reader of computer books soon realizes, many titles are of the moment, designed to give us the latest in technology quickly. Busy software developers and managers certainly need this kind of eBook in order to keep up with an ever-changing discipline. Some titles are generated from theory and academic research; others from actual practice and experience in the field. It is rare that a eBook draws so well from both types of expertise. James Cusick's *Durable Ideas in Software Engineering: Concepts, Methods, and Approaches from my Virtual Toolbox* is one such eBook. It's a compendium and review of major ideas of software engineering informed by the author's outstanding academic and practical knowledge of the field. Garnered from his experience at leading-edge corporations like AT&T and Bell Labs, with over twenty years of software development and successful project management, the author leads us through a tour of both theory *and* practice. Not only does it give us a perspective of designing, testing, managing and supporting software drawn from real experience, it also provides an overview of some of the major trends in software design, from the earliest software engineering methodologies to today's Agile methods and globally based development teams. Moreover, as an early adopter and researcher into the use of metrics to improve software reliability, the author has a lot to say about improving software from the ground up.

Much has changed in software engineering over the past few decades, but as this eBook argues, there are some tools and ideas that have endured. In many years as a colleague and friend, I have always valued the author's perspective on what's next in our field. With his experiences in leading-edge companies, where software methodology and process were clearly not an afterthought, and his extensive publications, James Cusick can offer us a unique perspective – a successful developer and manager of complex software projects who has drawn the best ideas from software process and development to inform our own work. *Durable Ideas in Software Engineering* is an invaluable resource for software developers and managers for both large and small projects. Throughout this eBook, you will learn what has worked in real projects, and you will see area of software process seldom covered, such as support and metrics for software defect management.

Strong coverage of topics like models of software development, system architecture, risk analysis, and managing software change will also prove invaluable to working software professionals. Ideal for any software developer or manager, *Durable Ideas in Software Engineering* is a readable, thorough, and engaging tour of some of the very best ideas from software engineering as applied to real-world projects.

Richard V. Dragan, Ph.D.
Contributing Editor
PCMag.com
Ziff-Davis, Inc.

PREFACE

This eBook has its roots in the many technical publications, lectures, and prior attempts at putting it all together over the last 15 years. In working with Prof. Al Aho at Columbia University I was challenged to convert my lectures on Software Engineering into a text which could be better than those available at the time. After repeated failed attempts at doing so I collected sufficient material to build this refocused document. When the opportunity presented itself to write and publish electronically on the tools that have worked for me over the duration of my career I decided to give it one more try. With the help of Bentham Science Publishers this is the result.

Software Engineering now occupies a central place in the development of technology and in the advancement of the economy. From telecommunications to aerospace and from cash registers to medical imaging, software plays a vital and often decisive role in the successful accomplishment of a variety of pursuits. The creation of software requires a variety of techniques, tools, and especially, properly skilled engineers. The enduring, lasting, and meaningful concepts, ideas, and methods in software engineering from the perspective of what has worked on the job for me will be presented and discussed. This exploration will not be exhaustive as the subject is immense in breadth. Instead the focus will be on those core concepts and approaches that have proven useful to the author time and time again on many industry projects and over a quarter century of research, development, and teaching.

The eBook covers the essential topics of the field of software engineering with a focus on practical and commonly used techniques along with advanced topics meant to extend the reader's knowledge regarding leading edge approaches. Some sections derive from lectures or presentations which received limited circulation thus are new in this format. The eBook was developed as a multiple chapter manuscript with figures, charts, tables, designs or source code examples where needed, and other supporting information. The voice of the eBook is certainly technical in nature but does not assume significant prior knowledge in the field.

Building on both the industrial, research, and teaching experiences of the author a dynamic treatment of the subject is provided incorporating a wide body of published findings and techniques, novel organization of material, original concepts, contributions from specialists, and clear, concise writing. Using over 20 years of lecture notes, transcripts, course notes, view graphs, published articles, and other materials, an overall framework was established for the book. New research was conducted to support the content development as well.

The core technical topics of the eBook include project organization, planning, and execution. Both CMMI and Agile methods are discussed so that the essence of each is understood for their key benefits. A generic process engineering approach is also provided that allows for the creation and adaptation of any future required process model. Architecture and design are highlighted by providing previously unpublished summaries of fundamental web software architectures and design approaches. A special section on the use of the Operational Profile and achieving reliable software designs as well as practical test methods balance the planning and architecture focus. Additionally, a discussion of useful software metrics in the areas of estimation, quality, test planning, and performance engineering and performance analysis is be provided throughout the book. Unlike many books on this subject, a detailed view of support engineering using a simplified, proven, and custom application of ITIL is provided. Finally, the latest trends in the software profession, offshore management, and global software development models are reviewed with an emphasis on cross boarder development oversight and governance taking into account culture, communications, and dispersion.

In summary, this eBook focuses on the core aspects of software development, planning, architecture, measurement, testing, deployment, support, and global cooperation that is vital to realizing complex software projects today. Each of the ideas presented here are practical and proven from my own experience and do not represent simply a catalog of proposed concepts or methods.

However, the author confirm that this eBook has no conflict of interest.

James J. Cusick

New York City

USA

E-mail: jcusick3@nyc.rr.com

ACKNOWLEDGEMENTS

The author wishes to thank Al Aho for inspiring the initial attempt at authoring this eBook. Also, the author has included some work in this eBook which was first developed in working with many colleagues including Prof. William Tepfenhart, Terry Welch, and Max Fine. The author is indebted to the teams he has worked with at AT&T, Bell Labs, and Wolters Kluwer over many years to gain practical experience in applying these methods. In addition his many students at Columbia University who participated in the lectures which help form a basis for these pages provided useful suggestions and questions over several years. The author also thanks Rich Dragan for taking the time to read the manuscript and for providing very comprehensive forward. Finally, the entire team at Bentham should be recognized for their role in making this eBook a reality.

Send Orders of Reprints at bspsaif@emirates.net.ae
Durable Ideas in Software Engineering, 2013, 3-32

CHAPTER 1

Introduction

Abstract: Sets the scope of the eBook. Explains what is meant by a durable tool in my software toolbox. Defines the meaning of Software Engineering. Introduces the first tools in the tool box including the Scientific Method, problem solving, abstraction, process, planning, programming, and more. Provides an overview of the eBook and lays out the topics to be covered.

Keywords: Programming, software engineering, process engineering, Scientific Method, technical writing, abstraction, project management.

In life, some things are more permanent than others. I have noticed that the same thing is true in software development and software engineering methods and tools. Just as a skilled woodworker may rely on a trusty adze or chisel for years I have come to learn of the enduring usefulness of a variety of tools, concepts, methods, and approaches to software engineering or to specific problem areas within software development. In these pages I hope to capture the essence of these more enduring elements so that others may compare their experiences with mine, look for elements that they may have missed, and provide feedback on where they might disagree or prefer alternative views.

This is not meant to be a definitive encyclopedia on the subject of software development methods. Such encyclopedic treatments of the subject exist and can be found in software engineering text books and the software body of knowledge project. Nor is this eBook supposed to be static. Things will change over time especially in particular implementation technologies. That is one reason that this is provided in a e-book format. However, in the 25 years of my professional career which has included time spent mostly as a commercial software developer, manager, or consultant, the topics included here are the most enduring and useful I have encountered. Since I have also played the role of teacher, researcher, and author, I have an academic interest and understanding of the context, value, and applicability of some of these methods in the light of industry and subject area trends. I will attempt to paint a balanced view of the industrial reality of software development with the proposed values of an academic awareness of best

James J. Cusick

practices. To be precise, the focus here is on practice not on theory. I may provide the concepts behind the practice but what is presented is what works.

In telling the story of software development 's enduring practices I will verge on telling my own story as an engineer and a manager. I do not see this as self-promotion but as a means of grounding the information in examples. Some of the concepts, methods, and tools that we will explore include Design Patterns, process models, estimation methods, Operational Profiles, heuristics, Pareto analysis, Gantt charts, Kaizen, algorithms, data structures, cyclomatic complexity, glass box testing, black box testing, and more. These various methods make up my virtual tool box which I carry with me from job to job and project to project. They are both (so far) timeless and extensible. They emerged in the time of mainframes and distributed systems, were perfected in the age of client/server architectures, and have lasted into the age of the Internet, mobile applications, and social media. In each case the techniques are well documented but I will venture to be precise and concise in my description of them so they can be applied easily by any reader with a base in computing. Let's begin.

1.1. SOFTWARE ENGINEERING INTRODUCED

Most people are introduced to software development through one or more programming languages. The first program attempted is often a simple variant of "hello, world". In their classic treatment of the C language, Kernighan & Ritchie [1] offer this simple working program:

```
#include <stdio.h>
main()
{
printf("hello, world\n");
}
```

By compiling and running this program we would get the output "hello, world" on our display. For most languages, this can be duplicated in much the same way. The syntax will vary but the effect will be the same.

However, the technology of 1975 and the technology of today is quite different. In 1975 mainframes and timesharing minicomputers ruled and were accessed by terminals of limited 80 by 40 character screens. Today, most computer users have PCs with graphical displays. They can process large sets of data locally or on network servers or over the World Wide Web. Additionally, smartphones, tablet computers, and embedded devices of various kinds now abound.

Yet, with all these advances, programming languages are much the same as in the early days of the C language. It takes a bit more effort to get the "hello, world" program up and running in some cases but the approach is virtually identical. Consider the "hello, world" program in Java by Arnold & Gosling [2]:

```
class HelloWorld {
public static void main(String args[]) {
System.out.println("hello, world");
}
}
```

We can see that a bit more work is required but we generally accomplish the same thing. This language is a 1990s Object-Oriented vintage. There are other languages that might be more recent such as Python or Ruby but in essence the same starting point would be required. For Ruby the basic form of this operation boils down to the fragment below (Flanagan & Matsumoto [3]):

```
puts "Hello World"
```

The simplicity of Ruby shown above is based on this example being based on an interpreted runtime while the earlier language examples like C, C++, Java, and C# require compilation. In choosing a programming language there are many factors to consider including language power, portability, features, extensibility, and more. There may be a plethora of reasons we need to consider when making this choice, however, at some level all languages begin to blur as implementation approaches and the complexity of software realization is pushed upstream into requirements and design and downstream in testing, configuration, deployment, and support.

Writing a piece of code in any language is not equivalent to software engineering and does not encompass the full scope of software development. Instead, software engineering takes a broad view of end to end development needs from requirements to architecture to design to implementation to testing and finally to deployment and support. In addition key topics such as process, planning, metrics, management, offshoring, security, object modeling, and more can play a role. For Software Engineering, the essence of the work we do in building systems has remained much the same over the last few decades, just as the programming languages have stayed familiar. However, the accumulated mass of technology and techniques developed since the coinage of the term "software engineering" in the late 1960s has reshaped the nature of the project team and the roles its members play. From the beginning there has never been a "hello, world" equivalent in software engineering. The closest one can come is perhaps a functioning prototype or a high level architecture drawing.

Software Engineering requires time and effort because it is used to produce real applications and usable products that are resilient to change, support mission critical functions for business and government, and require the coordination of large numbers of resources of both people and technology. Software Engineering is not limited to syntax, a set of semantics, or a grammar. It includes taste, art, negotiation, compromise, exactitude, judgment, and skill. To learn about Software Engineering or to improve one's skills in practicing the many aspects of the discipline requires exposure to both knowledge and the acquisition of experience. Typically, one person cannot master all of these elements. This eBook offers a condensed exploration of the essential content of the subject focusing on what works and at limited cost and effort (a managerial consideration). This set of chapters is also designed to support the instruction of Software Engineering. With the addition of a team-based laboratory this can help to provide the experiences critical to attaining the experiential depth required of a professional developer.

The focus herein will be on establishing the foundations for the software development field, end to end processes, planning approaches, and techniques that work. My preference is to work from real and well identified problems and then to abstract to reusable approaches. By doing so one can develop an engineering model which translates requirements into software by relying on standard architectures, design patterns, and routine methods. Problem examples will be provided at an architecture level and using implementation languages where required. Equal weight is placed on process, measurement, and test techniques. The sum of this exploration should provide the reader with a balanced set of real and repeatable techniques for approaching large-scale software development problems over many years. That is, technology fads may come and go, but these methods will by and large out last those trends.

1.2. SOFTWARE ENGINEERING DEFINED

Software Engineering now occupies a central place in the development of technology and in the advancement of the economy. From telecommunications to aerospace and from cash registers to medical imaging, software plays a vital and often decisive role in the successful accomplishment of a variety of pursuits. The creation of software requires a variety of techniques, tools, and especially, properly skilled engineers.

Upon asking my profession, people outside of the software industry have often asked me "well, what in fact is Software Engineering ?" Or upon learning that I have taught the subject they ask "and what is it that you actually teach?" With practice I have developed some stock answers to these questions. However, to deeply pursue the answers requires more time and more care.

As an undergraduate I was fortunate to have enjoyed the lectures of a professor of humanities who carefully defined each significant term encountered in the wide-ranging field of letters. He would, for example, start by saying "… 'Mythology', which comes from the Latin root 'mythos' which means story …", and so on. Then he would slowly and methodically build upon that definition until finally the entire tragedy at hand was linked to a dozen different concepts and premises. I have always admired this approach since it puts one brick on top of another. It is easy to follow this line of discourse.

In attempting to answer the question "what is software engineering " it is, in a similar vein, best to start at the beginning. At the NATO conferences [4] of 1968 and 1969 the original definitions of software engineering were offered and the field was officially born. Software Engineering grew out of a set of existing disciplines mostly from Computer Science and Engineering. Modern Computer Science can trace its roots to Babbage (and Joucard) but truly begins with the electronic age starting roughly at the birth of ENIAC in 1946 [5]. Engineering traces it roots to the dawn of human civilization in the form of building, construction, and tool making [6]. Thus the field of software engineering is half as old as the current electronic age of computation, and only a fraction as old as engineering itself. Software Engineering formally is currently just over the 40 year mark.

So the first thing we know about Software Engineering is that it is young. Taking a cue from my humanities professor, we can define software and then engineering separately. Before tackling our real goal, which is to consider what the entire phrase means and then proceed to explore its meaning step by step, let us first define software and engineering [7]:

> SOFTWARE: Written, printed (or stored), data such as programs, routines, symbolic languages, essential to the operation of a computer (including documentation).
>
> ENGINEERING: The science by which the properties of matter and the sources of energy in nature are made useful to man in structures, machines, and products.

So in essence, software is a set of symbolic artifacts which animate a computer and engineering is the approach used to convert natural artifacts into useful items. With this much said we know what software is and we also know what engineering is. Now let us consider the following relatively standard and accepted definitions of "Software Engineering ":

> *The establishment and use of sound engineering principles in order to obtain economically software that is reliable and works on real machines.*
>
> *Bauer, 1972 [8]*

The practical application of scientific knowledge in the design and construction of computer programs and the associated documentation required to develop, operate, and maintain them.

Boehm, 1977 [9]

(1) The application of a systematic, disciplined, quantifiable approach to the development, operation and maintenance of software, that is, the application of engineering to software. (2) The study of approaches as in (1).

IEEE Std 610.12 (Moore, 1998) [10]

Each of these definitions provides a clear answer to the original question "what is software engineering ". However, each definition also raises many other subsequent questions. Indeed the term "software engineering" is just wrapping on a stack of interrelated and interdependent concepts, technologies, and techniques. These layers can be approached from many directions. One may inquire about programming languages and find a set of answers. Or one may ask about performance quantification and find an entire practice established. Interestingly, nearly all of these questions can be answered with a set of methods or tools.

Engineering is a problem solving discipline but this is not taught in most programming language courses. Instead focus is placed on syntax, compilation techniques, and language aspects. Thus the "hello world" program from above is built on in ever increasing complexity. Typically, in introductory programming classes schools do not teach how to formulate a problem, structure a problem, solve a problem, represent the problem abstractly, test it, confirm that it is working correctly, and support it for many years. In later courses they may be exposed to this level of complexity but not in all cases. This eBook may not give you all the tools you need to solve all software problems but it will give enough context to have the required reference points and set your bearings on how to approach the problem solving activities required of software developers.

The material covered here is built for wide appeal. While the artifacts of system development include source code, this is only one thing that makes up a software system. From my experience in teaching these concepts the people attracted to software development came from many backgrounds including bartenders, musicians, teachers, accountants, finance people, hardware engineers, and more. During the 1990s and the *dot.com* boom, people of all stripes turned to software as a livelihood. There was an old saying at the turn of the 20th century that everyone would eventually need to be a telephone operator as switchboards became so large and complex. Eventually this was true as first the rotary dial telephone and then the DTMF (Dual Tone Multi Frequency) touch pad telephone were introduced shifting the switching responsibility to the end user. Many end user programming tasks are done today in businesses and at home including macro programming in spreadsheets (a recent study showed that 5 times more programmers exist outside of IT organizations than within [11]. Interestingly, companies are also pushing almost all data entry work to end users as well by exposing data entry and query forms over the Internet. This has implications for the role of software engineers. Specifically, human factors, load estimations, and usage profiling all have to be handled.

1.3. HOW FAR HAVE WE COME?

> *"... in those days ... one often encountered the naïve expectation that, once more powerful machines were available, programming would no longer be a problem ... now we have gigantic computers and programming is an equally gigantic problem". Dijkstra, 1956 [12]*

> *"As long as we have to translate laboriously every set of data into a separate program we do not understand information". Drucker, 1968 [13]*

In my course on software engineering I would provide a quiz to the students. I would give them quotes like the ones above (without any dates) and ask them what decade they were from. Amazingly, and perhaps sadly, these quotes could be said at any time. They could still be said today. They could have been said decades ago. Pick up any eBook or trade journal and these are the types of comments you will find. From the 70s, 90s, 50s, and today these issues have been around and not many have been solved. Those that have been solved have not been solved universally or in every application area or in every software development organization. In my experience, some organizations with lower maturity, discipline, or sophistication run into problems that have proven solutions but they are unable to resolve them effectively due to the complexity of the challenges and the high bar they face in getting their organizations aligned to meet the challenges. This regression to more primitive levels of software achievement in some organizations occurs especially when business factors press on teams and break up working methods. Whether you are experienced or a novice developer these are the types of problems you are likely to encounter.

Therefore, the idea is not to jump for the trends publicized as the solutions for the day, but look for the root causes of the real problems you are having in developing software and look for solutions that work and have proven cost to benefit ratio. Interestingly, the trend towards Agile development methods and away from "plan based" or waterfall methods (like the CMMI or Capability Maturity Model-Integrated) is a case in point. The CMMI model assumes an ability to predict [14]. Regardless of methods, vendor based solutions du jour or narrowly supported solutions from a particular author or a small set of "experts" should be avoided. Go for substance not hype. There is a lot of hype within the Agile community now which is not meant as a detraction, simply as fact. A recent author discussing Enterprise Agile methods claimed that Agile "in all cases" produces better quality [15]. I have been around the block enough times to know that anyone selling a sure fire panacea is not being fully honest or is unaware of the limits of their own methods. The trends reflected in the quotations above are endemic and enduring in the industry and could be found in arguments urging the adoption of Agile some 40 years after the advent of the software engineering field.

One of my favorite books on systems development which puts this into perspective is from the author Gall called "Systemantics" published in 1975 [16]. Some rules or axioms Gall describes for any systems development and systems behavior include the following:

1. *A complex system that works is invariably found to have evolved from a simple system that works*

2. *Systems are like babies: once you get one, you have it. They don't go away.*

3. *When a fail-safe system fails, it fails by failing to fail-safe.*

4. *Systems tend to grow, and as they grow, they encroach.*

5. *Complex systems tend to produce complex responses (not solutions) to problems.*

6. *Systems run better when designed to run downhill*

7. *A complex system can fail in an infinite number of ways*

8. *New systems generate new problems.*

9. *System delusion: A state of mind in which we believe that a misgotten product grudgingly produced by a system is what we wanted all the time.*

10. *The mode of failure of a complex system cannot be predicted from its structure*

In reflecting on these rules I can provide example after example from systems that I have worked on, watched, or used that prove these rules again and again. Nearly the entire methodological basis of Agile development can be derived from the first rule. The last three years of my career which included leading a large systems maintenance organization proves the second rule on caring for a baby. My many experiences in seeing a lack of a backup approach is reflected in rule three. And so on.

1.4. ENGINEERING AND THE FIRST TOOLS IN THE TOOLBOX

Software Engineering is different than other engineering disciplines in a few key ways. Some people define software engineering as work done in constructing operating systems, device drivers, or firmware and no other types of applications. In fact any software systems built economically that are efficient and reliable by the application of sound engineering can be viewed as the result of software engineering. Software Engineering as a discipline is a body of knowledge, practice, and theory that helps us to accomplish the construction of such systems. This is what will discuss in these pages and focus on what works, what is light-weight, practical, and extensible with proven results in the field. One such important set of knowledge revolves around what we mean by Science, engineering, and technology, and how these three intersect, stand apart, and support each other in creating new software methods, validating them, and extending them for future applications. It is through understanding these three areas (Fig. **1**) that we can better understand the tool box we are discussing, how the apparatus in the toolbox was found, and how those tools can be extended. In a classic case of pump priming, once the Science, engineering, and technology cycle is started it can be self-reinforcing. Thus for a good software engineer she must know what these terms mean in a real sense.

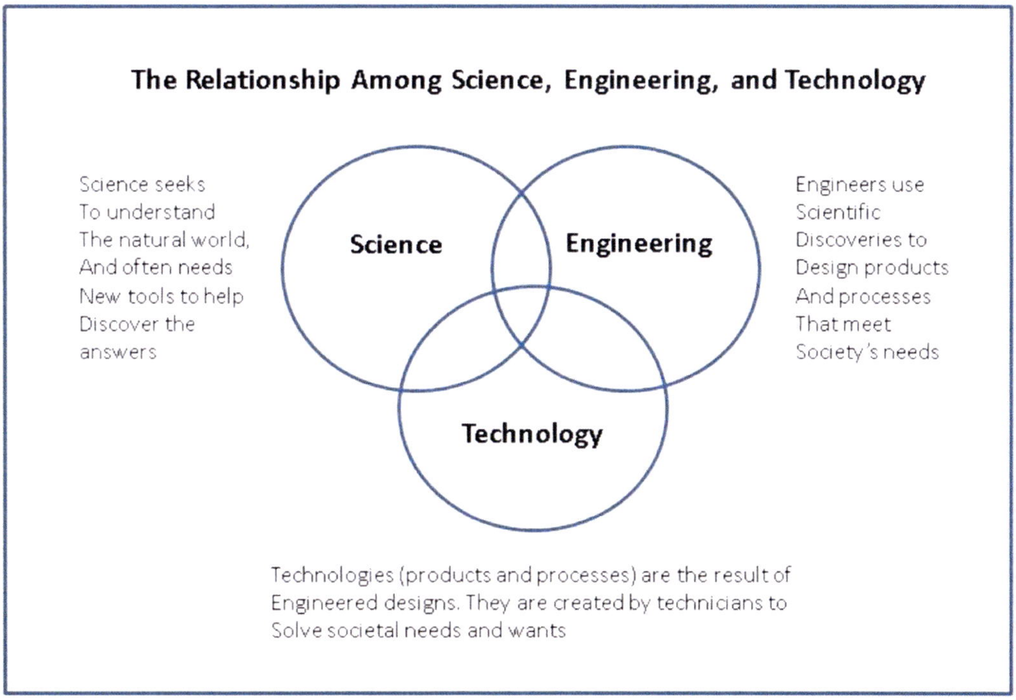

Figure 1: Relationship between Science, Engineering, and Technology [17].

Engineering is a familiar practice in terms of the artifacts it produces. We are surrounded by the end-products of engineering every day. Engineering is related to science in that they share some of the same techniques but have slightly different goals. Engineering focuses on problem solving, it is not theoretical as much as it is problem solving. Engineering has blossomed in the 20th century. Software Engineering has increased its scope in the economy but has not increased in terms of efficiency (this is of course still hotly debated) or its rigor of application broadly. It is up to all software professionals to demonstrate the improvements needed in our practice to earn a solid footing in the engineering world. So it is with this assumption, the assumption that the practice is emerging and constantly improving, that we start to dig into the specifics of software engineering.

The complete picture requires management, computer science, communication, and more as a base (see Fig. **2**). We also are dependent upon science and culture. In Japan Human Factors Engineers are needed more regularly as a higher quality focus from their cultural tendency and development for a wide range of export markets forces usability. US developers have access to the same engineering knowledge as Japanese developers but the Japanese have a culture that lends itself to the principles of quality more carefully (such as kaizen or continuous improvement). This affects software types and costs. Some software may be cheaper because of lower defect rates or they may be higher due to added quality

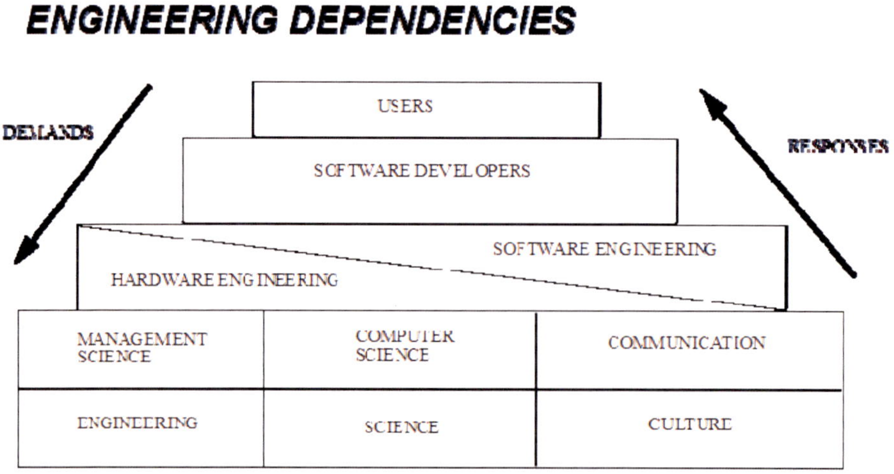

Figure 2: A Notional Model for the Relationship of Engineering, Science, and Software Delivery.

activities. In an Agile model quality is assumed to improve due to the integration of kaizen activities in every step.

Science looks for clues about the universe or the question at hand. Science wants to expand our understanding of nature. It tries to answer why something works. Engineering normally produces practical applications of science. That is, engineering relies on scientific knowledge and methods to develop applications of scientific, engineering, and heuristic or trial and error based knowledge. Most work must be guided by logical and disciplined approach to problem solving.

Engineering starts with a needs statement. These perceived needs come from users, market opportunity. In Science theory this is also the case. It is only when an investigator declares a need, such as Babbage looking for steam power to drive computations, that a path towards discovery is found. Drawing from theory and experience people apply their thought power to solve needs or problems. Some attempts fail and some succeed. We refine our understanding and try again (See Fig. **3**).

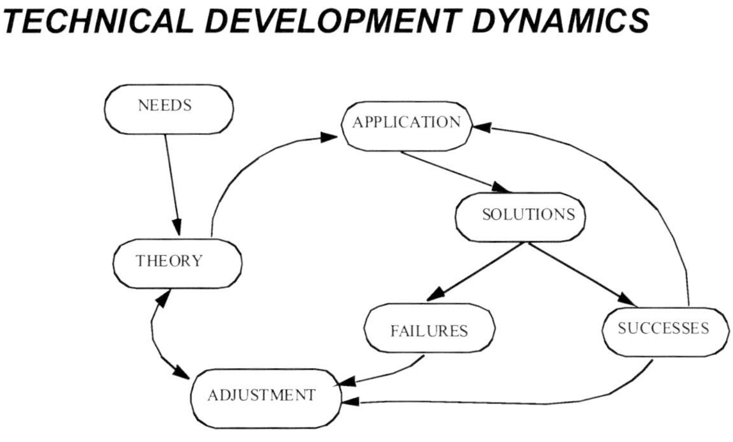

Figure 3: How Science, Engineering, and Technology are Driven by Needs.

The material presented here consists of my best current understanding of the theory and practice of software engineering. Not everything will be correct - it may be adjusted as further application attempts bring in modifications to the techniques. Not all techniques will work in every business or engineering environment. The concept may be sound but could require needs adjustment in localized application or if a different technique is needed for the current problem. My own understanding may also change or improve based on new experiences or work done in new environments or against novel problem sets.

Eventually, the interplay between scientific discovery and experience helped developed models, rules, and approaches to successful design, construction, and operations for structures, machines, electronics, and all other manufactured and processed goods and materials. In some cases engineering ran ahead of Science (such as early aircraft designs) and in other cases Science ran sometimes many years ahead of engineering [18]. Thus, writing became of vital link between the worlds of scientific exploration and discovery and the practical applications of ideas through engineering. Importantly, the Scientific method is then, the first of the tried and true tools in my virtual tool box. Without it none of the other tools would have been found, catalogued, sharpened, or provided with the context, integration, and applicability for use, extension, and leverage against practical problems.

Basics of the Scientific Method (empiricism) [19]:

1. Define the question
2. Gather information and resources (observe)
3. Form hypothesis
4. Perform experiment and collect data
5. Analyze data
6. Interpret data and draw conclusions that serve as a starting point for new hypothesis
7. Publish results
8. Retest (frequently done by other Scientists)

This cycle of critical thinking, analysis, planning, experimentation, data analysis, and publication of results is the empirical underpinnings of all of Science. Within the world of software engineering we use this method to bootstrap ourselves into new methods and techniques. With these techniques we can then apply them to business or real world problems and come up with working solutions. In the course of doing so we refine the engineering methods we have adopted. These steps allow us to isolate problems by factoring out causes (a controlled environment which will become more evident when we discuss testing). We eliminate variables and focus on root causes and impactful techniques or applications. These methods require clear thinking and careful planning.

There is much assumed in being able to do this. First there is the ability to read and write. I say this not in a basic sense but in the manner that is applied to scientific and engineering analysis. One must read to keep up with advances in the field, understand system requirements, review design documents, and apply technical frameworks. The writing required of an engineer is that of the technical report, requirements documents, and results. As part of this there are also research skills. These allow an engineer to find information relevant to a problem. Finally, an engineer will need to present ideas and results verbally and to listen to others to build requirements lists and related artifacts. Taken together reading, writing, and research gives us our second tool: communications. (A complete discussion on writing for science and engineering is provided by Cusick [20]).

One form of communication is mathematics. For both science and engineering mathematics plays a key role in understanding, representing, and predicting system behavior. Thus the third tool in our tool set is quantification. As we will see throughout our discussion and especially in architecture, performance, and quality, quantification techniques are vital. In my experience the primary field of mathematics which comes most into play is statistics and probability. Raw numbers or discrete series of data are often turned into sums and percentages and compared with each other to provide trending and comparative analysis. Also, data visualization is used in most engineering activities. These might include histograms, scatter plots, pie charts, and other standard tools. Occasionally, regression analysis has been useful in my work when trying to understand the interplay of two variables. As we will discuss later, reliability methods call on stochastic processes heavily.

The next tool required in the tool box is a proper headset. This includes critical thinking, analysis skills, problem solving, creative thinking, doggedness, pursuit of solutions, curiosity, persistence, tinkering, experimenting, a methodical approach, and focus on continuous improvement. This headset is not always in-born. It can be taught. However, some traits may be stronger in some individuals. In some cases there will be variability in terms of depth or emphasis in one or more of these areas which can be expected. This headset also grows into professional or engineering judgment. With enough training and experience one can make the right decisions due to being able to draw on years of having seen the same patterns repeated or being able to apply heuristics to novel problems. Youth and enthusiasm can do well for many straight ahead problems but sometimes the thornier problems require deeper understanding and a broader view. This is where the right headset comes in.

1.5. APPLYING THESE FIRST TOOLS

Engineering problems are solved through a generic engineering design cycle as introduced above. First of all we need to recognize that there is a problem. This is not always so easy. We look at similar problems and their solutions. We try to filter our irrelevant information. Once the problem is formulated we begin analysis where we consider what we will do about the problem. Sometimes we may elect to do nothing or discover that solving the problem is not feasible. Other times the problem has already been solved by someone else and a reuse of an earlier solution is all that is needed. This might require a tool or application acquisition requiring detailed evaluation (explored in Chapter 9). In other cases a simple solution might be all that is needed. If it is not we may then enter the use of our basic engineering tools.

First we need to define the problem carefully so that it can be solved. Then we search for a high level design concept to fit the problem. With this done, specifications will be drawn up to denote the specific functionality needed to solve it and what the solution will look like including measures to determine if the problem is actually solved. Based on the process being used this might be done up front or in incremental steps. The solution is then built and verified with the appropriate documentation and side artifacts such as operations guides. If bugs are found this indicates a problem in the design cycle. As most people who have used software know this is quite common. In the most mature organizations methods are in place to not only reduce the number of latent defects such as through the use of Agile and incremental methods and/or quality assurance methods but also there are methods to adjust the process so that future releases have fewer bugs.

This generic statement of engineering processes gives us a starting point for discussing software engineering. In the following chapters we will rename some of these steps more formally and embellish each step and try to put controls in place on the design cycle to optimize our more critical goals such as quality, cost, or features. We then instrument each step and measure our progress using one of our basic tools - quantification.

For most software engineering efforts, the work will be organized as a project. A project as we will discuss is a collective effort with a bounded set of goals and timelines. These goals help us direct efforts both small and large. In some cases a date serves as a primary goal and plans for each step of the way are made to get us there. It is important to take the time to plan what you need to do to solve your problem and meet your goal. In an Agile model this might be done in bursts or in flow and in a traditional plan driven model this might be done end to end. For any multiple team member projects such coordination is highly critical. It is typical that before programming actually starts the imagined solution is represented in a standard diagrammatic technique and quickly followed up with working prototypes. For Agile methodologists it is the working code that is the focus and the models that are supportive. A complete description of formal modeling techniques are presented by other sources such as UML (Universal Modeling Language) guides [21]. In this discussion we will incorporate basic modeling practices to illuminate a discussion on solution architecture. This will assist our discussion of the perennial tasks of engineering which includes understand the nature of the current problem at hand and selecting the most appropriate engineering techniques to solve them. This skill is more critical than knowing the latest trend technique.

One benefit of modeling with a standard language like UML is that others can collaborate on the solution rapidly. This is another example of communication at work and also brings us to abstraction as a tool. It is important to be able to represent lower level functional implementation details at a high level and not be stuck on semantics or proprietary modeling languages.

Thus we have now introduced several key terms which represent additional tools in our virtual tool box: 1) Process; 2) Planning; 3) Modeling; 4) Programming; and 5) Tool Selection. Each of these will be covered in some detail in future chapters. For most of these a full chapter will be devoted to exploring the topic.

1.6. CONSIDERING PROCESS AND INNOVATION

With these fundamental tools we can start stitching together a process to develop software. Process itself is one of the most powerful and flexible tools in my toolbox. Whether one uses and Agile approach, a plan driven approach, or any other model, integration of core development skills and steps is vital to success.

We will discuss process, process engineering, and process models in detail. For now what is important to point out is that to pull together the tools and human resources required to build software you need process to support any method or means to control the software creation. If these are not present you will most likely produce poor products. If there are problems with the software we can look at the process producing it we will find flaws. It is not our products against the competitor's products that matter but our process against their process. If we can produce things more efficiently, effectively, economically, and with higher quality then this will allow us to win in the long run in the market place.

Even in a blue-sky scenario - say investigating new technologies, without a proper process in place to do this, you will be awash in publications, reports, paperwork. If you have to investigate new technologies what are you going to do? Go out and buy all the software on the market and see what is new? This will not work. You need to have a method of evaluation and have a way of working in a structured manner to compare them and report on the results. Still a process is needed and in a later chapter we will discuss this in depth.

Even in the most innovative environments there will be a process. If we look at the Apple computer Steve Jobs travelled, played the guitar, and fiddled with hobby kits, which eventually led to the development of the PC. Later, in creating the original MAC he moved key development teams out of the Apple headquarters to focus on the new machine as a revolutionary product. There is process to this but is it repeatable, is it scalable, how do you tap into this. In mainstream development context will this work? When is this feasible? The home hobbyist or basement developer may be quite successful in developing games or even some breakthrough products. However, large scale software systems are a different matter altogether. Mission critical systems often require outside verification, professional documentation, and more. These cannot be slung together ad hoc. So even innovation requires planning and process. Innovation then is an additional tool in my tool box.

One of the key discussion points in software engineering was called the "software crisis". This had to do with the fact that software product development was typically over budget, late, and products were delivered with plenty of bugs. While this debate has toned down in recent years the struggle to meet the goals of software of good quality representing user needs and on budget and with predictable delivery dates goes on. Much of this debate centers on process. The tools I will cover will not talk deeply about products but will talk about underlying fundamentals of the software development process and how they impact projects and product development. Most readers will have had experiences with software products being delayed and buggy. Our job will be to understand all the factors to avoid these outcomes.

One common complaint that some people have of "methods and process " heavy organizations is that most of the time is spent in planning, modeling, and diagramming, and code ends up as an afterthought. I believe it was experiences like this that contributed to the rise in the use of Agile methodologies. Nevertheless, in some organizations rules and procedures may need to remain in place for how to develop software to insure compliance with regulations or contract requirements. Strong process models may also be motivated by a positive outlook on improving quality or time to market and at other times it may be a reaction to the disasters of the past. A combination may also be the best fit. A heuristic for design *versus* programming can be kept in mind. In my experience, the more time spent in designing a program with standard methodologies the less time is required to be spent programming before the program actually worked.

This is also the case with such methods as test driven development which dates back decades. I was trained in this method in 1990 at Bell Laboratories. This method calls for test cases to be built before code is developed. While I was trained on this method upon being hired at Bell Laboratories I never saw it practiced in the industry until recent Agile methodologists began endorsing it [22].

1.7. TRAINING AND EDUCATION

Another tool in the software engineer's tool box needs to be a lifelong interest in training and education. While university programs may prepare students for core capabilities demanded by the profession, technologies change rapidly and keeping up with advances is critical. Alternatively, if one cannot keep up with all the latest announcements, digging deep in a particular area can make them a specialist in an in demand discipline. In either case, being able to self-tutor, learn from training classes, or retool in additional formal education programs becomes essential.

The tools mentioned here in my virtual tool box will be explained in sufficient depth to understand them but in order to master them some additional research or training may be necessary. In years past many undergraduate degree programs did not offer a course in Software Engineering. They had courses in algorithms, Artificial Intelligence, operating systems, programming and so on. Eventually they added course work around software engineering. However, today most schools do not require project management or software measurement topics as part of core computing curriculums. These are skills that need to be developed on the job.

Many students enter software engineering with an interest in building solutions. What they discover on the job is that areas of Management Science are of equal concern to Software Engineering as any computing science area. This includes project definition, including what the project resources are, people, time, equipment. Costs are often determined by specific corporate guidelines that need to be understood. Contract decisions and sourcing approaches need to be understood as well. This leads us to yet another key tool in the tool box: project management. This encompasses process and planning which were already mentioned but also covers estimation, organization, costing, lifecycle design, and more. Getting training on these areas usually will require technical courses in addition to a computing degree.

We have already mentioned communications as part of the job: technical writing, presentations, as well as reading skills. Engineers tend to do a lot of writing to explain where they are going, what the design is, and what should be done next. This is an important though underappreciated area of software engineering: writing and reading even though this may seem a bit odd. Vic Basili offered an interesting set of conclusions around perspective based reading [23] which says that people will read documents differently based on their purpose. The same can be said for each area of communication. One must be trained to read, write, and communicate. This is an area that typically requires additional training and years of development. An interesting eBook in this area is "How to read a book" [24] and of course "Elements of Style" [25]. Pursuing these areas on a self-study basis may be necessary for most engineers. In any case, ongoing training, development, and education is a tool in my tool box that I use continuously.

1.8. ARCHITECTURE AND REALIZATION

So far in this introduction we have talked about many of the core skills leading up to the creation of a working solution. To get to such a solution we need to talk about architecture and then realization of that architecture. Architecture itself is a broad subject and is definitely a tool in the virtual toolbox. The system architect defines the context of the problem solution in terms of the hardware, software, procedural, and human components of the system to a business solution. Engineering is directed at problem solving and it requires a number of different disciplines to come in to collaborate on a solution. System engineers describe at the black box level what major components are needed and how they will fit together with support personnel to create a business system solution. The software architect will then go in and define what major software components will be required and where key functionalities will be placed and will then typically turn over the work to further definition by other software professionals. In some organizations the architect will also work on the realization of the solution.

If we look at other industries like construction it is the architect that brings vision to a project. There may be many people working on the realization of that vision but a unifying scope and approach needs to be provided up front. In an Agile model this initial vision may emerge over many iterations. In either case, the role of the architect is to define the three C's: components, connections, and constraints [26] within the solution. There may be a grand design up front or a gradual evolution of the design or a combination. But architecture and the three C's is a tool we will discuss in greater detail.

With the underlying principles of software engineering well in hand we can now begin to apply these principles to the problems business, individuals, and society face. Problems are all around us. How do we schedule airline traffic in and out of a busy airport? How do we control a spacecraft millions of miles away? How do we allow someone to draw a happy face for a birthday card?

These problems and many more call on the software engineer's skill, experience, and imagination. The imagination will produce many of the components to a problem's solution but it will require skill and experience to accomplish the complete task. While it is hard to influence someone's imaginative power's, skills and experience can be richly developed over time. The principles of software engineering strongly support both by providing proven techniques created through many experiences and by providing methodologies which guide one towards the requisite skills and procedures to solve problems.

When push comes to shove the real heart of software engineering is implementation. This is one of the tenants of Agile Development – focus on working code over other artifacts. With the theory translated into screamingly fast compilers and algorithms, with the business problem translated into specifications and data models, the software engineer turns programmer. The first programmers were scientists and engineers often working on basic computational problems, applied research in mathematics, or military systems. Today there are millions of programmers around the world working on widely diverse problems and using just as diverse languages for implementing these solutions. The interesting question faced in this realm is where does software engineering begin and end.

Should writing a solid piece of code be considered software engineering? Or are there thresholds to where software engineering applies in implementation?

We will investigate these and other questions that deal with taking our previously formed vision for a solution and translating that into a working solution. By looking at Program Construction we will cover such topics as languages and programming. We will also cover ideas around design approach and discuss the factors required to produce successful solutions. This discussion will also include software maintenance, performance engineering, and tools. Finally, we will focus on Producing Reliable Software. This will close the loop back to methodology and design principles while introducing the critical topics of reuse, testing, software reliability, and Software Quality Assurance.

Once we have produced a tested software product, engineered to meet customer specifications, we now need to make it pay. All good software eventually shines in a production environment where the peculiar methods, tools, and techniques used to build it are unknown and certainly of no interest. The only thing that matters at this point is the performance of the software in the hands of the customer. This performance is a vector of many factors including quality, ease of use, cost of operations, and more.

We will discuss the issues related to software packaging and release, maintenance and code evolution, support, and most importantly, documentation. While documentation is critical throughout the software development process, in production the documentation becomes a product in itself. In today's environment documentation is often produced in an on-line fashion employing hypertext. This requires both technical writing skills and hypermedia design methods. Interestingly, this brings us back to the top of our framework since hypermedia methods, due to the explosion of the Internet, are only now receiving the recognition needed to firmly establish them in the software engineering culture as part of standard communication techniques.

1.9. AN ENGINEERING EXAMPLE

This introduction has touched on a wide array of topics that reflect many of the tools in my virtual software engineering toolbox. I would like to talk through a simple example of how some of these tools are used before closing this chapter and diving into more detail on each of these tools.

Earlier we looked at the generic engineering design cycle. In this cycle we had a need and we incrementally built out the solution using feedback. This was guided by the Scientific Method including planning, documentation, quantification, and more.

Let's consider that we have a need to build a paper airplane. This may seem like a trivial example but in fact if you look at it deeply it provides a lot of detail in the problem solution cycle. The problem recognition in this case could be that we wanted to demonstrate some concepts and fill in some of the boxes of the problem solving model. Let's start with that as our need statement.

So what are some of the kinds of considerations that would come up in a very simple problem of building a paper airplane if we take if from an engineering perspective? Well the recognition of the problem is that we want to demonstrate some concepts. We could solve this problem with one sheet of paper and assuming we know how to fold. Instead, as a thought experiment, what we really want to do is focus on the process of solving the problem in a very structured way and not really solve the problem in actuality.

As we stated, a starting point can be to look at what solutions are similar in the past. Look at toys you have made, or go to a hobby shop – this is the research component of the toolbox. Before going in to an application domain you want to do some research on the problem area. For example, when I worked in the telecommunications domain I read books in the area because I needed to understand what the problems were and I needed to be able to talk with the customers and to know if my solutions made sense in that domain. You may want to read a chapter in the encyclopedia on that area - or if you have experience in finance you may be valuable in developing financial applications. For paper airplanes perhaps a quick check of Wikipedia might help.

We may also want to look at engineering processes in our case. What is misleading is that building a paper airplane has nothing to do with software - or so you would think - it is also quite simple. Whereas most software problems are very complex either in terms of technology or in terms of organizations. Here we are just thinking through a simple problem but many of the steps will echo for larger problems.

Typically we would start out with a mission statement or statement of purpose. Ours could be "We need a compact engineering task to demonstrate a full development cycle". We want to define the details of paper airplane construction and we want to have such a definition that we could then follow in order to accomplish the task of building a paper airplane. That is our statement of purpose. This is the wording you need up front - if you can't state in one or two lines what it is that you want to do then maybe it is something that you can't accomplish anyway. That is where some people get into trouble. If you start writing chapter after chapter then you may not really be on the right track. If you can't state it succinctly then maybe it is something you do not understand. But we do want enough detail to flush out the engineering steps in the process.

So what is our goal? To have fun? Life and death? To request help? Let us say we are trapped in flood and want to escape so our plan is to send a message *via* a paper airplane. In that case you probably would not want to spend a lot of time talking about the process of building a paper airplane - you would just build it. And that is the point. Development is based on goals. You may want to solve a problem immediately without regard to process or if you are trying to build life critical systems you may want to take all care.

For example, on the Apollo 13 mission where an oxygen tank exploded in the command module on the way to the moon they had a very interesting problem. They had no calculations for how to maneuver the command module and LEM around the moon and back to Earth as configured. Usually they would not do it this way so they did not have the software ready. They called upon the support team and informed them of a need for an algorithm and working program within 7 hours or these guys will be lost. If they did not hit that navigational window then they would not make it [27]. This is a real pressure situation where life is on the line. In my case recently I was on call and there was a problem with the system - I also was about to go on vacation and did not want to leave the problem for someone else on the next Monday - so my goal was to fix it fast and go on vacation by 5. So it depends on your goals what kind of development technique you use.

If we analyze this problem - that is we list out the characteristics of the problem that we will need to consider to come up with a solution this is what we need to specify. We may not know all the answers right away. But here are some of the parameters we need to know. Are we talking about a handheld airplane or a Wright Brothers glider - which was mostly built of paper. How heavy does this thing need to be? Is there a propulsion system? Perhaps a propeller and rubber band involved. And so we may need to look at structural integrity. Durability is an issue, how many flights are called for? One flight, what if it gets wet. What speed are we trying to attain. As you can see, once we start asking questions we start hitting lots of paths to consider.

This can also lead to a problem know as paralysis by analysis. Some people are data gatherers and they will spend an unlimited amount of time up front if left to their preferences. They just want data and more data so that they are comfortable. Some people never move on to the next step. However, once we have analyzed all the parameters going into the problem now we can make decisions. Let's assume this will be a hand held plane and it will fly across a small room and that is it. Now what kind of materials do we need? If instead we want to get it across the street we could probably do it but the materials and design will vary. This may indicate the operating environment for the solution, a key requirement. The same thing holds true for software - it works fine in a certain environment (like a test lab) but change the environment and all of a sudden there are problems (like going into a user environment). Why is that? Because the design process optimizes for a given environment as well as application areas. Test methods also create success for the given environment but may not predict success for the true production target environment, this is a classical problem [28]. That will be a decision point in the engineering process - you know what your problem is, you have communicated it to your team, you have analyzed all the factors that go into building a paper airplane, you have made your solution choices and are ready to construct.

Before we started we would have wanted to look at some of the process issues. What is our schedule, perhaps we want to buy the airplane. That is economical and could save time. In software this is quite interesting. We build some tools but it is more economical to buy other tools instead because our core business is banking for example and not software tools. This is the key build *versus* buy decision which will discuss later.

Once the solution is agreed upon then we want to begin the detailed design. Do we begin with a rectangle or a square? What is the folding pattern? With Origami you can build cranes and flowers. Not me, but others can. They can do this because they know the folding patterns. Design drawings are echoed in these Origami books - they say step 1, 2, 3 on how to fold all this paper. That is how you learn how to do it. Either someone shows you or you look at available design patterns, known solutions, and examples. You may want to add something, scotch tape or glue. We may need to specify an assembly order. We may also want to think about ergonomics, is the plane easy to hold and launch. What about maintenance? Is it going to require refolding after each flight? How long will it hold up?

To finish the problem we will test it and perhaps we will document it. What were the original specifications, design drawings, work plan, charter, user manual, and so on. Software needs documentation. It is usually not much good if you do not know how to turn it on. These days you have on-line help engines. In many cases training or users will be required. Imagine if we had to give our paper airplane to someone how had never seen one before and did not understand the principles behind launching it. You may have to demonstrate its use first and then let the user practice for a while. In a recent business situation the majority of a small team of developers decided to resign from the company. The left behind no documentation and a system working without proper automation in some cases. The incoming team had to trace back from the application to the code with minimal assistance to be able to slowly move forward again.

When we look at this example we can expand it to all the tools in our virtual tool box. We used design principles, trial and error, research, training, architecture patterns, and more. This simple example can now lead us into the deeper discussions of each of these tools and more. This is how you could look like to build a system.

CONCLUSION

This eBook provides fluency in the core Software Engineering concepts I maintain in my toolbox. By reading this eBook you will learn dozens of concrete an applicable concepts and approaches. This eBook will also allow you to understand when someone says to you that a system architect is going to do some specifications what options they have for that and which way to organize effectively to accomplish that work. You will know the key Quality Assurance methods available. You will be exposed to a little bit of the theory - why things are done a certain way - but this eBook will also show you how things are done in a more practical sense. I will look at historical trends and how they reflect on persistent problems in the technology challenges of the industry. This eBook also develops a vocabulary for discussion engineering problems as we have already seen in this introduction. So for example if you come across a reference to UML you will know what it is or if you are asked how to calculate McCabe Cyclomatic complexity you will know what someone is talking about. Think about professional skills and growth areas. Once you finish this eBook you will still need to read constantly and not be afraid to build up you knowledge base. Importantly, this eBook provides a list or working framework of essential and durable ideas in software engineering. It may not provide all the ideas and methods you need but it will provide enough of a guide to allow you to build on.

Prior knowledge of hardware, operating systems, programming languages, and databases will help in understanding the concepts presented here but no assumption of this knowledge is made. If a new concept is introduced the basic preliminaries will be provided as well. When you finish this eBook you will understand the development process, development management, have analysis and design techniques to employ, and be aware of testing and quality issues. Perhaps you will come up with some ideas on where to advance your skills in the future. We will look at theory, practice application, problem solving, economics, management of software projects economically, and reliability - just as the definition of Software Engineering states. The most durable ideas I have seen applied will be the ones I focus on. To paraphrase Archimedes "*Give me a lever and I will move the world*".

REFERENCES

[1] Kernighan, B.W, & Ritchie, D.M., **The C Programming Language**, 2nd Edition, Prentice Hall, 1988.

[2] Arnold, K., & Gosling, J., **The Java Programming Language**, Addison-Wesley, 1996.

[3] Flanagan, D., & Matsumoto, Y., **The Ruby Programming Language**, O'Reilly, 2008.

[4] Pressman, **Software Engineering: A Practitionner's Approach**, 4th Edition, McGraw-Hill, New York, 1997.

[5] Goldstine, H. **The Computer from Pascal to von Neumann**, Princeton University Press, Princeton, New Jersy,1972.

[6] Pacey, Arnold, Technology in World Civilization, MIT Press, Cambridge, MASS, 1991.

[7] Webster, The American Heritage Dictionary, 2nd College Edition, Houghton Mifflin, Boston, 1982.

[8] Bauer, F. L., **Software Engineering: An Advanced Course**, Springer-Verlag, 1977.

[9] Boehm, B., **Software Engineering Economics**, Prentice-Hall, Engelwood Cliffs, NJ, 1981.

[10] Moore, J., **Software Engineering Standards: A User's Road Map**, IEEE Computer Society, 1998.

[11] Larman Craig, and Basili Victor, "*Iterative and Incremental Development: A Brief History*", **IEEE Computer**, June 2003, Volume 36, Number 6.

[12] Cusick, J., **Software Engineering Student Guide**, Edition 2, Columbia University Division of Special Programs, New York City, September 1995.

[13] Drucker, P., **The Age of Discontinuity: Guidelines to our Changing Society**, Harper & Row, New York, 1968.

[14] Konrad, M., *et al.,* **CMMI for Development®: Guidelines for Process Integration and Product Improvement**, SEI Series, Addison-Wesley Professional, 2011.

[15] Schiel, James, **Enterprise-Scale Agile Software Development**, CRC Press, 2010.

[16] Gall, J., **SYSTEMANTICS: How Systems Work and Especially How They Fail**, Quadrangle, 1975.

[17] Cusick, J., Writing for Science and Engineering: A personal account of methods and approaches, January 2010, viewed July 24, 2011, www.mendeley.com/profiles/james-cusick

[18] Tomayko, James, "*A Historian's View of Software Engineering* ", **13th Conference on Software Engineering Education and Training**, pp 39-46, Austin, TX, March, 2000.

[19] Crawford., S., Stucki., L., "*Peer review and the changing research record*", **Journal of American Society or Information Science,** vol. 41, pp 223-228, 1990.

[20] Cusick, J., Writing for Science and Engineering: A personal account of methods and approaches, January 2010, viewed July 24, 2011, www.mendeley.com/profiles/james-cusick

[21] Booch, G., *et al.*, **Unified Modeling Language User Guide, The (2nd Edition),** Addison-Wesley Professional, 2005.

[22] Astels, D., **Test-Driven Development: A Practical Guide**, Prentice Hall, 2003.

[23] Basili, V., *et al.*, "*The Empirical Investigation of Perspective-Based Reading*", **Empirical Software Engineering,** 1, 133-164, 1996.

[24] Adler, M., & Doren, C., **How to Read a Book: The Classic Guide to Intelligent Reading**, Touchstone, 1972.

[25] Strunk, W., & White, E., **The Elements of Style**, 4th Edition, Longman, 1999.

[26] Garlan, D., and Shaw, M., "*An Introduction to Software Architecture* ", **Advances in Software Engineering,** Volume I, eds., Ambriola, V., and Tortora, G., World Scientific Publishing Co., New Jersey, 1993.

[27] McDougall, W., **The Heavens and the Earth: A Political History of the Space Age**, Basic Books, New York, 1985.

[28] Cusick, J., & Welch, T., "*Developing and Applying a Distributed Systems Performance Approach for a Web Platform*", **30th International Conference for the Resource Management and Performance Evaluation of Computing Systems**, Las Vegas, NV, December 10, 2004.

CHAPTER 2

Methods, Process & Metrics

Abstract: Introduction of software lifecycles, development of process models, review of existing development approaches. Introduction of software metrics and their uses. Comparison of several models of development from waterfall to spiral to incremental to rapid application development to Agile. Establishment of metrics explained as the basis for managing development lifecycles and projects.

Keywords: Software process, software process engineering, software lifecycles, waterfall development, spiral development, incremental development, Agile development, domain modeling, CMMI, software metrics, GQM, estimation, complexity measurement, reliability, availability, performance.

2.1. INTRODUCTION

Typically, when people mention "process", programmers run for the hills. However, if you define process as a transform of inputs to outputs then software itself is a process as is the creation of software also. Process provides the "what-to-do" for software development while methods and techniques offer the "how-to" and languages and tools provide the "with-what". Some may say that everything is a process.

As a tool in my virtual toolbox, process and the creation of process (called process engineering) are both vital to putting all the other tools in the tool box to work. In nearly any case we can think of process is a transformation of inputs to a set of outputs (Fig. **1**). However, my interpretation of the need for process is a bottoms up approach from an identified problem to a defined methodological solution and finally to an end to end process of these discrete methods. Viewing process, methods, and process engineering in this way provides fantastic leverage in organizing and managing resources of any type.

From a simple process on how to handle support calls to a complex process of how to develop end to end solutions, basic tools in the process engineer's tool box include abstraction of tasks, interviewing impacted or involved parties, and developing flow diagrams and procedure descriptions. There are also standard

James J. Cusick

frameworks for many problem domains which offer a means to jumpstart the process definition and build on the work of others. Typically, these frameworks are meant to be tailored or customized to fit a particular organization's needs. Good examples of popular frameworks include CMMI (Capability Maturity Model Integrated) [1] and ITIL (Information Technology Integration Library) [2]. What these process frameworks provide are a robust model within which the process engineer can organize a view on a process area like development (CMMI) or support (ITIL). Any model like this is usually not prescriptive but lays out a path for the practitioner to follow. Within these models many useful concepts are presented and typically in a step wise arrangement of inputs and outputs.

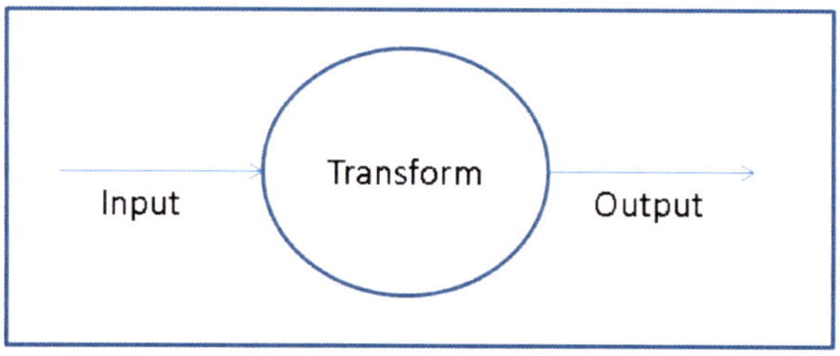

Figure 1: An Input Output Diagram.

However, in my experience, the more common need is the point procedure or process for which a framework may not exist or which one may not address adequately (or in some cases may be overkill). This is why I prefer to work from problem statements to methods and finally to processes. Building up a process from the micro methods within them aids in deriving only what is needed to get the job done. Working blindly from a prescribed framework can force too much unnecessary procedures into a process solution.

A useful way to think about process is through 'cybernetics' which is the science of aiming. Weinberger [3] uses the concept of Cybernetics to explain process. In this view process is the means by which the software development organization aims its efforts (Fig. **2**). The development process has inputs and outputs and is subject to randomness and variation. Overall, process tends to be a fuzzy area of software engineering in terms of attaining concrete and repeatable processes. Of course this model is a simplification of the process and does not explicitly show the users of software. However, nearly all processes can be viewed in this abstract view including Agile processes. This cybernetic view adds some additional complexity to our understanding of the simple input/output diagram above. The next level of complexity has to do with lifecycle models built around these basic process concepts. These layers of abstraction add useful tools to our toolbox. We can see each problem from an input/output perspective and solve for the integrated approach.

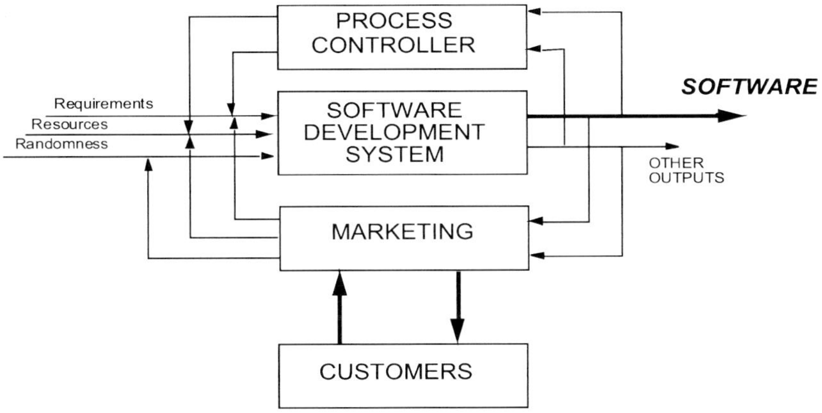

Figure 2: Cybernetics and Process Aiming.

Processes and their sub-processes support the attainment of the prerequisites of making software such as attaining and organizing staff, computing resources, and requirements. Standard business practices and common sense govern the decision making process around the development of the capital and revenue resources needed to sustain a software development operation. Initial development may come from venture capital, partnerships, or loans. IT based development is typically fully funded by internal corporate R&D budgets. When existing products are to be expanded or modified current revenue streams are taxed to underwrite development. Most of this part of launching a development effort fall outside the traditional sphere of software engineering but can often be the responsibility of a project manager who might actually be a software engineer. Once funding is established, a site for development must be established or selected from existing options. In today's environment distributed teams are common as are global teams. For both capital and the establishment of a development site, standard business practices often prevail. These fundamentals create the scene for software development itself and it is at this point when process becomes a factor.

Process is essentially a description of the tasks that must be carried out to accomplish a well-defined objective. According to Humphrey [4], process should be used when you want to perform some repetitive task such as writing documents or programs. Process helps one to plan and track work, to guide the performance of tasks, and to evaluate and improve the way a job is done. Process can include scripts, standards, forms, or measures [5]. Process is also valuable in that it leads to order, stability, schedule control, predictability, learning, measurement support, and makes software visible [6]. In today's environment two general families of process are often followed, either plan driven processes like CMMI or Agile methods like Scrum. For each of these there are defined concepts, steps, methods, terms, approaches, and lifecycle models. Before looking at them it will be useful to look at an abstraction of process for software. This abstraction of lifecycle and specific process orientation proves to be a useful tool as well.

2.2. A SOFTWARE PROCESS META-MODEL

A fine grain treatment of process which dissects the elements of software process provided by Brownlie [7] offers a view of the underlying information model of software process. This is represented in Fig. **3a**. In my own work of extending this model a concentration on the highlighted elements of template, work product, method, tool, and task was undertaken [8]. We also added to the model with a design pattern element (Fig. **3b**). This information model of a process provides an underlying structure to the discussion of process artifacts, their relationships, and usage scenarios. This abstraction of the underlying concepts in a generic process model offers a reusable tool for any process problem.

Software Engineering in practice is much more relative in nature. Depending on the individuals involved, the problem to be solved, and the organizations involved, the appropriate engineering mix will be selected. Home built software is fine if you are going to use it yourself and no one else. Once you try to package systems and market them many other issues will present themselves. You then will enter the world of support which requires a different level of preparation. At that level exposure to all the concepts in the field will help you in building a product because you will be able to use your engineering judgment to put an entire process and a resultant product together.

In developing process there are three general stages [9] beyond not having a process at all:

- Defined Process: A coherent set of steps for creating and evolving added-value products or services.
- Well Defined Process: The interrelationships among the steps, and their overall effect, can be reasoned about.
- Process Engineering: Rigorously describing a process and assessing its suitability for some purpose.

We need to look at the types of process models people have used and then where these models are going today. In general, the trend is away from plan driven models and more toward Agile development models. Agile does bring with it a disciplined process approach just like planned models but a key difference is that it anticipates and expects changes where plan driven models adapt differently. Process is prized today as a measure of quality and the maturity of processes are a topic of widespread interest in the industry.

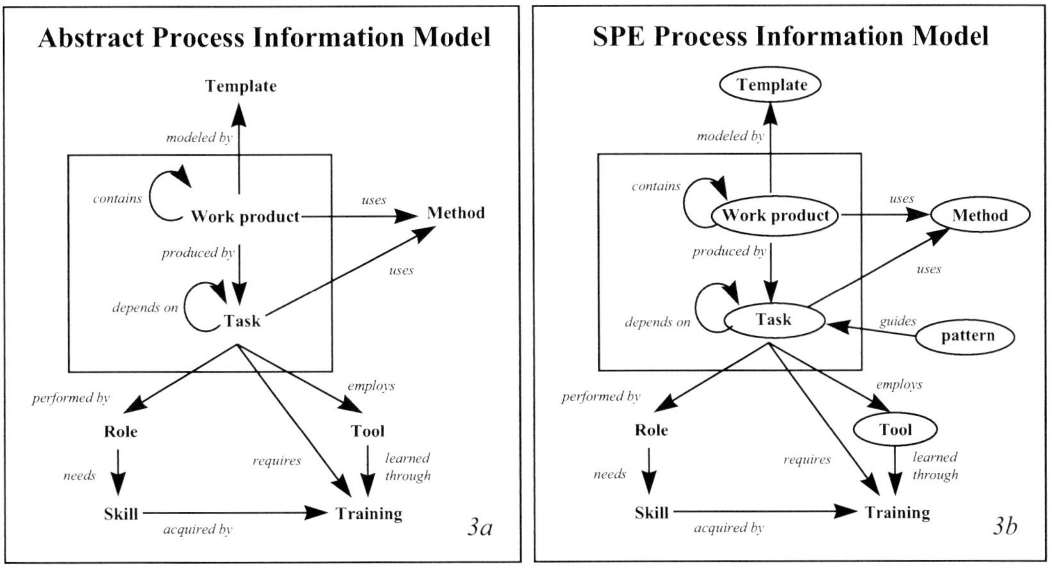

Figure 3a & 3b: Process Information Model: Brownlie [7] offers a compact view of the essential elements comprising a process in Figs. **2-3a**. The generation of work products is guided by a template and a method. Tasks call for the individual to work within a role using specific tools and skills developed through training. For the purpose of the SPE only a subset of these elements take on priority as indicted by the bubbles shown in Figs. **2-3b**. Also, patterns are added into the process model to guide tasks.

Such an understanding of process, as presented by Brownlie, goes far to help design and deploy custom processes. Unfortunately, when software process is discussed, an assumption is made that a large and complex project is being considered. Somehow, when a project consists of only 2 or 3 engineers, or the purpose of the project is experimental, or proof-of-concept, process is often ignored. Incredibly, process is often not formally applied for *development* projects let alone software research projects. In fact nearly 80% of all software projects in the U.S. are developed without a defined process [10].

2.3. PROCESS EVOLUTION

Process models did not emerge overnight. It took decades for people to invest the sophistication into these models that they required to be helpful. From style guides to methods and from life-cycle models to process paradigms process models improved (see Fig. **4**). Missing from this prediction was the rise of the Agile movement. In the Agile metaphor, working code is preferred over defined processes and customer collaboration is preferred over negotiated requirements. This evolution has turned the tide of industry practice from CMMI to Agile in a brief 10 year period. From my own point of view my work has always relied on agile concepts within a planned framework. Many of the projects I have worked on have called for the basic tools of process engineering, the input/output model, applied at a micro level and to fit into a larger planned framework environment. Today what is faddish is to work incrementally within a constantly adjusting paradigm called Agile. This is not significantly different than solving for point processes and then scaling up.

The quality of the software being developed can be predicted if you understand the level of sophistication of the organization which is doing the development. By looking at the maturation of the development approaches, instead of talking about the technical generation of the project (in terms of programming languages), we can learn more about the organization. Obviously, language choice impacts productivity or sometimes feature sets, but of more interest is the maturity of the organization. An immature engineering organization can be expected to produce poor quality products. If you have a very mature organization with experience in the application area, the technology, and in engineering itself, then you tend to get much better products. That is why some organizations come out with very nice products all the time and others go bankrupt. There are reasons for this - and some people believe this has to do with organizational maturity. Most software projects fail due not to technical problems but due to sociological or project management problems [11]. This is very critical and is driving a fad to rank organizations in terms of maturity.

DECADE	*PROCESS*	*ASSESMENT*
1960's Individuals	Style Guides	
1970's Small Teams	Method Definitions	
1980's Large Teams	Life Cycle Models, Standards	Post Mortems
1990's Companies	Process Programs & Agile Methods	Capability Maturity Models
2000's Coalitions	Formal Process Models	Formal Process Analysis

Figure 4: Process Evolution [12].

2.3.1. Life Cycle Models

Flowing from this high level abstraction of what a process is are the standard lifecycle models used in industry. These include the Waterfall, Incremental or Spiral development, Agile development, and more. These lifecycle models represent key tools in the software engineer's toolbox as they provide a means of organizing work. Let's explore some of the key lifecycle models. The first model to discuss is the Waterfall (Fig. **5**). Introduced by Royce in 1977 [13] this model was a reflection of traditional hardware engineering approaches. What is of interest in this model is that it provided distinct phases, gated progress, and feedback at each phase. Some authors may describe the Waterfall as a "big bang" approach and that can be true in the sense that development efforts following this model would release results only once. In alternate models, often called incremental models [13], software is built, tested, and released in steps. This is the preferred approach for the currently preferred Agile approaches. The Agile approaches find their roots in the incremental model (Fig. **6**).

It is helpful to start with a clear understanding of the core steps of the waterfall as most other models derive from these elements. In the Waterfall the following phases are typically discussed:

- **FEASIBILITY**: Defining preferred concept, its life cycle feasibility and superiority to alternative concepts
- **REQUIREMENTS**: Complete, validated specification of required functions, interfaces, and performance.
- **PRODUCT DESIGN**: Complete, verified specification of hardware-software architecture.
- **DETAILED DESIGN**: Complete, verified specification of control structure, data structure, interface relations, key algorithms of each component.
- **CODING**: Complete, verified set of program components.
- **INTEGRATION**: Properly functioning software product.
- **MAINTENANCE**: Fully functioning operational system
- **PHASE OUT**: Clean transition of product functions to successors.
- **VERIFICATION**: Are we building the product right?
- **VALIDATION**: Are we building the right product?
- **IMPLEMENTATION:** Deployment of the system.
- **OPERATIONS:** Ongoing usage and support of the system.

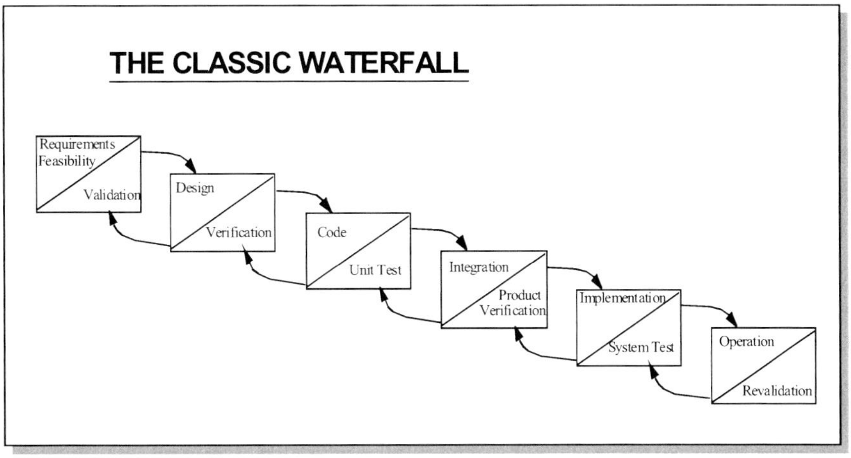

Figure 5: Waterfall Model [14].

Some of the limitations to the Waterfall are that we often do not know the full set of requirements ahead of time. Also, those requirements may change during the life of the project. Further, getting user feedback is important and with the Waterfall this is typically at the far end of the process making adjustments costly or impossible. The Waterfall is sometimes the only process tool that can be followed, however, such as in a cutover of a major infrastructure or software element. There may be a phased approach possible in some cases but not in all.

The realization of these limitations by early software engineers led to the next model, incremental development. In this model, used as early as the 1960s, software is built and deployed in phases and continuously improved upon. The assumption being that one cannot know all the requirements up front and that user feedback received early and often will drive the product to a better outcome (Fig. **6**). In this approach the phases remain the same but there are multiple passes through the waterfall.

Both the classic Waterfall and the Incremental model integrate internal feedback from phase to phase (a point some authors leave out) and they allow for testing at each phase. To be more precise they allow for verification and validation at the appropriate stages. In Fig. **7**, we can view the progression through the waterfall (or the incremental approach) through a “V” shaped process model. In this view, we can see that a paired verification or validation step occurs for each design or creation step. Regardless of approach, this concept of validating or verifying requirements, design, and development will remain a constant theme in process engineering. Within my toolbox, both verification (did we build the right thing) and validation (did we build it right) will be central themes.

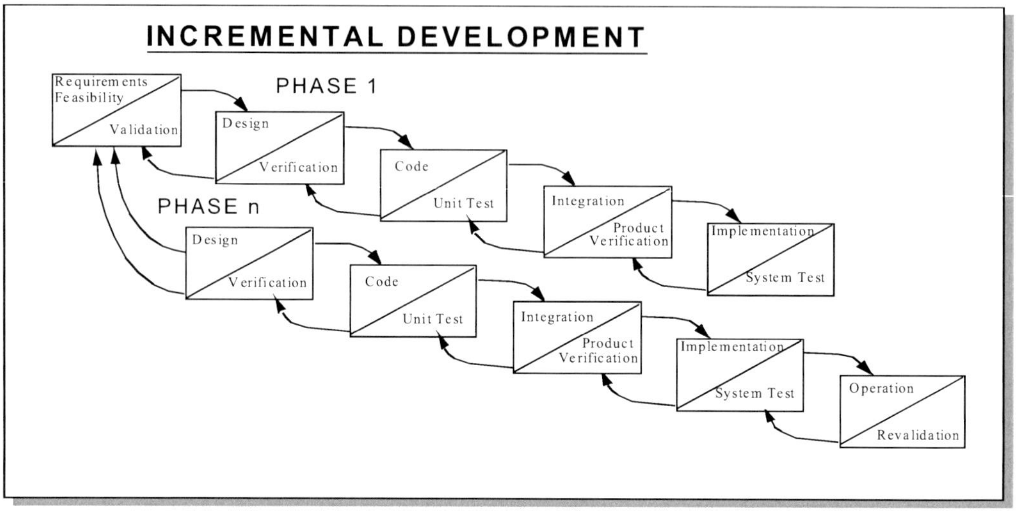

Figure 6: Incremental Development [15].

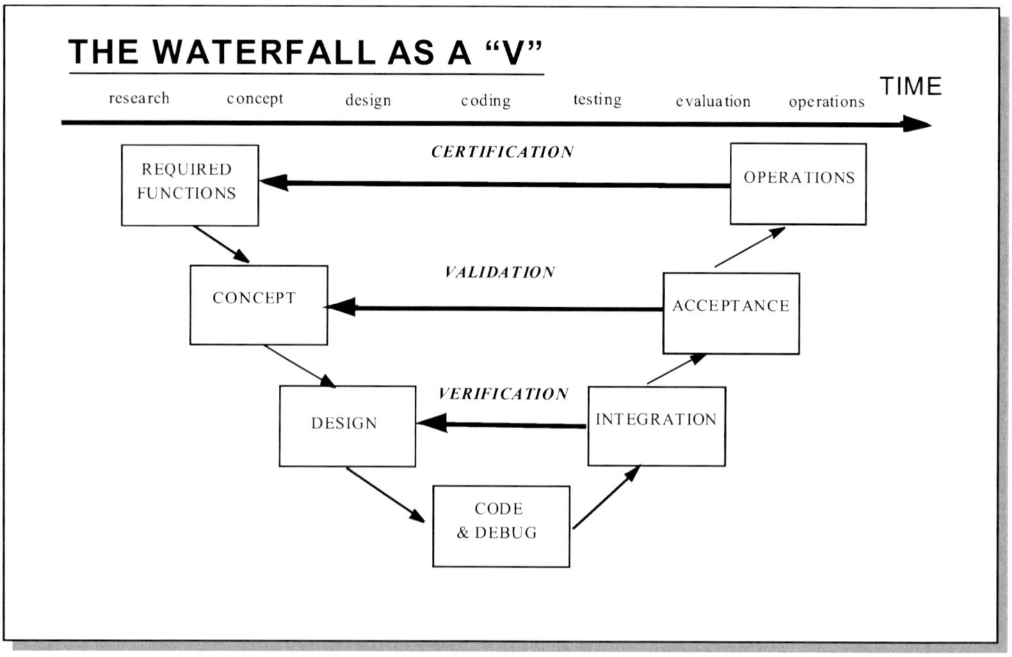

Figure 7: The Waterfall as a V [16].

A further improvement on the incremental model came from Barry Boehm [14] in the form of the Spiral model (Fig. **8**). In this model, which is also incremental, a built in risk analysis phase is added. Thus, as development progresses, a quantified risk assessment is conduced and helps guide the next increment of development. This model also formally includes a customer feedback phase.

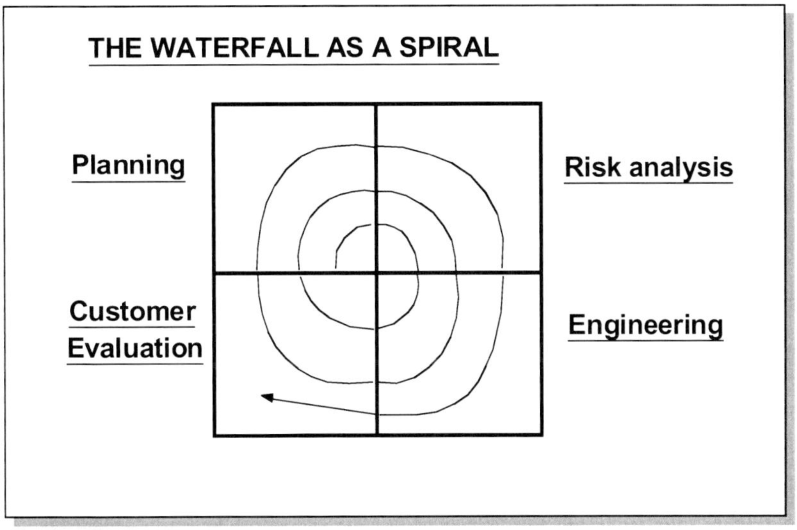

Figure 8: The Spiral Model [15].

There are numerous other variations on the Waterfall and the Incremental or Spiral models. One is called the Whirlpool model which separates some work into iterative clusters (Fig. **9**). Dozens of other models have been proposed, used, published, and in some cases abandoned. The key point in looking at these standard models is that they allow for customization to your particular needs through process engineering methods.

The waterfall has been criticized because of the large time lag from concept inception to product deployment and the separation and relative isolation of technical specialists up and down the waterfall. Thus we can also view the development life cycle as a spiral. Here we incorporate a prototyping (RAD – Rapid Application Development) stage in the development approach. In this model customer feedback is built into each cycle of development. We move from early concept to an engineering phase which results in a working version of the system - perhaps some key interfaces or functions - for the customer to review. This model represents one of the earliest forms of Agile development.

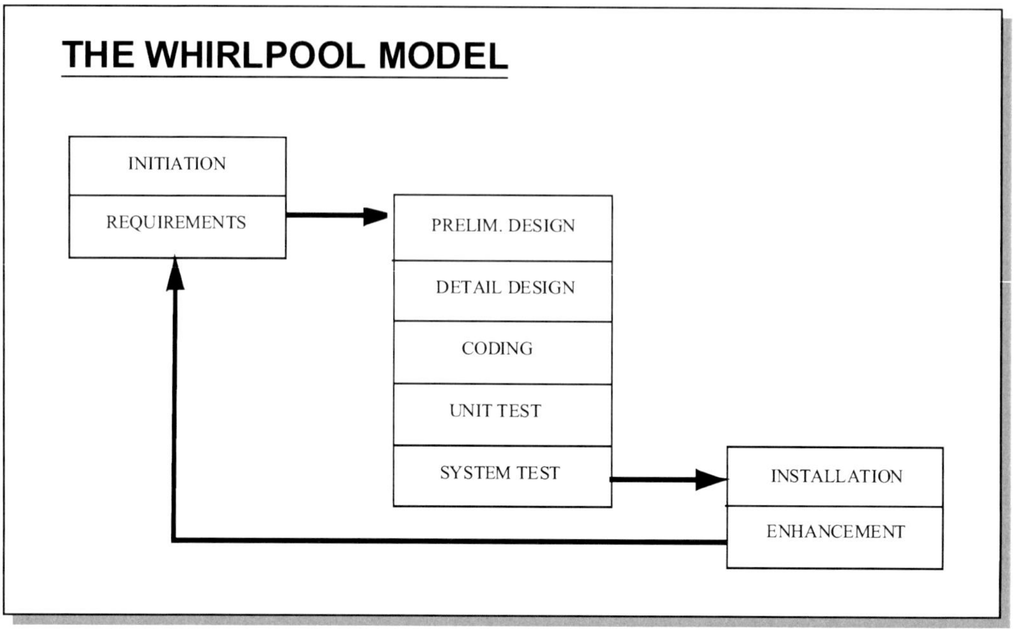

Figure 9: The Whirlpool Model [15].

Using the Waterfall model typically would require in the range of 1-2 years to produce an operational product. Using a Spiral technique you could see a partial system that is operational within about 6 months or less from inception. This is really quite different. Here you produce a core system and continue to refine it until you reach full feature deployment instead of waiting for all the features to be available prior to use akin to an Agile approach. Planning is different here as well because you need to architect the system such that features can be introduced piece-meal and not all at once. In other words more feature independence must be engineered and feature inter-dependence must be avoided (a concept formally known as loose coupling).

Incremental or RAD is also related to the Spiral method as is Agile. What we must do is recursively visit the feature list and build the software mechanisms required to support each feature - sometimes across multiple processes. This must be done in tightly controlled engineering cycles. Each one can culminate with a release (thereby improving release velocity). The Agile development camp has bought into this model heavily and built on it. Within Scrum methodology this is what is meant by the term backlog.

The experiences from using these lifecycle models also led the development of several methods collectively known as Agile methods. The family of Agile methods owes much to the early work in incremental and spiral methods. However, they also introduce some novel concepts.

The benefits of the Scrum model include lightweight process, limited extraneous artifacts, early and often software builds, and an ability to adjust product development after each sprint. This model falls into the incremental category of software process methods but adds some unique aspects including continuous builds, tight test integration, and heavy product management involvement.

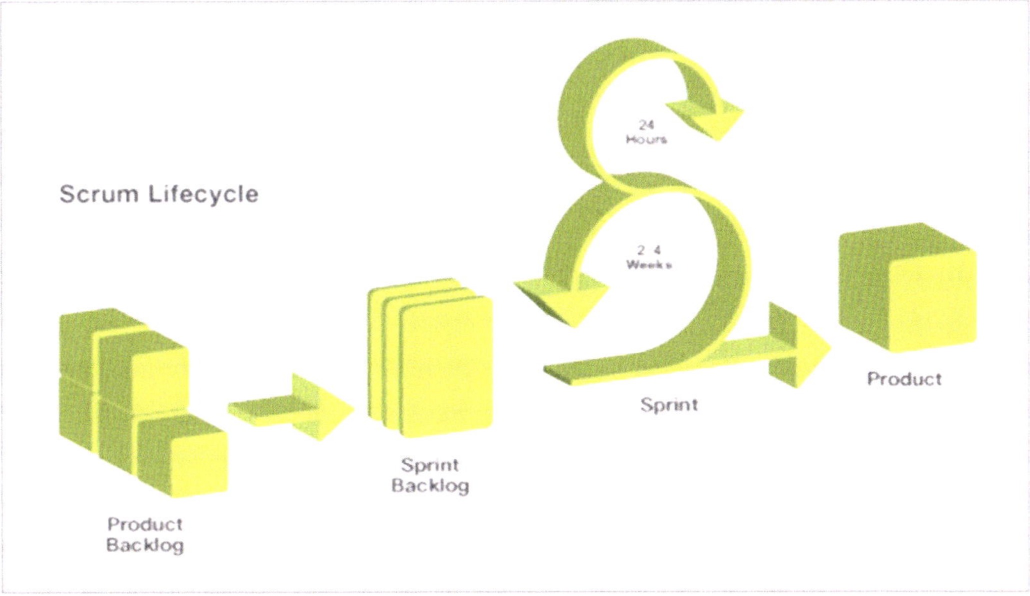

Figure 10: The Scrum Model of Agile[1]. Note the similarities with the Spiral and Whirlpool models of development.

The core ideas behind Agile methods are that working code is the preferred artifact and that anticipating and planning for change is more effective than trying

[1]Compliments of http://www.softsearch.com/

to plan for all eventualities in advance. One of the most popular models for Agile development is Scrum. This method has its own lifecycle model (Fig. **10**). In the Scrum model a product owner organizes requirements into a product backlog. Development teams meet to plan a specifically time bounded (or time boxed) work effort known as a sprint, usually about a month in duration. A Scrum Master runs the activity using daily meetings and other methods. At the end of each sprint a working and usable (customer shippable) output is produced.

2.4. CURRENT SOFTWARE DEVELOPMENT APPROACHES

2.4.1. Incremental Development

Knowing which features to build first can act as a beacon when spiraling through development. The concept of incremental development has been well understood and documented starting at least with Brooks [17] and Boehm [14]. Recently Microsoft reports frenetic rates of integration and automated regression testing [18]. Such incremental development, with early integration testing, can be even more beneficial when coupled with Operational Profile driven testing (also termed "operational development" [19]). One approach used with a client/server version of a telecommunications system was to develop the overall architecture of the system using Object Oriented Analysis and Design. We then built up functionality recursively across the entire system using Object-Oriented Programming [20]. This approach foreshadowed the current Agile and Scrum models quite well (See Fig. **11**).

Using this approach, key components are given structural integrity and minimal functionality prior to the initial integration. Load levels selected from the Operational Profile (a statistical representation of system usage patterns) are then used to drive early testing. Successive iterations introduce additional features and functionality in priority as derived from the Functional Profile. As seen in Fig. **11**, each component's overall scope is understood prior to the initial cycle (C1). As transitions are made to successive cycles (C2, C3, C4), the system soon becomes robust in lab conditions which closely mimic field operations following the Operational Profile. A side benefit is that the system quickly forms into something deliverable from a product standpoint. With relatively short lead time a working system can be delivered to system test. In C1 the basic structure of each subsystem is created represented by the large opaque box. This provides the process structure and fundamental behavior of the subsystem (initialization, error handling, key algorithmic capabilities). At this point a working skeletal system is in place. In C2 additional feature bundles are added as represented by the shaded boxes. These components are developed in descending priority order thereby assuring that as early as possible in the development cycle the highest number of required features are available. At each transition point between cycles (as indicated by the arrows) an integration test phase is conducted where reliability and performance goals can be assessed.

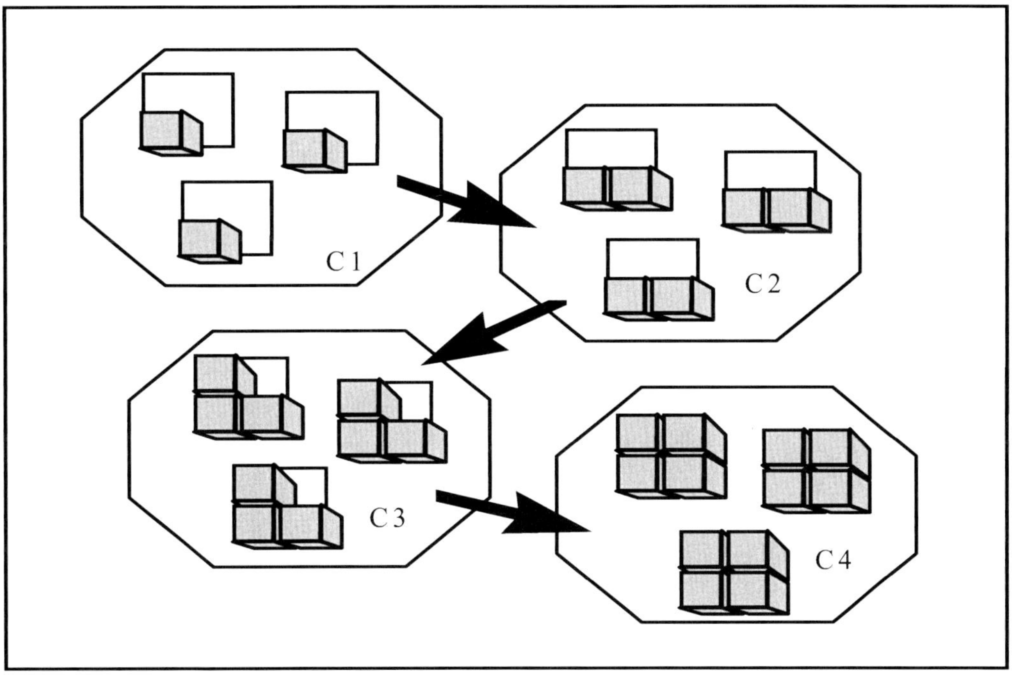

Figure 11: Incremental Development Driven by Operational Profile: In This Diagram the Octagons Represent the Entire System at Different Stages of Completion (C1, C2, C3, C4) [20].

Initially, we attempted to implement several features in parallel across subsystems. This became unwieldy. Midway through development when the number of existing features was relatively high the incremental approach was modified. Instead of grouping several features for development in a fixed time interval, feature-at-a-time development across all system components was followed for each incremental cycle. This was found to be easier to manage even though it required more cycles.

2.4.2. Process Maturity Models

In the past twenty years process for software development was driven heavily by the work done at the Software Engineering Institute (SEI) around maturity models. Recently the alternative camp, Agile, has taken a much bigger focus. However, it is beneficial to review the basic tenants of the maturity models as they do provide a useful tool in understanding the evolution of process within an organization whether they might follow Agile or not.

Watts Humphrey introduced the CMM (Capability Maturity Model) based on years of experience in developing large scale software at IBM [4]. With the help of many others at the SEI and in the industry the basic maturity model was developed:

- INITIAL: Ad Hoc or Chaotic
- REPEATABLE: Process in Place
- DEFINED: Documented and Standardized
- MANAGED: Projects carefully Measured
- OPTIMIZING: Continuous Process Improvement

The primary idea behind this model is that an organization must put some fundamental building blocks like requirements management, configuration management, and project controls in place before being able to succeed at higher levels of process sophistication. In later models like the CMMI (CMM Integrated) [1] a discontinuous view of process model was introduced. This allowed for the formal evolution of process in both basic and advanced areas at the same time. This allowed for more flexibility in reaching higher levels of process.

As a tool in the software engineer's tool box this type of thinking and abstraction can prove very useful. The idea is that you need to understand what the pre-requisites are for success, what are the foundations to be a healthy software producing organization and what steps do you need to take to get there. The CMM and CMMI are not prescriptive but instead provide a framework for quality improvement. Within the Agile world view this remains an important topic and so the tool of process maturity modeling is a useful tool for us. Agile has not thrown out the ideas of maturity but tends to approach growth differently and in a more incremental fashion.

2.4.3. Process Selection and Improvement

There are many types of development models and selecting between those discussed above and others requires some thinking. In today's environment, where component development is possible current development technology allows for a greater concentration on abstraction and specification and less of a reliance on custom development. Using commercial components for algorithms and data structures the work of implementing an application moves up the lifecycle chain.

Not every application and not every environment is suitable to have an engineered development process. For small applications of short term use there may not be any need to have an engineered process. But even in organic mode development, or small team environment, there may be a need for a documented process at some level to prevent communication problems. Typically, if there are more than three people working on a project some level of process will be required.

In selecting a process it has been my experience, as mentioned, that it is best to start with point problems and solve them and let the process evolve around those working solutions. This approach starts with identifying real problems, coming up with solutions, and measuring results. If you have done anything good the measurements should reflect that. This process is then repeated again and again. This is known as the Shewart Cycle (Plan, Do, Check, Act). This is also known as kaizen in a Japanese quality context. We will discuss this in more depth later, however, this basic strategy is how problems are solved, methods developed and overall process is generated. This is a bottom's up approach as opposed to a top down framework driven approach like CMM or CMMI. This iterative approach is how we get better process and products. As a comparison, look at consumer electronics, autos, or other products. How do they get better? They constantly look at their design process, fabrication methods, manufacturing techniques, and always look for improvements. Not only from the end of the production line but from the bottoms up view of what is not working right. Within a true quality environment there is a de-emphasis on inspection processes and a focus on tuning the entire process as well as the point processes and methods that make up the macro process. Thus a key tool in my tool box is the combination of quality improvement methods with process design and evolution. It is through these combined tools that one can solve an engineering problem and continue to improve on that solution.

2.4.4. An Emerging Approach

Over the years I have proposed various process models. One approach which I have lectured on centers around Object Oriented repositories. This approach was based on the reaction to the development of new Object based technologies while software engineering will continue to evolve away from linear and from scratch models to component based iterative models. New concepts in Pattern theory will drive development towards repository browsing models. These models have great potential for organizing new software engineering support environments.

Such a process model might begin with establishing domain models and cataloging frameworks (both commercial and custom). With this amount of infrastructure in place an entire process could evolve where architects browse for existing solutions (Service Patterns, Architecture Patterns, Design Patterns), and then integrate or generate the instance required. This process might look like Fig. **12** below. It is only from an integrated approach where process, environment, and repositories come together can the most be gained from modern development. Today this conceptual approach is found as realistic development environments to support a variety of platforms including web applications like. Net and mobile applications.

Essentially, this process represents a model for systems integration and development that relies on a sophisticated infrastructure and skill base. This process and environment has never been created anywhere in the industry to date. Nevertheless, such a process and environment could deliver the types of characteristics needed by leading edge development organizations. For example, to assure non-duplicate efforts the Application Instance repository could be cross referenced with new architecture requests. Automatic analysis of design similarity could trigger a warning to the analyst. To prevent mistakes from happening early in the development process, this environment (coupled with an architecture review process) would provide proven solutions to designers. Naturally, any such environment and process would require much additional development prior to serious consideration.

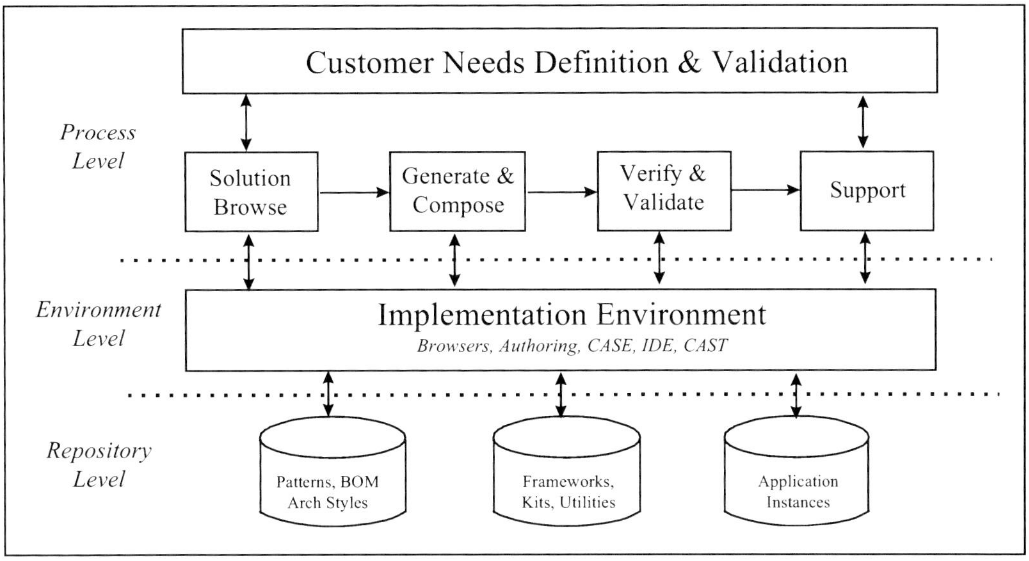

Figure 12: A Pattern Based Development Model.

2.4.5. Domain Modeling to Support Enterprise Development

To populate the repository layer of the process model above will require work by a standards group to pull in vertical and utility frameworks as well as pattern mining by the architecture group. For the Domain Modeling group lies another challenge. The concept of enterprise data modeling in not entirely different than object-oriented domain modeling. Fundamentally, the domain modeling effort will attempt to establish the business objects most resilient to change (such as a subscriber line or customer account entity) and the relationships between them. These may come from analytical efforts from first principles or may be derived from established object models built by development organizations. These models (along with frameworks, patterns, and commercial objects and components) will make up the enterprise object repository. The next Figs. (**2-13**) demonstrates how the domain models and the enterprise objects exist beyond the time frames of the transient projects. These particular concepts are well established and frequently attempted by world class development organizations.

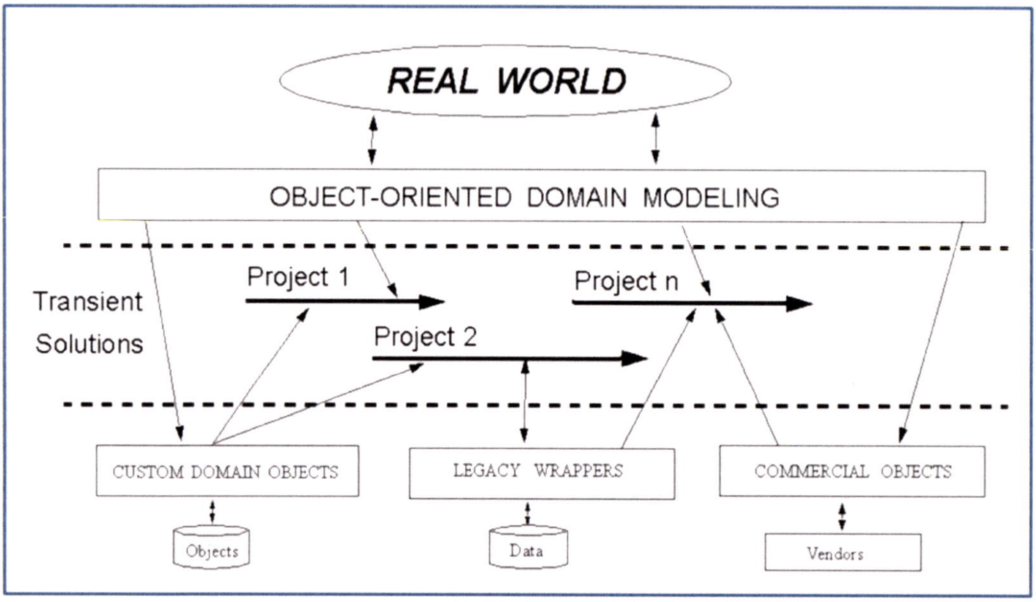

Figure 13: An Object Modeling Based Development Model.

2.4.6. Internet Software Development

At its core, creating web applications is no different than creating any other software application. The only difference is that things change so much more rapidly. There is an architecture to consider, an information model to be constructed, databases to build, and code to write. And there is always testing. However, when we look closer at Web development there are significant differences. With Internet applications, initially documents and then forms, graphics, and other content approaches were provided in a browser as the primary interface. These documents require more than the usual visual design effort. Complex page navigation routes must be considered and maintained. Finally, the document components can include text, graphics, data entry forms, video, and audio. Clearly, in the beginning these applications introduced new demands to most development teams. After more than 15 years of maturation of technology these demands are less troubling. However, the problems of software development have not disappeared. They are still with us but within the new environment. Once again, process is a key tool in managing these challenges.

In reaction to the demand to merge new content creation activities into the more established development processes a new process model is needed. Such a process might merge a traditional spiral model of software development with the additional steps required for hypermedia production. This would need to be augmented with a "content life-cycle " model as well since documents can go stale or otherwise need evolution (such as technical or stylistic improvement). Beyond this we need methodologies for information analysis that can transform information to hypertext document representations.

In terms of life cycle duration, many Internet applications currently take from less than one month to about 3 months to complete. These timeframes are considerably shorter than most traditional software projects would expect. However, maintenance costs can introduce higher costs due to the often rapid and sometimes undisciplined approaches to Internet development.

At first, few development process models were offered for application development on the Internet. In looking for parallels from other work, traditional film and video production process can offer some help in understanding the activities that make up traditional hypermedia development. These techniques incorporate steps including story-boarding, content acquisition, theme design, programming, testing, and production [21]. However, Internet development has unique properties much more aligned with software development.

An early overall model for an Internet development process in Fig. **14** is provided by December and Ginsburg [21]. This model is interesting for the experienced development manager in that there are several new steps involved in the process and new deliverables. For Internet development it becomes necessary to promote the site and to rapidly innovate new content and reengineer the site. Furthermore, audience analysis must be worked into the process much as user centered design techniques recommend. Further, SEO (Search Engine Optimization) becomes a key factor in the process as keywords, content, and search listings drive visibility on the Internet. The process resembles a spiral and also introduces some additional content related development steps. Over the years this thinking has by and large been subsumed by the Agile community.

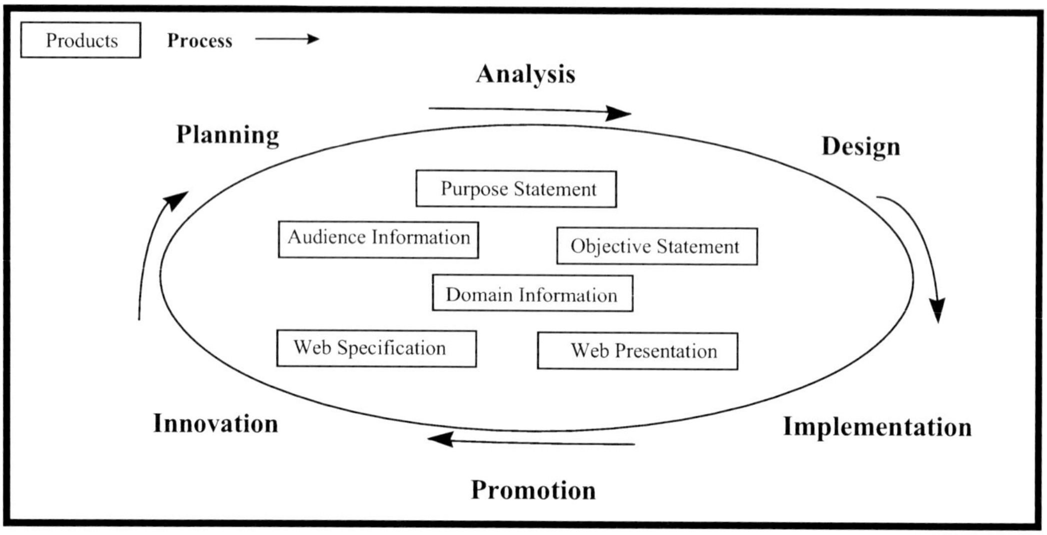

Figure 14: Internet Development Process.

2.4.7. Skills for Internet Development

With changes in process and technology it is not a surprise that new skills may be required as well. At a minimum, these are some of the skills required to build Web applications:

- Project Management
- User Interface Design
- Writing
- Graphic Design
- Video and Animation
- Human Factors
- Application Programming

- Database Development
- System Testing
- Systems Integration
- Systems Administration

Some of these skills will be in more demand than others on any given project. For example, if no video will be included in the application then this skill will not be needed. In any case, a successful process for developing on the Internet must make sense of these different skill requirements and tie them together as appropriate.

2.4.8. Other Impacts on Development

One of the major differences between traditional software development and Internet application development is the rate of change and the rate of delivery. With traditional development technologies cycle times for large-scale innovation can be from 18 months to three years. In other words, longevity of the underlying software construction technology was usually stable enough for products to be put into production prior to their obsolescence. In the Internet sphere this is no longer the case. Content itself can go stale in a matter of hours or days. The tools used for content creation and development are becoming obsolete in a matter of months while the sheer volume of technology introduction is difficult to track. These realities force the development teams to carefully architect applications for rapid *rebuild* as well as initial development.

Think of the development of an encyclopedia. Older software development practices were similar to those required to deliver large scale, infrequently updated information products like an encyclopedia. Wikipedia has shattered the old model of encyclopedia development. Now consider a newspaper publisher. The format changes slowly but the content changes rapidly, in fact overnight. A software process must be aimed at this pace of content and function delivery. This is a large challenge when the underlying technology is also in flux. As a result it is important to design for rapid rebuild but also to balance new techniques with the risk of missing the daily headline. In other words, consider targeting a technological status quo that is somewhat trailing the leading edge since you will be there in 3-6 months anyway.

Once again, process engineering and process design remains a useful tool in the Internet age. For whatever problem one may be facing there will be tasks that have relationships, precedence, and inputs and outputs. This means that process engineering will still be a valid and useful tool into the future.

In discussing process as a tool the purpose is to find the right balance between process and development focus whether the development is for an Internet application or not. Agile is all about this balance. There is discipline within Agile methods such as Scrum. There is also true agility in the one off app development of a hit game like Angry Birds. The Apple application store has changed development process to some degree. There is now a market for smaller and less complex software building on the object base and APIs (Application Programming Interfaces) provided. A focus on working software can be seen as the new mantra as opposed to a focus on the process that produces the software. Still, process as a tool remains valuable when presented with larger problems like integrating multiple Scrum teams or solving operational problems like data center functions or support.

Software Engineering in practice is much more relative in nature. Depending on the individuals involved, the problem to be solved, and the organizations involved, the appropriate engineering mix will be selected. Home built software is fine if you are going to use it and no one else. Once you try to package the systems and market them many other issues will present themselves.

Process can be mix and match, thus, exposure to all the concepts in the field will help you in building a product because you will be able to use your engineering judgment to put an entire process and a resultant product together.

2.4.9. The Earliest Process Approaches

Prior to the world we have today there was a time and a place without PCs but with computer systems being built. Early engineering comes from the engineering world where people have been building dams, bridges, and pyramids for centuries. They knew how to build things and they knew how to solve problems. So when it came to building early software systems the same engineering approaches were applied to meet the problem solving and organizational challenges that they had seen in the past and had used for other engineering efforts.

There are many large scale engineering artifacts that were built before the use of computers. Hoover Dam is a good example. The dam, which will last for centuries was not built with any PCs involved. No computers were involved at all. The tools used were brains, paper and pencil, and slide rules. The point is that if you have a problem to solve, software is not the only issue, you have to understand what the problem is, you have to be able to state it clearly and come up with some design solutions and perhaps a selection process to find the one that best fits. This must be specified so that not only you but others can solve the problem from these descriptions - not only today but in the future so that someone can look back and see what you have done and why. This is true for problem solutioning and for process design. In fact we can think about process design as creating a means to repeatedly solve additional problems.

It is helpful to review problem solving and process methods from the dawn of computing. Below is a description of the techniques used for solving systems development problems more than 40 years ago [16]. The beginning would be a survey where they would look at available technologies to solve the problem at hand and collect data on the system they were trying to build. They would look at what the expectations were of the system. They would do the design and programming, build files, define clerical procedures, and develop the testing required (See Fig. **15**).

The focus in those days was on output. This follows from the approach of Output Centered Design. If you have a problem to solve where do you start? You can start with the output. Find out what people want the system to produce. Many early systems were mostly reports or transactions so that wanted tabulations, calculations, or sorts as outputs. This drives timing and the other things you wanted the system to do.

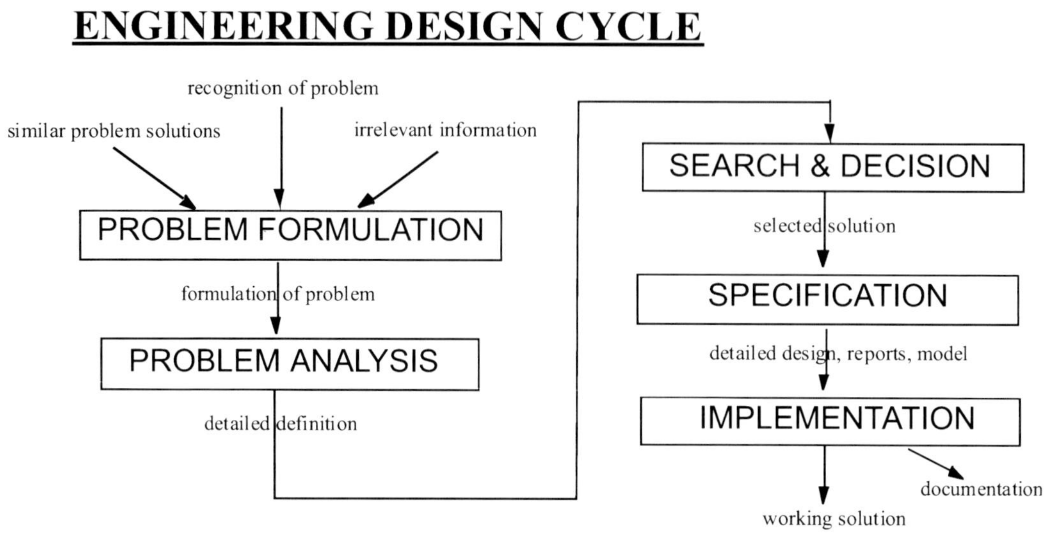

Figure 15: Early Engineering Lifecycle Model.

In the design phase they used process charts and flow charts. They would work from a block diagram and then go down into some specific detail.

They also had to consider the input formats like reels of tape or machine interpretable documents. They also had to consider keyboard insertions to produce reels of tape, punched cards. The documentation abstraction for this is shown in Fig. **16**. Also part of the programming assignment included tape handling instructions. Memory was more of a concern where today we have the luxury of more or less ignoring many size restrictions. Run books also had to be developed - instructions on how to use this program. This is how the systems were developed in those days. Some of these approaches remain valid today based on the system. If batches are involved, for example, run books are still used.

In those days they talked in terms of data item which we can also call a data field. They had to be concerned with every data element in the program and what size it was and what type. This has not changed so much. We build systems today we need to have a complete data schema. This has not changed.

To design a process, process charts are often used. A basic flow charting technique will be useful to any process design task. Once the process is created (see Fig. **17** for a process example [22]) we then move to programming. With a written flow chart we can then write a program or develop the procedures needed to follow if the process design is for a non-programming task like information routing or management.

PROCESS CHART SYMBOLS

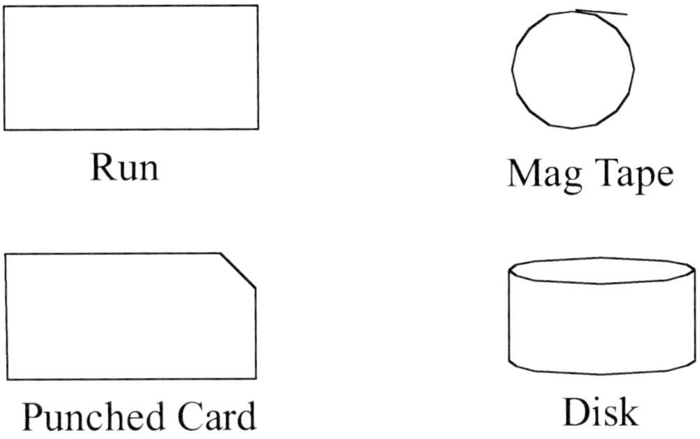

Figure 16: Basic Flow Chart Symbols.

PROCESS CHART EXAMPLE

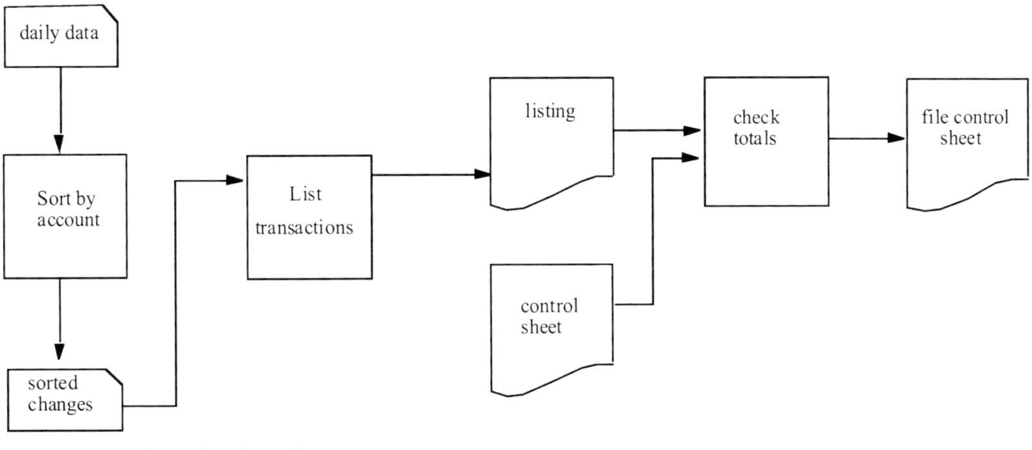

Figure 17: A Sample Flow Chart.

Process charts like those above came from the engineering world in the early days of software engineering and flow charts grew out of them to encompass some of the new issues related to software development. Process charts and flow charts were in fact the first type of modeling notations used for doing software design. There are some limitations to these models and they have fallen somewhat out of favor. However, even in Agile methods one will find process charts still being used. Some of the decision flows or architecture diagrams on projects find their roots in process diagrams and flow charts. Flow charts are still useful for scenario molding or decision flows. However, the concept of using symbols to represent what we are doing remains popular. When we look at SASD (Structured Analysis/Structured Design) [23], or OOA/OOD (Object Oriented Analysis /Design) [24], it is the same kind of thing. These boxes, circles, and arrows are the syntactical and semantic building blocks of our software design task. Today's design tools like Visio or PowerPoint all maintain design stencils for flow charting. It remains a staple tool for systems and software designers.

2.4.10. Process and Metrics

Closely related to process are metrics. If process is a tool for organizing work then metrics represent the tools for keeping the process on track. We have already mentioned the Shewart cycle, a core concept in quality. Within this cycle: Plan, Act, Check, Do is an embedded concept of measurement. Objective and scientific measurement of work as driven by process is assumed. Software measurement techniques have been built up over the decades and there are many key metrics which can be used as important tools in developing and perfecting process and for managing software projects. There are also functional metrics such as reliability and performance which tell you how your software is behaving. All of these metrics are critical to succeeding in bringing software to life and maintaining it. As a tool in my virtual tool kit, qualitative, quantitative, direct, and indirect measures are all vital to achieving results and to knowing when to adjust a process.

A classic eBook on design quality by Card and Glass [25] introduces the concept of improvement as measured objectively. In Fig. **18** we can see that with any process there may be non-conformances. The idea is to manage the rate of non-conformances to an acceptable level through the introduction of new technologies or process changes. The basic ideas from statistical process control of managing to an upper control limit and lower control limit can be used again and again from process area to process area. Throughout my career this one diagram has proven to be the most useful of any metrics diagrams outside of the normal distribution curve which we will also discuss.

Considering metrics per phase we can see that up front we want to know cost, schedule, and ROI. In design we are concerned with reliability, performance, and complexity. As such a good metric is constant in its application across systems. We want the metric to behave the same way and produce comparable information from software target to software target.

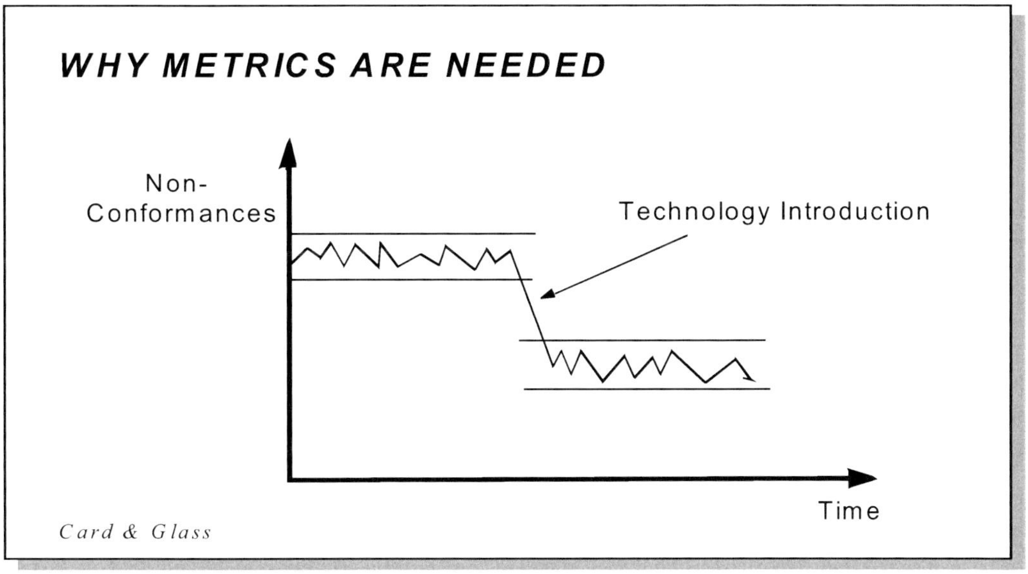

Figure 18: Metrics Fundamentals (this chart is also called a run chart).

There are many kinds of metrics we might want to consider in our process work. In general we talk about end to end process measures and in-process measures. The in-process metrics might be the number of test cases executed in unit testing. An end to end metric might be the total staff effort for the entire project. Other useful metrics might be cost, schedule, ROI (return on investment), and more. For development purposes we might want to know the number of lines of code (LOC) produced, or the number of defects detected. These are raw metrics. When put together, for example defects per LOC, we now have a measurement. These measures can be tracked and base-lined, they can also be benchmarked against industry standards to understand if our performance makes us competitive. Overall the most important thing in measurement is that we can observe trends, set and track goals, and observe deviations in performance. Eventually, we hope to be improving the outcomes of our process.

The point of metrics is that even though these things are difficult to track, or are somewhat subjective, or leave certain factors unaccounted for, if we establish a pattern of how a particular piece of software behaves, or how a particular development organization is able to produce, in terms of productivity or error rate, if we have a method to measure that reliability over time, then if we introduce something like a new technology, or new software release, if the metric can indicate to us what the delta has been the metric has succeeded. This is the key point to applying software measures - tracking changes. If you are not measuring the development process you are not in control of it.

2.4.10.1. Custom Metrics

To establish usable metrics we need to consider many factors. We want the metric to behave the same way and produce comparable information from software target to software target. Key metrics to collect by any means should include efficiency, cycle time, defects, product size, cost, and reliability. A metric is built from direct measures on a process or an activity or on the software itself. There are many kinds of custom metrics one may be interested in, for example, the numbers of orders per hour that a system processes. Or the number of screens of an application that have been implemented out of the total planned. Or the performance level of a database in terms of transactions compared with a benchmark level. These custom metrics will play a role in my toolbox based on need. It is through metrics that we know how our process is faring.

A classic software measure is lines of code (LOC). You can measure some of key variables by LOC but this has certain draw backs. There is no standard on code counting. LOC are not the only products produced, graphics, documents, *etc.*, are also produced. The exact amount of code produced is also hard to predict in advance. Finally, users do not care about LOC they care about functionality.

For these reasons LOC have been critiqued to such an extent that they are somewhat out of favor as a primary software measurement. However, in practice I use LOC in addition to other metrics because they are so easy to collect and has multiple direct uses like sizing, estimating, and defect prediction. Also, many models have been built based on LOC and so there is an extensive set of operations that can be conducted using LOC as an input. So LOC measurement is still one of the tools in my tool box.

2.4.10.2. Goal, Question, Metric

In getting to any metric a useful method I have learned to apply is GQM (Goal, Question, Metric) developed by Vic Basili [26]. This method starts the process by defining what goal you are trying to achieve and then what questions you would have to answer in order to know if you had achieved that goal. Only after that will the metrics you need be obvious. The basic pattern for this method is shown in Fig. **19** below.

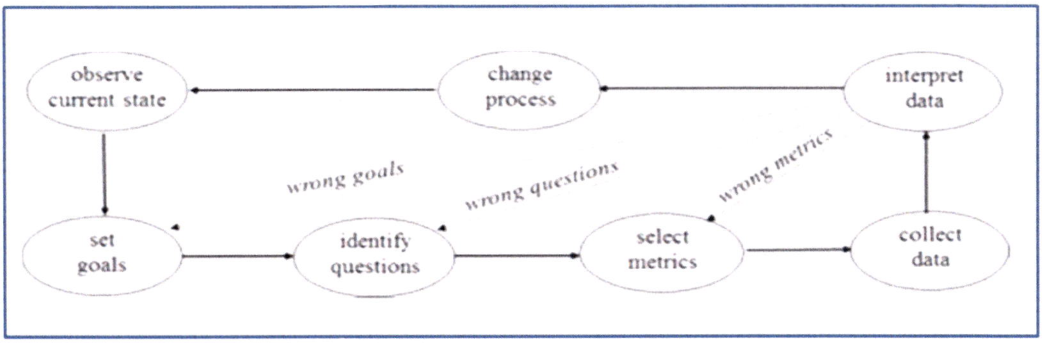

Figure 19: Goal, Question, Metric Technique.

2.4.10.3. Estimation Metrics

A starting point in most projects is an understanding what it will take to execute the project. Estimating is a key step in project planning as discussed in the next chapter. In an Agile model this is done essentially in one day during each Scrum cycle. In large scale projects estimation can be a more significant up front effort. Either way, an estimate must be derived and metrical techniques are useful for this.

2.4.10.3.1. Analogy & Heuristics

With LOC or complexity stand-ins an analogous estimate can be derived. This has its drawbacks as not every project is the same. Too many variables will differ from project to project. However, in the absence of other methods this is a basic metric that can be applied.

2.4.10.3.2. Function Points

FP (Function Points) are a synthetic measure of software. Whereas LOC is a direct measure of software, FPs have been invented to measure software externally. You can look into an editor and see a LOC but you cannot do that and see a FP. FPs are derived from the software. Just as temperature is a synthetic metric. FPs are used to find productivity and other measurers. Thus, Function Points provide an alternative that can be used to measure functionality across multiple programming languages.

Albrect invented the FPs at IBM 's Palo Alto Lab in the 70s [27]. Capers Jones became the most well-known champion of FPs [28]. The practice of FP has developed considerably but has not generally caught the interest of software developers. The use of FPs is guided by standards and there are numerous industry studies on their successful use but they have struggled to stay relevant.

The reason they remain a tool in my toolbox is due to the utility of the data collected around software using Function Points and due to a technique known as 'backfiring' which allows one to estimate FPs using LOC. FPs are a measure of functionality as delivered to customers. They represent a realistic assessment of the level of functionality provided by the software. Basically, FPs require a count of inputs, outputs, files, interfaces, and complexity.

Early FPs did not address certain types of systems well. Criticism of FPs continues to center on this point. However, these shortcomings were mostly resolved and have little claim in fact compared to today's FP. For example, relational databases are well supported in FP counting today but not in the first set of counting rules. Also, algorithmic complexity was added to provide a more balanced measure applicable to communications and systems level programs. For example, a scientific application for calculating air flow over an experimental wing shape might take as input a vector and produce a pass-fail result. This program would have virtually no storage or user interface. Early FP counting would have penalized such a program but today it would be represented fairly.

To run any business requires information about that business. Companies depend upon the delivery of software to run its business but often times they know surprisingly little about its own internal software business. Surprisingly, with software few people know how many systems might be owned or what they look like. Questions such as how much software is in place, what is it worth, and how much effort does it take to maintain or enhance it cannot generally be answered easily. Questions covering the rate of new system introduction, the average size of a system, or what are the typical implementation languages are hard to determine at times.

Lines of Code represent a direct physical artifact of software construction. Each line must be written or generated and represents the functional base of any software application. However, LOC have a number of deficiencies as a software metric as mentioned. Thus mixed language comparisons are very difficult to conduct.

Backfiring was invented by Jones. This technique allows for an approximation in Function Points from LOC. The process for conducting the Backfiring was carried out using the following steps modified from the original technique of Jones [26].

1. Separate multi-language system data into unique rows per language
2. Sort all rows by language
3. Sum LOC per language
4. Assign complexity value per language
5. Assign language power per language
6. Calculate Function Points per language
7. Sum all Function Points per organization and across company

The steps requiring explanation are 4 - 7. Backfiring is calculated in the following manner:

$$B = C\left(\frac{S}{P}\right) \tag{1}$$

where

$B = Backfired\ Function\ Points,$

$C = Complexity,$

$s = LOC$

$p = Language\ Power.$

In traditional backfiring scenarios complexity ranges from 0.70 to 1.30 and is determined by a summation of problem, code, and data complexity. Both complexity and selected language powers are given in Table **1** below as a sample. Full details for many program languages can be found in Jones [28].

Table 1: Complexity Factor and Relative Language Power.

Language	Complexity		Common Languages	LOC per FP
COBOL, PL/1, Shell, 4GL	0.8		Assembly	320
C, SAS, Mixed	1.0		C	128
C/C++	1.1		COBOL	91
C++	1.2		C++	29
			SQL	12

Now we can replace the LOC based calculations of productivity with the same measures in FP without doing the full FP count which can take significant effort. What is interesting about this is that with the Backfiring technique if you have a LOC count or an estimate of a LOC count (perhaps from an analogous analysis) you can use a "pocket planner" provided by Jones to understand many factors of the project (see Table **2**). So for example you can see if we have a project estimated at 320 FPs this would take 55 staff months and about $275K to execute. There are many other predictions that can come from this database as well including defect rates. Since this calculation is fairly straight forward and a comparative database exists and is published this technique is very useful in calibrating estimates and process progress. This method remains one of the handiest tools in my tool box to this day.

Table 2: Function Point Pocket Planner.

Size in FP	20	80	320	1,280	10,240
Staff	1	1	5	20	200
Schedule	0.75	6.5	12	22	53
Effort SM	0.75	6.5	55	450	10.5K
FP/SM	25	12	6	3	1
Cost $	3,750	32.5K	275K	2.25M	52.5M
Potential Defects	30	200	1K	4.8K	51K
DRE%	98	95	88	82	72
Delivered Defects	1	10	120	860	14.3K

2.4.10.3.3. COCOMO

A method to triangulate your estimates is by using COCOMO (Constructive Cost Model). This model was develop by Boehm (1981) [27] and relies on an estimate of LOC. COMOMO is calibrated with hundreds of real projects but tends to produce estimates on the high end compared to Jones' tables and my own experience.

The primary assumption here is that LOC drives the cost of system development. If you disagree with this COCOMO is not the best model. This includes the entire lifecycle costs including management, feasibility, *etc.* This is calibrated to include all these other costs even though it is based on only LOC. This requires a full work break down structure and a means of knowing the source code to be produced.

COCOMO provides multiple levels of complexity to the estimate based on team structure and system complexity. The standard formula for COCOMO looks like this:

$$\textit{Effort Applied (E)} = a_b(LOC)^{b}{}_{b} \qquad \textbf{(2)}$$

The coefficients applied to the LOC estimate are supplied by Boehm. There are three levels to the model: basic, intermediate, and embedded depending on system complexity and approach. There is also a COCOMO II model with many more parameters but I have not applied this model. Instead, I recommend using the basic model of COCOMO if it suits your needs as it is much simpler and well proven.

In using any of these models or techniques iteration and approximation may be required. If for example we have a simple software architecture and a matching set of requirements we can derive LOC approximations. We may have a data base with several input processes, processing modules, and communications routines. We can approximate the LOC for each major component 1K for database interface, 3K for input processing, and 1K for computation. The total may be 9KLOC based on my experience, knowledge of the language, effort required for implementation of the requirements, and analogous systems. I can then use this in a model to estimate. You can also reverse engineer code from earlier systems. Importantly, estimation is an iterative estimate where we have a feasibility estimate followed by a commitment estimate. We do the best job we can up front and as we go along and collect data and see how the project is going we can recalibrate the estimate as long as the customer is willing to accept the change. One thing that I do is conduct up front estimates based on requirements or a box count from the architecture then as soon as implementation begins compare running code counts to the completed requirements.

In my experience these techniques can be highly accurate. The interesting thing is that these techniques are not widely understood by experienced professionals and often such professionals do not buy into the estimates because they do not understand the methods. But when the estimates turn out to be accurate they wonder how it was done. At the same time start-up I worked for when I explain these methods respond by saying they do not have time for these methods. The ironic thing is that better methods require time up front to understand and deploy but will in the end save time.

2.4.10.4. Complexity Metrics

Another major category of software metrics are static code analysis techniques like source code complexity. There are several metrics such as Halsted's Software Science based on how many operands, operators, and unique expressions are there in a particular piece of source code. I have not found these metrics to be very applicable to concrete project work. However, McCabe's Cyclomatic Complexity [29] has proved very useful. Complexity as per McCabe is highly applicable in unit testing by providing complexity measures for test case design. Cyclomatic Complexity is provided by the following formula:

$$V(G) = E - N + 2 \quad \textbf{(3)}$$

We will discuss the use of this measure in Chapter 7 for use in testing. Here E represents edges in the graph and N represents nodes. The meaning of this formula comes from graph theory. Essentially the complexity of a program can be derived from the edges and nodes contained within its structure. A program with a complexity of less than about 12 is considered maintainable and above 12 is hard to maintain. The complexity level also represents the exact number of unit tests required to exercise all paths within the program. This is a critical piece of information and represents a very practical tool in my tool box which we will touch on again later when we discuss testing methods. In this context it can be applied for quality control purposes in the upfront implementation phase of a project especially during spiral or incremental development. If any module or method on a class (a function assigned to an object) exceeds the guideline the method is a good target for refactoring or simplification of its design.

Taking complexity one step up we can also discuss system complexity as formulated here [30]:

$$Ct = St + Dt \quad \textbf{(4)}$$

Where

Ct = System complexity

St = Inter-module system complexity

Dt = Inter-module data complexity

The purpose of this metric is to allow for an understanding of the scope of a system and the interdependencies within the system that add to program complexity. Higher complexity values will indicate potential challenges in maintenance and quality. These two straight forward complexity measures are tools that I use often.

2.4.10.4. Reliability, Availability, and Performance

Quality is fundamental to software development and is very apparent to the customer but is quite difficult to measure. In Chapter 7 we will focus on reliability techniques and in Chapter 8 we will discuss Availability. To summarize, reliability is the probability of failure free operations and availability is the actual percentage of uptime in relation to planned up time. These metrics are core to understanding runtime quality of a system. Naturally, correctness is also a primary judgment of program quality. Producing a correct program is the key responsibility of the developer. If it is not correct it will not work properly and is not going to be used by the customer. Perhaps correctness comes second to reliability. If the program works correctly but fails often then it will not be used by customers. Thirdly, programs need to be available and performant. Without both, users will not make use of an application.

In terms of tools in this area we will discuss the Operational Profile [19] (which is a statistical model of system usage), reliability models, and support methods to achieve availability. From a performance standpoint metrics that are relevant include throughput and resource utilization measures (*i.e.*, percent of CPU in use). The field of performance engineering is rich and extensive. A good eBook on this topic is "Guerilla Capacity Planning" by Gunther [31]. The models presented there are useful in managing any system from a performance standpoint.

A basic tool I use in trying to understand performance on a system or a platform is the relationship between the resources on the platform and the thresholds or limits they must stay within (Cusick, 2003) [32]. The initial relationship of platform elements above was developed further into the following "*figure of merit*" measure called the Platform Performance Index (PPI):

$$\begin{array}{l}Platform\\ Performance\\ Index\end{array} = \sum_{i=1}^{i=n} \left(\frac{Actual\ Device\ Utilization}{ThresholdAmount} \right) \quad \textbf{(5)}$$

This measure assumes that the components of each device can be measured as a proportion of utilization as it relates to a stated threshold. The specific metrics and the calculations required to compute the number are discussed in Cusick [32]. The fundamental use of this figure of merit is in understanding the scope of the system under management and its overall performance. This is a dynamic metric which measures the end result of the process – how well does the system behave for the customer.

CONCLUSIONS

This chapter covers a lot of ground. From the definition of process to lifecycle models to metrics. Regardless of whether you might be developing an app for a mobile device in your basement or developing a large scale enterprise application under Agile or traditional process models a process will be involved – implicitly or explicitly. Understanding these processes is what this chapter has been about. What models have traditionally been defined and more importantly how to define your own new processes when that is necessary.

Further, we discussed process metrics. If you are not measuring the development process you are not in control of it. The point of metrics is that even though software activities are difficult to track, or are somewhat subjective, or leave certain factors unaccounted for, if we establish a pattern of how a particular piece of software behaves, or how a particular development organization is able to produce, in terms of productivity or error rate, if we have a method to measure that reliability over time, then if we introduce something like a new technology, or new software release, if the metric can indicate to us what the delta has been the metric has succeeded. This is the key point to applying software measures within a process - tracking changes to understand if we are improving.

REFERENCES

[1] Konrad, M., *et al.*, CMMI for Development®: Guidelines for Process Integration and Product Improvement, SEI Series, Addison-Wesley Professional, 2011.

[2] Taylor, S., Foundations of IT Service Management based on ITIL, ITSM Library, itSMF International, Van Haren Publishing, 2007.

[3] Weinberg, G., Quality Software Management: Vol.1 Systems Thinking, Dorset House, 1992.

[4] Humphrey, W., A Discipline for Software Engineering, Addison-Wesley, Reading, MA, 1995.
[5] *ibid.*
[6] Aho, A., Conversations with the author, 1997.
[7] Brownlie, R., *et al.*, "*Tools for Software Process Engineering* ", Bell Labs Technical Journal, Winter 1997, pp. 130-143.
[8] Cusick, J., "*A Pattern-Rich Process Definition Environment*", TechNote Pre-pendium, OOPSLA`98, Vancouver, Canada, October, 1998.
[9] Riddle, William E., "*Integrated Information and Process Modeling and Analysis*", 4th International Conference on Applications of Software Measurement, Orlando, FL, November, 1993.
[10] Frese, R., & Sauter, V., Project Success and Failure: What is Success, What is Failure, and How Can You Improve your Odds for Success?, December 16, 2003, viewed 11/5/2011, http://www.umsl.edu/~sauterv/analysis /6840_f03_papers/frese/.
[11] Demarco, T., & Lister, T., Peopleware, Dorset House, 1987.
[12] Cusick, J., Software Engineering Student Guide, Edition 2, Columbia University Division of Special Programs, New York City, September 1995.
[13] Larman, C., & Basili, V., Iterative and Incremental Development: A Brief History, vol. 36, no. 6, pp. 47-56, 2003.
[14] Boehm, B., Software Engineering Economics, Prentice-Hall, Engelwood Cliffs, NJ, 1981.
[15] DeGrace, P., & Stahl, L., Wicked Problems & Righteous Solutions: A Catalogue of Modern S.E. Paradigms, Prentice-Hall, Englewood Cliffs, NJ, 1990.
[16] Jensen, R., Software Engineering, Prentice Hall, Engelwood Cliffs, NJ, 1979.
[17] Brooks, F., The Mythical Man-Month: Essays on Software Engineering, Addison-Wesley, Reading, MA, 1975.
[18] Booch., G., "The Microsoft Effect", Object Magazine, SIGS Publications, Inc., October, 1995.
[19] Musa, J. D., "*Operational Profiles in Software-Reliability Engineering* ", IEEE Software, March 1993.
[20] Cusick, J., & Fine, M., "*Guiding Reengineering with the Operational Profile* ", ISSRE 97 Case Studies, IEEE Computer Society Chapter 1, pp 15-25, Los Alamitos, CA, 1997.
[21] December, J., & Ginsburg, M., HTML & CGI Unleashed, Sams Publishing, Indianapolis, IN, 1995.
[22] Gildersleeve, H. N., & Landen T. R., System Design for Computer Applications, John Wiley & Sons, Inc, 1967.
[23] Page-Jones, Meilir, The Practical Guide to Structured Systems Design, Yourdon Press, 1988.
[24] Rumbaugh, J., *et al.*, Object-Oriented Modeling and Design, Prentice Hall, 1991.
[25] Card, D., & Glass, R., Measuring Sorfware Design Quality, Prentice Hall, NJ, 1990.
[26] Basili, V., *et al.*, "*Goal Question Metric Approach*", Encyclopedia of Software Engineering, pp. 528-532, John Wiley & Sons, Inc., 1994.
[27] Albrecht, A., "Measuring Application Development Productivity", Proceedings of the Joint SHARE GUIDE and IBM Application Development Symposium, October, 1979.
[28] Jones, C., Applied Software Measurement: Assuring Productivity and Quality, McGraw Hill, New York, 1991.

[29] McCabe, T., "*A Complexity Measure*". IEEE Transactions on Software Engineering, pp. 308–320, December, 1976.

[30] Kearney, J., *et al.*, *Software Complexity Measurement*, Communications of the ACM, November 1986, Vol 29, No 11.

[31] Gunther, N., Guerilla Capacity Planning, Springer, 2007.

[32] Cusick, J., & Welch, T., "*Developing and Applying a Distributed Systems Performance Approach for a Web Platform*", 30th International Conference for the Resource Management and Performance Evaluation of Computing Systems, Las Vegas, NV, December 10, 2004.

Send Orders of Reprints at bspsaif@emirates.net.ae

Durable Ideas in Software Engineering, 2013, 74-103

CHAPTER 3

Project Planning, Risk and Management

"In preparing for battle I have always found that plans are useless, but planning is indispensable".

Eisenhower [1]

Abstract: Discussion of project management, risk management, and planning of projects. Additional focus on management topics including organizing, staffing, leading, and controlling IT teams. A conceptual model for project management is presented and discussed. Details of project planning, project planning templates, and tracking methods are presented. A focus on scheduling and estimating is also included.

Keywords: Project management, project estimation, scheduling, organization, staffing, project plans, project phases, quality measures, work environments.

3.1. INTRODUCTION

In building software it may seem counter intuitive that planning is a topic that should come early and take up a significant focus. However, most software is constructed in the context of a project as are many related IT functions like support activities, technical transformations, and analysis activities. Thus, planning in general is a key topic area and approaches to planning represent a core tool in my toolbox. In addition, risk management plays a key role and we will spend time on this discipline also. Finally, management of and by itself is important to anyone engaged in a software project as there will be a hierarchy of staff and management even at the smallest companies and the smallest of projects. Managing well is a key to successful software development in the short and especially in the long run. I will attempt to summarize some of the guidance I have been given in learning how to manage and transfer some of my own observations on this topic as it relates to running projects of many types. This chapter will tie together the processes discussed in the previous chapter along with some additional focus on applying metrics and will illuminate the relationship between project management and management itself.

Any project can be difficult to pull off. Think about projects that you have organized and run. You may have remodeled your kitchen or bath, refinished an

James J. Cusick

old piece of furniture, or restored an antique car. Each of these projects have a beginning a middle and an end. There are perceptions about the project prior to starting and there are the roadblocks you might face in the middle and steps you have taken to get around them. I once refinished an old desk from approximately the 1930s. I found out that the 2 ½ inch centers of the drawer handles were very rare and difficult to replace. What I thought would be a simple task of buying 4 drawer handles turned into a protracted hunt for materials lasting weeks. When remodeling a bathroom we had finished everything but when the town inspector came by he did not approve the wiring and we ended up having to tear open the wall, run a dedicated circuit with a GFCI outlet to the basement, and replacing and upgrading the entire electrical panel which cost thousands of dollars and delayed the completion of the project.

These are all real world and relatable experiences. You will have your own such stories. In software development the same kinds of unpredictable events can occur. That is why planning is so vital. One must plan in sufficient detail up front but remain agile and adaptable throughout the project by expecting and responding to changing circumstances. This does not remove the need for up front planning. It also does not eliminate the need for a defined process. Actually, a defined process (whether Agile or not) will accommodate changes in a more balanced manner.

In software development there may be many kinds of projects. There can be small projects or massive projects or anywhere in between. Some projects are based on new or bleeding edge technology, some may call for new hardware to be deployed, and some may call for extensive design efforts breaking the mold or prior software capabilities. Managing these varying projects, meeting objectives, and delighting customers is what everyone's goals should be. More formally projects can be considered as any individual or collaborative effort to attain a specific aim.

3.1.1. Project Planning

In Rock-n-Roll there is a famous lyric:

> *"You can't always get what you want,*

but if you try sometimes,

you just might find,

you get what you need". (Rolling Stones) [2]

For project managers in software engineering getting a portion of what you need is normally the case. The project manager usually must choose between what they would ideally prefer and what is possible to achieve. This is known in engineering circles as "The Triple Constraint" (Fig. **1**). The Triple Constraint [3] reflects the reality that in striving to deliver a system a development team will be bound by three inter-related factors: time, cost, and features.

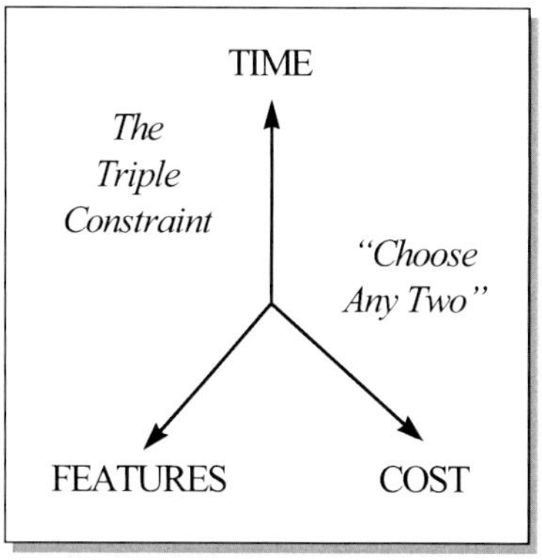

Figure 1: The Triple Constraint.

The oft heard comment is that you have to pick two of these three factors to optimize. You cannot have it all. A project may deliver on time and within budget but typically this will require skimping on features. Or the project may deliver tons of functionality within the boundaries of the deadline but will require additional staff costs. The project manager must find a way to balance these competing demands.

The work required to produce industrial grade software often exceeds the capacity of one individual. In order to manage this work projects are created to decompose and execute the necessary tasks of creating software. Projects are one of the fundamental constructs in managing software development. What is a Project? Projects have specific goals, constraints, and discrete time boundaries. In developing software, projects typically produced include applications, systems, documents, or platforms as outputs. More specific features of projects are discussed below. But first, let us discuss the context of a project in terms of the model shown in Fig. **2**.

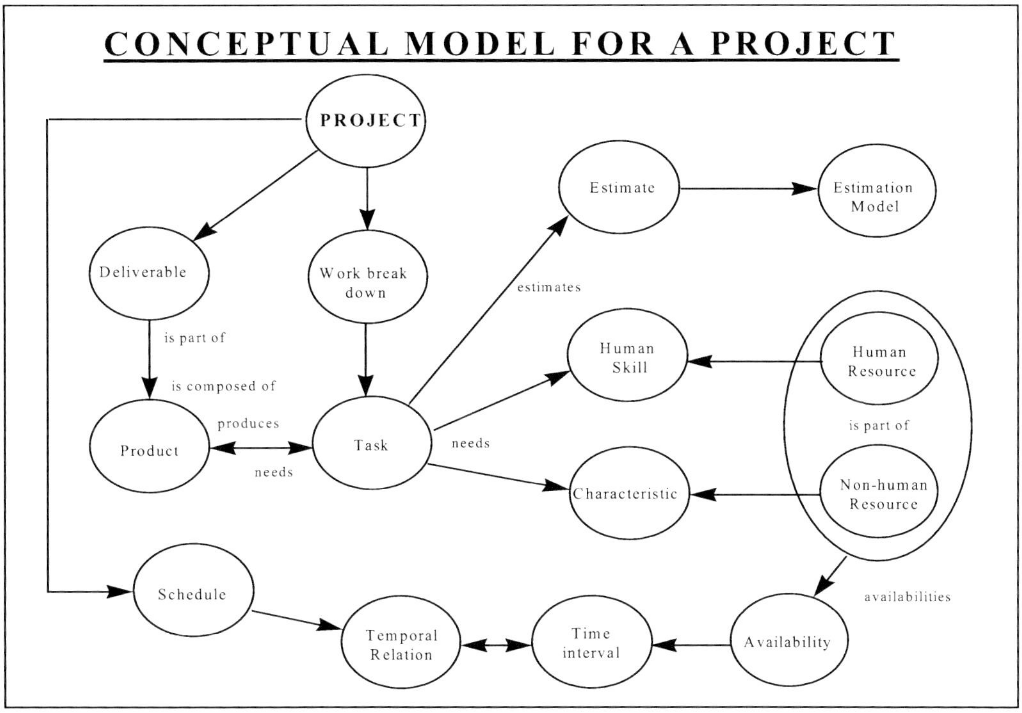

Figure 2: A Model of What a Project Looks Like [4].

This model can be read from the project node downward. Thus projects are made up of deliverables which are comprised of products. These products are created by work tasks -that can be organized in a work-breakdown structure. Each task must be estimated using estimation techniques and each task requires certain resources. The resources for each task may be human skills and/or technical equipment or other resources (*e.g.*, products, services, financing). Based on the list of required resources and their availability, a schedule can be developed using the estimations for each required resource.

This brief overview of the dynamics of a project will provide the starting point for a detailed description of each node in this model. In this chapter we will focus on the structure of development management, project planning, team organization, estimation, and scheduling. To discuss estimation will require the review of software metrics which we began in Chapter 2 regarding process metrics.

3.1.2. Development Management Tasks & Techniques

Software development is normally conducted in the context of a larger organization. The organization may be a commercial software vendor, a hardware manufacturer, a government agency, or any number of corporations requiring software development for business operations. Each of these organizations will have a management structure tuned to their organizational goals whether it is profit, research, or public service. These goals will shape the manner in which software development is conducted and how projects are formed, funded, and executed. We will briefly discuss some of the general management context which creates software development projects.

3.1.3. Software Technology Management

At the highest level management is concerned with several key functions including [5]:

1. Planning - objectives, forecasting, decision making
2. Organizing - delegation, decentralization, theory
3. Staffing - Recruitment, training, appraisal, career development
4. Leadership - motivation, communication
5. Controlling - budgeting, IT, operations

Each of these issues are reflected at the organizational level, such as a corporation, and at the subordinate organization level, such as the IT or R&D departments of a corporation. The planning function at the corporate level will concentrate on strategic issues which will drive the tactical projects of the development project. Other high level management functions such as budgeting for development will have a significant impact on engineering efforts.

Roughly speaking, the technology development leadership in an organization will be concerned with how IT supports the needs of the business and the twin issues of setting strategy and monitoring costs. For the technical department charged with carrying out the corporate technology strategy the primary concerns are how to translate the stated needs into concrete technical solutions and how to coordinate this transformation into executable tactics or projects. For project managers which are oftentimes handed a project which is still in a fuzzy state of definition the concerns will center on clarification of the goals of the project, securing adequate funding and staffing, and then developing the low-level plans and sub-projects to fulfill the strategic vision.

3.1.4. The Role of IT Management in Software Engineering

The responsibilities of IT management in setting strategy and overseeing the translation of business needs into operational systems merits some discussion as it relates to the formation of projects requiring software engineering expertise. Most corporate projects (or products) today require systems and software development. These systems may support sales initiatives, customer service, telemarketing, or product manufacturing. The management activities which are required to organize and plan for these projects starts with establishing fundamental roles.

The fundamental roles of software or technology management departments include:

- Establish & document corporate applications
- Establish & document corporate information requirements
- Define & cost IT projects to meet requirements
- Plan & manage IT projects in development and operation
- Advise users of systems

Once these roles are established technical direction is developed using strategic planning. Strategic planning will precede the creation of projects that will execute on the direction. Strategic planning is conducted using the several steps targeting strategic analysis, systems appraisal, and the creation of a technical evolution plan.

Long range planning steps include:

1. Planning kick-off
2. Application definition
3. Data area definition
4. Current assessment
5. Document situation
6. Response and solution
7. Prioritization
8. Recommendations
9. Presentation of results

In recent positions as Director of IT I have used this type of strategic planning framework effectively to map out the needs of the broader customer organization, technical trends, opportunities, and challenges using a SWOT method (Strengths, Weaknesses, Opportunities, and Threat matrix). The effort spent on these strategic planning exercises has paid off handsomely in team development, work focus, alignment of tasks, and overall governance capabilities for the organization. Working through a shared framework of action has also allowed for a clear enunciation of the services and projects offered or planned by the organization.

The outputs of this process include:

1. Scope/charter
2. Application/architecture structure

3. Data/information structure
4. Systems relationships
5. Requirements
6. Action plan

With an action plan in place new projects can be established to achieve the goals uncovered in the high level requirements for the organization. This might call for the development of all new products, systems, and software. It may require the consolidation of several systems to simplify customer service. No matter what the recommendation, the technical organization must now translate these requirements into functioning projects that can fulfill the needs of the business. To do this the will need to overcome the quandary of the Triple Constraint and the other reefs and shoals of software development.

3.1.5. Technical Management Problems

Prior to discussing the techniques of project management in depth it is important to consider some of the realities of software development. Studies indicate that between 1/4th to 1/3rd of all large projects are canceled. Some researchers argue that the root cause for these failures is not technological. Programming languages and algorithms are not the source of these failures. Instead sociological problems often related to communication tend to undermine many projects [6]. In a study at AT&T researchers reviewed technical review findings for hundreds of projects and found that half suffered from project management issues [7]. For the would-be development team, it is vital to consider the importance of good planning with frequent and frank communication.

Another important element of software development management that bears pointing out is that the nature of software development, even if governed by solid software engineering practice, is more akin to the creative work of an architect than to the repetitive work of a production line. Unfortunately, most U.S. management texts and approaches tend to rest heavily on production oriented methods and reward systems which in effect run counter to the required behavior of successful software development. Whereas in production the steady state is optimized, in software or technology development new approaches to product creation must always be sought. Naturally, with a mature, optimizing, process these two forces can be marshaled productively. However, it is worth a caution that the nature of software development calls for a non-traditional management style.

Finally, the true purpose of management is to maximize the useful output of any process and to limit wastefulness or friction (see Fig. **3**) [8]. The software engineering manager must always look for ways to smooth out the process they are managing and strive to support their project team in achieving to their best ability [9]. To do this a clear understanding of projects and project management techniques are required.

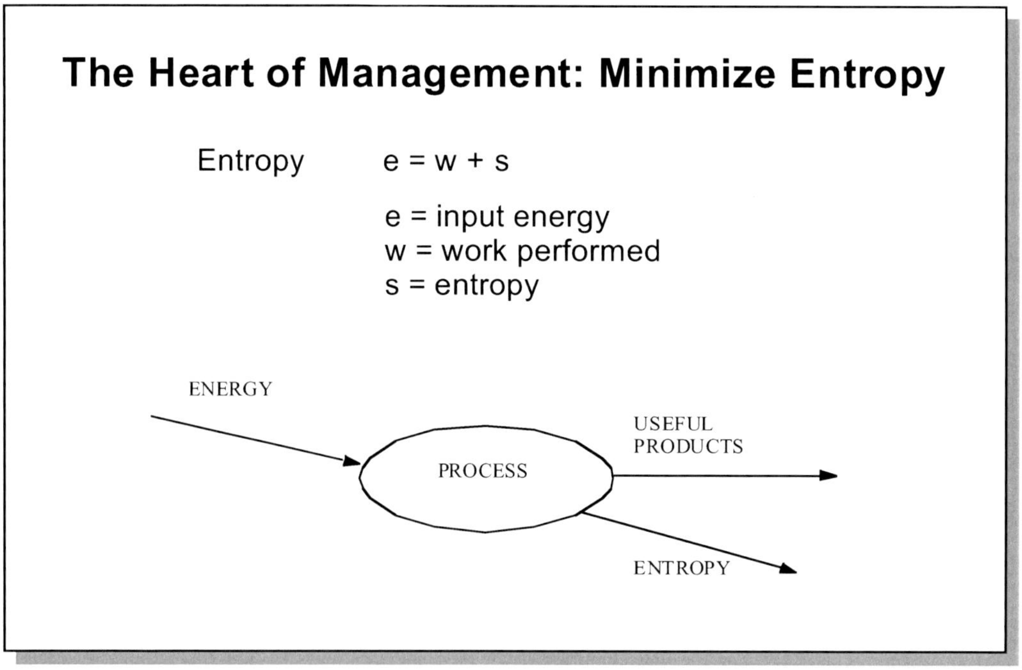

Figure 3: The Essence of Entropy in Projects.

3.1.6. Project Planning & Execution

Projects can be formed to pursue goals of many kinds. For software engineers the project is the typical working context. Projects have goals and constraints and are normally bounded by a discrete time interval. Often, software development projects are formed to produce a new system or to port, modify, or repair an existing system. Systems, in contrast to projects, have their own goals, users, and lifecycles. Systems and software products are typically the output of one or more projects.

3.1.7. Projects

What is a Project?

Projects have specific goals, constraints, and discrete time boundaries. As mentioned above, development projects can produce applications, systems, documents, or platforms as outputs. More specific features of projects are discussed below.

The project cast, the members of a project, can include:

- Management
- User Management
- Working Level Users
- Peer System Project Teams
- Vendors
- Internal Subcontractors
- Test Teams
- Quality Assurance Auditors
- Support Groups
- Consultants

The project activities, the activities of a project, can include:

- Presentations

- Reviews
- Interviews
- Interface negotiations
- Subcontracting
- Product delivery
- Memos, phone calls, meetings

Project Kick-Off

When beginning a project one must take into account numerous factors relating to the goals of the project, the strategy and resources to attain those goals, and the time it will require to complete. On top of this is the task of solving the technical problems in between.

Some starting points [10]:

- Check the contract carefully if there is one
- Prepare some preliminary diagrams quickly to visualize the potential system and project tasks
- Spend time with the customer(s) and develop good working relationships
- Anticipate that requirements will continue to appear during the project not just once up front
- Get something working as soon as possible and keep it working (this is a main plank of Agile methodologies)
- The activities that will need most attention include:
- Needs Identification - what does project/system need to produce/do?

- Planning - how can the project meet its goals
- Requirements Definition - capture, represent, review, agree on requirements
- Estimates - what will it take to meet the requirements (staff, time, resources)
- Schedule - when can it be done, when must it be done
- Closure – projects do come to an end, need to close out all activities

3.1.7.1. Preparing Techniques

For all the activities of the project make sure you have a sound method. No matter what you need to do in running a software project, in general, other people have been there and done it before. Typically, they have also written it down if it worked. Seek out proven methods for each important step in the project such as: Requirements, Design, Coding, Testing, Documentation. If you plan to follow a specific process such as an in-house process, review it for applicability. Perhaps some parts may be more valuable than other parts. Some areas may need adjustment. As discussed earlier, every problem needs a method to resolve it and the combination of methods (or procedures/practices) becomes a process. Such a collection might already be available in the form of a process or within the context of an Agile model you might have to document it as you go along. In either case understanding the problems you are facing and solving them effectively may be just as important as solving the customer problem in the form of working software as not doing so could prevent success.

3.1.7.2. Project Planning

Planning a project requires careful consideration of many factors. To start off with one must:

- Determine user needs
- Select a technical approach

- Analyze requirements
- Establish design to meet goals within constraints (cost/schedule/operating environment/features)
- Develop technical infrastructure for system development
- Manage group

Once these items are begun the ongoing needs of the project begin to dominate, including typical management challenges like:

- Providing rewards
- Running interference to protect developers
- Selling project to funders and others
- Keeping project on track
- Resolving problems fast
- Showing commitment to project
- Dealing with people problems
- Allowing for time-off

3.1.7.3. A Project Plan Outline

To get the project up and running, use the following template as a guide to building a project plan:

- Project Overview
- Project Scope
- Project Objectives

- Description of System
- Project Costs
- Project Returns and Benefits
- Project Risk Assessment
- Assumptions and Constraints
- Project Development Schedule
- Project Development Strategy & Methodology
- Project Quality Plan
- Test Plan
- Documentation Plan
- Configuration Management Plan
- Staffing and Organization
- Training Plan

Within an Agile context this may not all be done up front. Instead, as the project proceeds it will determine which of these artifacts are necessary to produce.

3.1.7.4. Scheduling for Software Development

If the time leg of the Triple Constraint has already been fixed with an end-date by the customer or by management scheduling can be almost academic if not problematic in realization. You look at the calendar and work backwards from the delivery date marking off the major milestones. If the project must deliver in August and it is March now that means you need to conduct testing in July, coding in May and June, and requirements and design immediately. While this situation seems farcical it is too often the case. In fact, scheduling software projects has always been difficult:

> *"One of the more serious - and more commonly encountered - data processing and systems management problems has been in setting up realistic schedules and project completion dates. In many data processing programs, this difficulty can be traced to inability, early in the work, to properly define all the elements of the program and the systems design effort required to put the program into operation".*
>
> *Gallagher, 1961 [11]*

This inability to define all the elements of a program is still common today. If we assume that we are not going to be unilaterally handed a ship date for our project there are some techniques we can use to rationally schedule projects and also to combat the problems Gallagher and others have commented on in the past. Fortunately, with the rise of Agile methods, a focus on incremental scheduling has emerged. This allows for time boxed development of feature sets. Such an approach reduces the waterfall negatives and big bang deliveries.

3.1.7.5. Scheduling Basics

In principle there is nothing complicated about scheduling a project. Keeping it ON schedule is the hard part. To conduct scheduling consider the following steps:

1. Identify work items
2. Break work into phases
3. Divide work into tasks and activities
4. Identify relationships between tasks
5. Estimate the time each task will take

Projects normally deliver something, for example software, documents, or hardware. To create any deliverable will require someone to carry out a task. They will either have to create, copy, borrow, or otherwise manufacture the deliverable and its components. All the steps to do this must be determined up front and estimated. With the advent of Agile methods this approach is modified by the creation of increments. Thus the planning is done in stages along with the development of the code base and working artifacts. Instead of planning lock, stock, and barrel for everything, the planning is done step-wise.

3.1.7.6. Work Breakdown Structure

If a traditional schedule is required, try breaking up your project into work phases and steps before estimating. Good Schedules are related to good designs. A well drawn architecture helps in planning its construction. A highly modular design makes development easier and produces more reliable software. We will discuss architecture and design in the chapter 5.

3.1.8. Basic Planning Tools

When it comes to planning tools there are some basics that need mentioning. The first is the trusty Gantt chart (named after its inventor). This is simply a histogram which reflects tasks in horizontal orientation (see Fig. **4**). The chart can also show relationships and dependencies between tasks. This same information can also be reflected in a PERT chart. While I have seen very few real world applications of the PERT chart its concepts are embedded in practical project planning and the Gantt chart. PERT analysis represents each activity in a project as a bubble which includes the predecessor time and the time in the task. Using this method the "critical path" or the longest path through the chart can be determined. It is this path that can then be optimized. For example, if the path through implementation (or coding) is the longest path then more developers might be added or the task can be further broken down into smaller pieces of work until it is no longer the longest path. In the simplest projects a task list without a chart might suffice. However, for any project of size analysis of the work required will usually call for a graphical representation of the work. Planning tools are now available to support the creation of these plans.

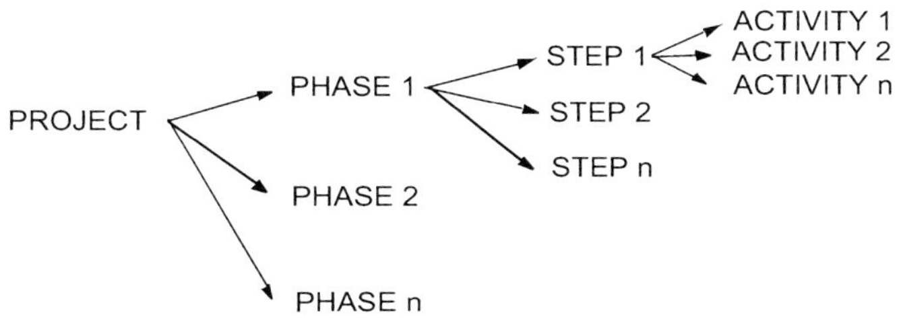

Figure 4: Project Task Decomposition.

3.1.8.1. Estimation

Once the tasks of a project are known, the tasks need estimating. In Chapter 2 we discussed process metrics that lead into estimation models. Estimation is key to any project. This is true of any lifecycle model including Agile techniques. To conduct an estimate there are several tried and true methods including expert analysis, metrical analysis, heuristics, historical comparison, and more as introduced in Chapter 2. Selecting among these methods is sometimes easy as one may have no other choice if only one method is available. However, whenever possible it is useful to employ more than one technique. As a tool, I view estimation techniques as a critical one.

The traditional estimation process for software projects runs as follows [12]:

1. Establish Objectives
2. Plan for Required Data and Resources
3. Pin Down Software Requirements
4. Work out as much Detail as Feasible
5. Use Several Independent Techniques and Sources
6. Compare and Iterate Estimates
7. Follow-up

Fundamental estimation approaches were identified as follows [13]:

- Algorithmic Models: for example COCOMO
- Expert Judgment: find someone who seems to know a lot
- Analogy: compare effort used to build similar existing system
- Parkinson: cynical view that work expands to fill a vacuum
- Price to Win: find out the lowest bid and beat it

- Top Down: analyze requirements to the lowest level and not estimated effort
- Bottom-up: individuals estimate their parts and then sum it up

3.1.8.2. Estimation approximations

The Brooks Classic [14]:

- 1/3 Planning
- 1/6 Coding
- 1/4 Component Test
- 1/4 System Test

This method was described by Brooks decades ago and still is useful as a guide.

Boddie on Bottom-Up [15]:

Estimate for each module:

- 1 day easy
- 3 days moderate difficulty
- 6 days difficult
- Sleep on the estimate, repeat, and compare.

Project Impacts of Under-Estimation

About 50% of all software projects are delivered over budget and late. If you get into such a state remember:

Options when late [16]:

1. Reduce requirements

2. Push out date

3. Cancel project

NON-Options when late:

- Add more staff (project will become more delayed)

- Stir-up motivation (people are already working hard)

A useful way of looking at estimation is also to keep in mind that estimates, like requirements, may become more accurate as time progresses. Steve McConnel introduces that idea of the "cone of uncertainty" around estimates (see Fig. **5**). In this approach estimates become more accurate as the project proceeds. The earlier in the project the less accurate the estimate. It can swing from too conservative to too aggressive. It is only with sufficient detail available that an accurate estimate can become available.

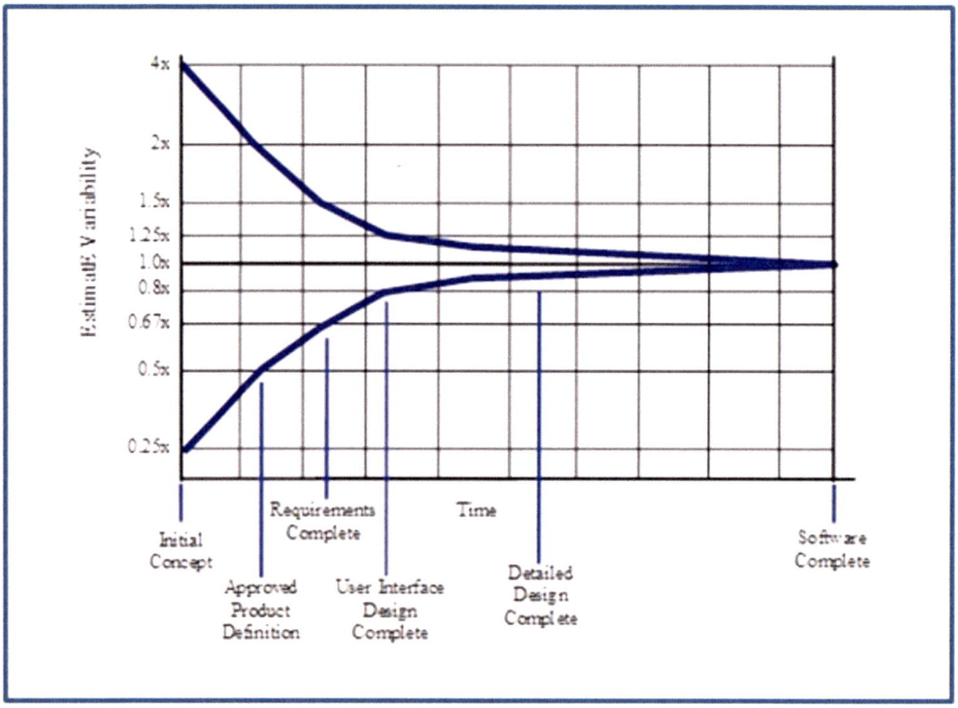

Figure 5: McConnell's Cone of Uncertainty [17].

3.1.8.3. COCOMO for Estimation

In Chapter 2 we introduced COCOMO (COntructive COst MOdel) [18] which was developed by Barry Boehm of USC. A new version, COCOMO II, is also available. COCOMO is an empirical LOC based algorithmic estimation model as previously discussed. The model can be used to predict and control software projects.

3.1.8.3.1. COCOMO Assumptions

The primary cost driver in software development is newly developed source instructions as assumed in COCOMO. COCOMO covers the complete life cycle costs of a project and you must have a detailed work breakdown structure to conduct estimate (Fig. **6**). This will include all labor (even management). For planning - one month equals 152 hours. Also, project is run with sensible management practices and stable requirements.

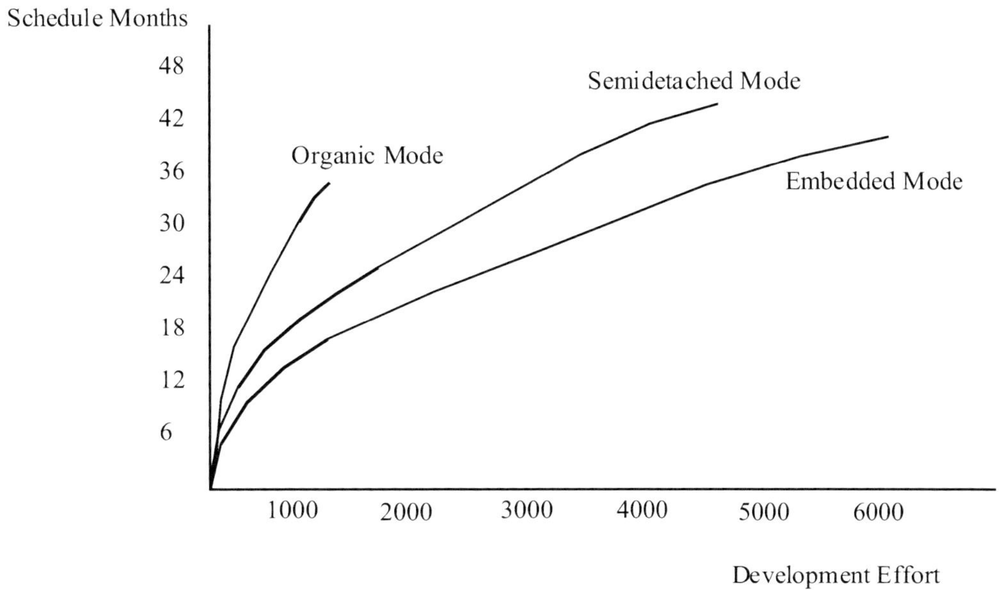

Figure 6: COCOMO Estimation Models.

3.1.8.3.2. A COCOMO Example

A project of medium complexity with 33.3KLOC would be computed to need 152 staff months to complete:

AN EXAMPLE:

$$E = ab(KLOC)\ exp(bb) \tag{6}$$

$$= 3.0(KLOC)\ exp(1.12)$$

$$= 3.0(33.3)1.12$$

$$= 152\ Staff\ Months$$

COMOMO is calibrated with hundreds of real projects but tends to produce estimates on the high end compared to the Function Point tables we will cover and my own experience.

Notice that 500 KLOC systems should not be built in organic mode. That is, a small team of loosely organized people that are not familiar with standardized development techniques should not be trying to build a large scale system. But a smaller application would be fine.

On large systems - communication overhead, management overhead, and complexity, are factors which drive down productivity. It is not that the team has suddenly turned into negativists but that there is more to do and more things to consider to make large scale applications work. Documentation requirements are much higher under military system development approaches and similar standards. This does not really add to delivered software functionality. But on the other hand it will typically drive quality up. The standard techniques or following ISO processes will not just add to paperwork but should improve software quality. However, evidence for this is contradictory. Some projects use heavy weight processes and produce reams of documentation but software quality is poor. This has been one reason that has driven the adoption of Agile methods.

Once you apply these metrics based methods with some basic data collection efforts, a reference eBook or database, and a calculator or spreadsheet you can generate estimates and later record observed data to build your own localized expert decision support data. This will give you time bounded and reasonable estimates.

Similar to using COCOMO, we can use Function Points as introduced in Chapter 2. With Function Points we can estimate the size of an application by using the planned number of screens, inputs, outputs, and interfaces. With that we can use baseline data to predict the effort. Jones [19] has provided a "pocket planner" for just this purpose. It can tell you that for a project of a certain size you may need 5 people, 12 calendar months, 55 staff months, at a rate of 6 FP per staff months, which will cost $250K and contain 1K potential defects, delivered with 88% of the defects removed. Using such a planning guide (as introduced in Chapter 2) has been useful to me in the past in real world project scenarios. I view this method as a particularly useful tool.

3.1.9. Feasibility & Risk Analysis

For any project, feasibility is an important topic and for all projects risks are a given. Feasibility in this instance means the "life-cycle" feasibility of the project and especially its superiority to other alternatives. We need to focus on the economic, technical, and legal issues plus the alternative solutions. A typical question is "can we build system-X with our team?"

This can be hard to answer early in the lifecycle since we are often not sure of the requirements yet. How can you conduct feasibility without complete requirements? Normally, you can identify the risks which may have the biggest impact and the highest probability of occurrence and try to understand how to minimize these. In actuality, following proper analysis, design, and test processes drive these risks down. Agile methods in and of themselves reduce risk and prove out feasibility due to the incrementalism involved. That is, by building out the system in steps the overall lifecycle risk is reduced.

3.1.10. Risk Management

For any method, you have to identify the right risks in order to protect the project. Some risks you can manage and some you cannot manage. For example, few software vendors have control over the major operating systems and their availability or popularity. They have to decide which platforms to develop for but really have no way to manage the risk that the OS they decide on will return the most benefit to them. In confronting the situation we look at the risks and try to decide upon the course to take. The risks are documented and monitored. In such cases, and many others, it is not the risk that is managed but the impacts.

The questions to ask include: what are the relevant risks we are facing, what is our exposure and likelihood of occurrence, and what is the level of risk that we want to take. Typically, software projects have large risks in their schedule. Either too little time is planned for or slips to the project begin to imperil the chances of success. Most risk in software is either in failure of delivery or failure of operations. Proving the required software which works are typically the failure points.

The mitigation of risk is based on the understanding of the risks being faced and then balancing them with proven engineering techniques.

Formal risk analysis uses failure analysis methods to try to provide an optimal level of risk where the cost of potential loss is low and also the cost of aversion is low. You do not want to spend a lot of money on protecting against a project risk for a low probability risk. But you would consider spending some extra money to avert the introduction of too many defects in your delivered software product, or being late on the delivery commitment. Here you many apply resources or increase resource, invest in tools for better analysis support, new computing equipment for faster compile times, more people for testing, or more funding for education and process. Investing in these areas properly brings down the potential loss from the risk of delivering late, or delivering a system with a high failure rate. This is how we combat risk.

> *Risk, more formally, is: "Chance of injury, damage, or loss including the value of the loss. In software, risk generally stems from the probability of failure.*

Risk areas include:

- Project plans have risk factors including the wrong team, bad relationships with product team, *etc.*
- Functional Risk - customer is expecting something which cannot be built or we are expecting too much from our design.
- Political Risk - sinks many projects, social issues, stonewalling, management never funds project, *etc.*

- Technical Risk - mistakes, inappropriate platform selection, subcontractor failure, *etc.*

- Financal Risk – poor controls on the project leading to overspending or misallocation of funds.

- Systemic Risk - AT&T inventing microwave telecommunications and then MCI using it to become its major competitor.

We have already covered project issues - now we will present concrete methods to bring these risk levels down - the risks in the technical and functional areas include specifications, design, and implementation. Also, testing is a source of risk based on how substantial the test approach is. To manage project risks we can use standard project planning techniques. For functional/technical risks we need to understand tech and do not charge into unknown territory.

In terms of tools from my virtual tool box, when it comes to risk a simple tool which is very effective is the act of questioning. At each step of the project the question is asked, what risks are we running and how can we minimize them. Or, are the risks so small that we can afford to take them since the impacts are also small. This form of active questioning serves a strong purpose in ferreting out risks and adequately compartmentalizing them.

As an example, during implementation the translation from design to a target programming language has many inherent risks. You can lose information, you can be imprecise or wrong in your translation. You can also have domain errors. The domain is the area being automated or solved. If the implementor is not aware of the domain the system may be compromised. To build a banking support system the programmer must understand the concept of debits and credits as well as the nuances of the programming environment. These risks can be averted through such techniques as abstraction, functional decomposition, standard design methods, reviews, testing, and external verification.

The mitigation of risk is based on the understanding of the risks being faced and then balancing them with proven engineering techniques (see Fig. **7**).

1. Risk Identification: What can go wrong?

2. Risk Measurement: What is the consequence?

3. Risk Evaluation: Prioritization of risk?

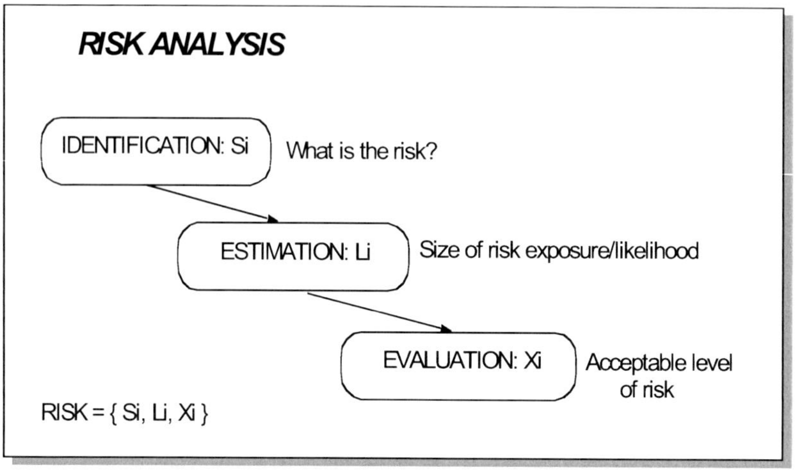

Figure 7: Risk and Risk Analysis in the Lifecycle [20].

Formal risk analysis uses failure analysis methods try to provide an optimal level of risk where our cost of potential loss is low and also the cost of aversion is low. Investing in these areas properly brings down the potential loss from the risk of delivering late, or delivering a system with a high failure rate. This is how we combat risk … the cost of aversion *vs.* the cost of loss --- seek the optimal balance (Fig. **8**).

As an example: what would be the perfect environmental system for your workspace, how much will you pay to prevent injuries or illness? You may but new chairs and upgrade lighting but not replace the entire air-flow system with expensive filtration materials.

3.1.11. Organizing for Software Development

Depending upon the organization, a project manager may play the role of manager or there may be a resource manager in a matrix role aside from the project manager. In either case, the engineering staff will be led by the project or program manager and perhaps by a technical manager or director. It is imperative that the leadership provided by these individuals is effective. This leadership is both of a technical nature and an organizational nature. Specifically, when decisions are needed around technical direction there is a protocol as to how those decisions are made and by whom. Also, the team structure and its norms are established in part by the leader. The team itself will also contribute to this. As a set of tools in my tool box, those around leadership, management, and communication are critical. Years ago I read the now classic Peopleware by Lister and Demarco. In that eBook three basic principles to team leadership were put forth:

1. Get the right people
2. Make the happy
3. Turn them loose

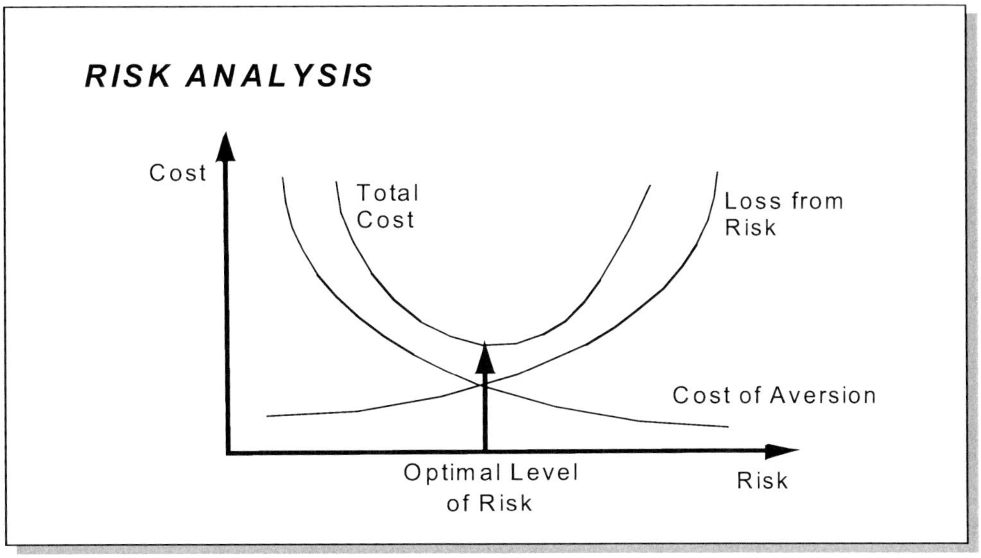

Figure 8: Understanding the Optimal Level of Risk to a Project [21].

I believe these ideas in all their simplicity works wonders. I have seen organizations struggle because they held onto people who were not committed to the success of the team or despite strong technical skills were not effective or interested in the work. There is nothing that kills morale quicker than such an individual on the team. In contrast, when everyone on the team is enthused – from the leader down – then great things can happen. There is a saying that teams move at the pace of their leader. I believe this to be true and so a key tool is enthusiasm and the effective communication of that enthusiasm.

When it comes to making people happy, it is important to get the "hygiene" factors right, like pay and working conditions but those are the minimum requirements. To really make people happy you have to invest them with responsibility, opportunities for achievement, and true recognition and rewards. Not everyone is motivated by the same rewards so you have to determine what is important to the individuals. In many cases, consensus building or inclusive decision making is a key tool to making people happy. When people feel like they are part of the solution they will buy into it more.

The final step of setting people loose can be difficult for some managers especially those that fall into the micro management camp. This has never been my downfall; I have always erred on the side of providing too much discretion to the team. I set a direction, a vision, and then encourage people to run with it. It is sometimes difficult to watch because people may take a different course or at least not a straight line but they are the owners of their work and a better result will be achieved in this manner (or so I have observed).

No Programmer is an island.

Lister and Demarco [22] also provide additional tips on what you need to do to keep a team together and keep it healthy:

- Foster a cult of quality

- Provide lots of satisfying closure
- Provide a sense of eliteness (esprit de corps)
- Allow and encourage heterogeneity
- Preserve and protect successful teams
- Provide strategic not tactical direction

Environmental conditions enabling flow or the intellectual grove of the knowledge worker which must be developed also plays a part in keeping people happy and achieving higher levels of productivity. Concentrating on your work and producing good software artifacts is difficult to attain in a busy office with interruptions, ringing phones, *etc.* To judge a work space consider yourself as a potential employee and evaluate the space where you would sit. Is it a private work space? Shared? Private offices? As a manager you cannot always control the space conditions within a company and have to make do. You can always adjust by allowing for think time, reading time, or creating one shared quite space or small library. The jobs are not production oriented they are problem solving jobs. It is ok to allow engineers to lay back in order to solve problems but not to lay back all the time. There needs to be balance.

If you do not consider these aspects of the workplace and the nature of people on teams our engineering metrics cannot tell the whole picture. These things are hard to quantify but do have an impact. I have worked in some environments where individual or paired offices were the norm. Where possible, higher quality environments can serve to achieve higher levels of productivity.

For productivity measures in technical work that does not actually produce software such as support jobs other measures need to be employed. For example, the rate and number of problems handled by day. It may be hard to tell the size of an answer - sometimes one answer can save $1,000 in time or expense for the client. Other answers might have a much smaller impact.

CONCLUSIONS

In looking at project management there are many models and standards available to work from. Experience is also a valuable teacher. By combining the two we can get to the best of all worlds, a practical and conceptually well informed approach to running projects. Of note is the fact that project management is not just a text eBook exercise. It requires constant course adjustments, frequent communication, and well informed decision making.

REFERENCES

[1] Eisenhower, D., **Brainy Quote**, viewed August 6, 2011, http://www.brainyquote.com/quotes/authors/d/dwight_d_eisenhower_2.html
[2] Rolling Stones, **Keno's Rolling Stones Web Site**, viewed August 6, 2011, http://www.keno.org/stones_lyrics/you_cant_always_get_what_you_want.htm
[3] **A Guide to the Project Management Body of Knowledge**, 3rd Edition, Project Management Institute, 2004
[4] Cusick, J., **Software Engineering Student Guide**, Editions 2, Columbia University Division of Special Programs, New York City, September, September 1995.
[5] **A Guide to the Project Management Body of Knowledge**, 3rd Edition, Project Management Institute, 2004
[6] Demarco, T., & Lister, T., **Peopleware,** Dorset House, 1987.
[7] Weyuker, E., Avritzer, A,, Elaine J. Weyuker: *Investigating Metrics for Architectural Assessment*. **IEEE METRICS** 1998: 4-10
[8] Jensen, R., **Software Engineering,** Prentice Hall, Englewood Cliffs, NJ, 1979.
[9] Weinberg, G., **Quality Software Management: Vol.1 Systems Thinking**, Dorset House, 1992.
[10] DeGrace, P., & Stahl, L., **Wicked Problems & Righteous Solutions: A Catalogue of Modern S.E. Paradigms**, Prentice-Hall, Englewood Cliffs, NJ, 1990.
[11] Cusick, J., **Software Engineering Student Guide**, Editions 2, Columbia University Division of Special Programs, New York City, September, September 1995.
[12] Boehm, B., **Software Engineering Economics**, Prentice-Hall, Englewood Cliffs, NJ, 1981.
[13] ibid.
[14] Brooks, F., **The Mythical Man-Month: Essays on Software Engineering,** Addison-Wesley, Reading, MA, 1975.
[15] Boddie, John, **Crunch Mode: Building Effective Systems on a Tight Schedule**, Prentice Hall, 1987.
[16] Thomsett, Rob, **Third Wave Project Management**, Prentice Hall, Englewood Cliffs, NJ, 1993.
[17] McConnell, Steve, **Software Estimation: Demystifying the Black Art**, Microsoft Press; 1 edition, March 1, 2006.
[18] Boehm, B., **Software Engineering Economics**, Prentice-Hall, Englewood Cliffs, NJ, 1981.

[19] Jones, C., **Applied Software Measurement: Assuring Productivity and Quality**, McGraw Hill, New York, 1991.

[20] Charette, Robert N., **Application Strategies for Risk Analysis**, McGraw-Hill, New York, 1990.

[21] Charette, Robert N., **Software Engineering Risk Analysis & Management**, McGraw-Hill, NY, 1989.

[22] Demarco, T., & Lister, T., **Peopleware,** Dorset House, 1987.

Send Orders of Reprints at bspsaif@emirates.net.ae

 Durable Ideas in Software Engineering, 2013, 104-128

CHAPTER 4

Requirements Analysis: Getting it Right Eventually

Abstract: Understanding problem exploration, analysis, and description. Use of standard analysis and design techniques including structured analysis and design, information engineering, Object Oriented Analysis and Design, and more. Examples of analysis problems are discussed. Use cases and scenarios are introduced. Essential systems requirements and analysis methods explored.

Keywords: Requirements analysis, problem analysis, structured analysis, structured design, Object Oriented Analysis, Object Oriented Design, Use Cases, scenarios, essential systems analysis.

4.1. INTRODUCTION

In software, knowing what to build can be as challenging as building it. This challenge increases with the scale, scope, and desired characteristics of the target solution. Managing the requirements and the process to derive and define the requirements is a major part of any development project. To define system requirements the engineer must accomplish the following:

- Define the problem that must be solved.
- Analyze the associated problems and alternatives.
- Write clear and concise description of what the solution must do.
- Alternatively, they may build a prototype or incrementally demonstrate the functionality desired.

These steps are best done incrementally. In fact, the most successful approach is to conduct prototyping of early requirements, review this implementation with users or sponsors, and modify the requirements to suit the results of this discovery process. Today, the Agile methods of Scrum and related techniques follow this incrementalism successfully in many cases.

Importantly, no matter what approach is taken, requirements specification is a communications based task. The analyst must build a model of the user or

James J. Cusick

customer needs that can be further refined and eventually built. It is incumbent upon the analyst to elicit the appropriate information from the client. The information gathered in this way must be presented for review in an organized manner. Again, in an Agile model, the customer or customer representative is on the project team and is involved in constant revalidation of the requirements.

4.1.1. Describing Problems for Solution

The starting point for traditional requirements analysis is putting the system in some operational context. This means that the engineer essentially draws a box around the system and logically separates the system from its environment. The important questions here are what aspects of the solution are part of the system and what attributes are outside the system solution space. As an example we can go back to our paper airplane the example from Chapter 1. The paper, paper clips, tape, and markings of the airplane are all considered part of the system. The environment is the air we fly it through whether that is within a room or across the street.

These starting requirement borders also begin to describe an architecture. The details of system architectures will be dealt with in detail in Chapter 5. For the purpose of requirements analysis suffice it to say that the form of the solution will generate a solution architecture eventually. In Fig. **1** the evolutionary or incremental interplay between understanding requirements and specifying a solution architecture is shown [1]. Several key concepts are shown in this diagram. The first is the incremental nature of system specification. The second is the use of modeling. And the third is the oscillation between abstraction and implementation specific representation. Finally, requirements specification moves from less detailed to more detailed. This final dimension can be provided over time or *via* "progress chunking" in an Agile approach.

Regardless of the method used or the timing (phased or incrementalist approach) the conceptual representation of the solution needs to be envisioned, captured, synthesized, and realized. Doing this can draw on several key methods: flow charting, structured analysis and design, and object oriented analysis and design depending on the problem. We will touch on each of these as they provide some useful tools for our tool box.

The types of models that we might develop in these double helix include:

- Information Model or an Object Model, this represents the information or data managed by the application.

- Feature/Functional Description, this represents the capabilities of the application.

- Processing Model, Limits, Performance Requirements, this leads us to the area of system constraints, as we will see in talking about architecture all systems have constraints and within requirements these constraints should be established.

- System Behavior, States, Events, Actions, another plane of system description dimensionality is behavior; if a system is stateful then these behavioral aspects must also be represented.

- Validation Criteria, for a complete set of requirements, the engineer should also define how the system can be validated.

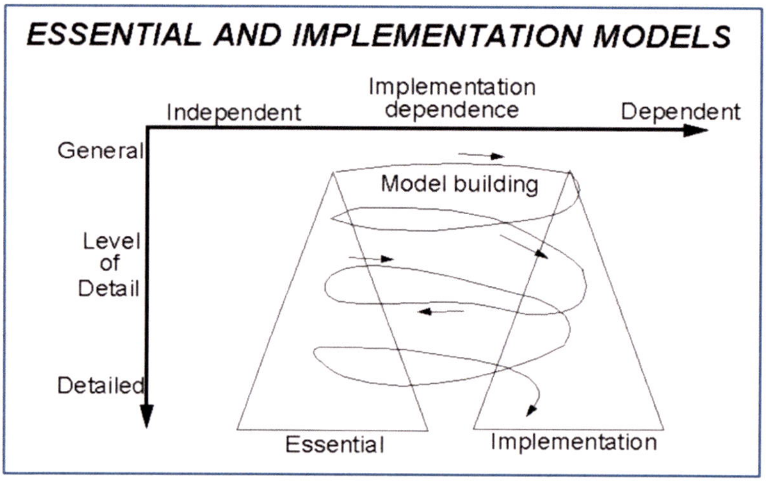

Figure 1: Essential Systems Design Concept Model.

Today, the requirements space itself is well represented by such methods as UML (Universal Modeling Language) which I will not attempt to provide a tutorial on. However, one can employ UML concepts and notation in talking about requirements, architecture, and design concepts, tools, and approaches. One interesting starting point in this area is to look at early traditions in requirements specification and model building. Of these I found Jensen's work the most practical and useful. He recommends the following models to be necessary in specifying a system:

- High level user communication model - state problem and goals.
- System Solution Model.
- High Level Design Model.
- Control Structure of Software.
- Data Flow Representation.
- Unit Level Model.
- Implementation in Code.

In UML and Object Oriented terms these models still exist. We can see a mapping between the system model and the package diagram. We can see that a high level design would map to an object model, a control structure diagram to sequence and state diagrams [2].

In an Agile mode, with the focus on working code, models may be de-emphasized. However, to layout overall system flow and boundaries these models remain useful.

In my own toolbox I keep these structured design techniques including the classic flow chart as well as the UML diagraming techniques depending upon the problem. The basics of flow charting can be summarized in the diagrams below (Fig. **2**).

Going further into requirements analysis which remains a difficult area, let us explain the context of the task of requirements (defining what a software system needs to do) further, and then outlining some of the techniques for doing this in some

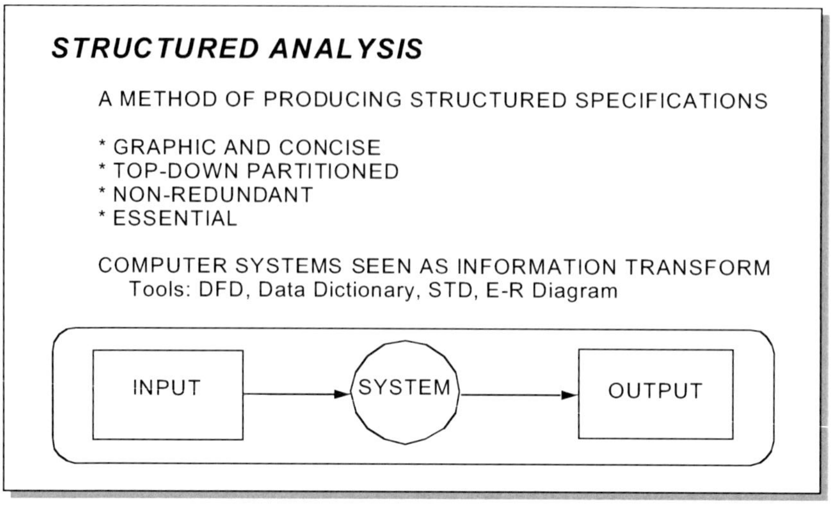

Figure 2: The starting point of any analysis is the description of the major boundaries of the system, what is in and what is out. Structured Analysis and Design introduced notational forms that became standard in the industry in the 1970s and 80s and remain useful today for some problem sets especially relational database design.

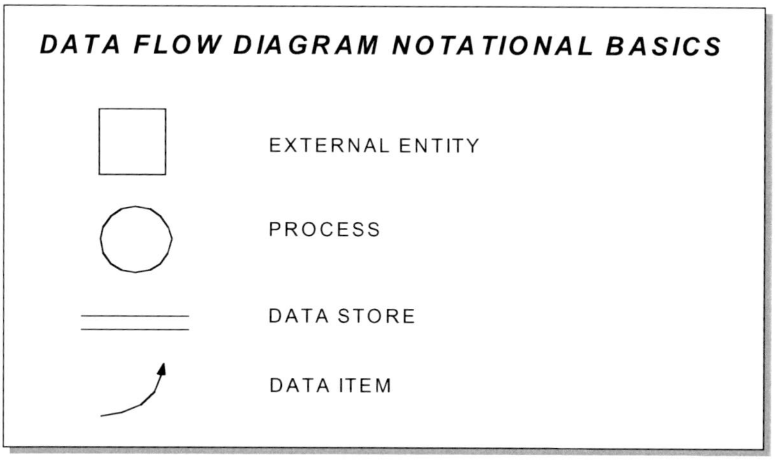

Figure 3: Data Flow Diagram (DFD) – a tried and true analytical tool which essentially represents the core ideas we discussed of process input, transform, and output but with a focus on data storage and transformation. This analysis tool remains useful but can also be conducted with a simple flow chart or a UML based data flow [3].

more detail. Within my toolbox we are making a transition away from scientific concepts, process, and project management per say, and more into analysis techniques, design techniques, and problem solving concepts. However, these techniques will be presented in a process oriented way - that is, what is the subprocess for analysis within the overall process of development? Once again, process is a tool we can use for understanding the approach to problem representation, problem solution, and validation. A problem leads to a method and a set of methods leads to a process. Execution of the process leads to solutions again and again.

Success in Software Engineering requires taking a task, breaking it down into its composite steps, and organizing for it as a process to achieve the results you are looking for. For requirements definition the issue is how does this fit into the sequence of tasks that produce the deliverable of interest (as in Fig. **2**). Drilling down into more specific analysis steps requires additional tools. The DFD (Data Flow Diagram) presented in Fig. **3** is one such tool. This allows us to quickly map out processing and data store elements of an application.

Building upon our life cycle process models we can now start filling in the details of what happens in each ordered phase. We can look at these tasks and provide examples. Some tasks will be harder to provide explanations for. Nevertheless, we hope to provide an understanding of each step so that these are not just boxes on a chart but they are well defined and rich process steps that relate to each other, communicate to each other, and in the end produce software.

We will skip systems engineering but in a sense it is defining the context of the application that you are going to build. A system is a complex unity of diverse parts. Many diverse parts are assembled into one single system which of itself has some kind of uniformity or elegance in operation (in concert with all of the different parts of the system). The system engineer is concerned with all these parts in coordination; it is the software engineer's job to focus on the software solution within the broader system. Most systems in this world are constructed from existing or fabricated parts and components. They have integrity, are complex and non-linear, semi-automated, and governed by stochastic inputs. Finally, these systems are competitive (one overnight package delivery system competes against another).

People often use the term software intensive system to reflect applications that are more software based than hardware based but today most systems from automobiles, to rice cookers, to music players are all based on a software component. So for practical purposes today's systems engineers need deep understanding of software and so too do software engineers need broad understanding of the systems environment where their software will be used. Nevertheless, as a software professional (not a systems engineer) I will outline the concerns of the systems engineer but focus on requirements analysis as practiced by a software engineer and leave the systems flavor to others. After all, there has to be some limit to how many tools can fit on my tool-belt.

As we began to discuss, the core tasks within systems and software analysis start with:

1. Problem Recognition.

2. Evaluation & Synthesis.

3. Modeling.

4. Specification & Architecture.

The idea at the beginning of an analysis task is to think in terms of the essential systems solution without constraints:

- Assume the Perfect Solution.

- No Technical Limitations.

- Work Towards Reality.

This step is often called a blue sky or green field session. What is possible without any constraints? What we are trying to do in reality is move from this blue sky scenario to build one complete system that is responsible for a particular set of functions. This will be done incrementally moving between the essential and abstract to the detailed and specific. There may be several identical systems, or a replication of systems, or perhaps just one. But a computer system - such as the global telephone network - is a massive system made up of people, software, and equipment. Another big system is a 747 airplane. One of the characteristics of a system is that it has some level of reliability and it has some consistency - when you take off from NY and land in LA you hope the whole plane makes it there. You can disassemble the system (in this case an airplane) into its consistent parts - doors, frame, wiring, computers, chairs, *etc*. But once it is assembled it behaves in a certain kind of manner and we can predict how it will behave. We can modify this system, improve it, or even cause it to deteriorate or malfunction.

Software can be seen in exactly the same manner. We use the term architecture in software development because we need someone in the process to provide a vision for how the overall complexity of the software system will be built. The developers of the NT operating system for example, followed an interesting process. There were about three Operating System (OS) gurus at Microsoft who were reported to have spent about 12 months with notebooks and talked about how to build an ideal operating system. They did not use computers or other tools - just their minds and paper and pencil. They had built major OSs before and had experience and ideas about what to do with a next generation version. (Interestingly, most other engineering fields rely on computers for design - autos, textiles, aerospace - but software generally does not.) One person came from DEC and had been the architect of VMS. The second from Carnegie Mellon and had invented the Mach OS Kernel.

At the end of the year they ended up with a set of notebooks which were the raw specifications for the new NT OS. They had developed a complex and unified vision for a full scale OS. However, this process is not really repeatable. A similar story can be found in the development of Apple's Macintosh. This is where Steve Jobs worked under a pirate flag across the street from the Apple headquarters and pursued a pure vision for the way a computer should really be - again not very repeatable but a great story and a great product. In Silicon Valley, projects are begun with a vision and people "sign up" for the project and basically put everything they have into it. This often produces breakthrough or leading edge technology solutions characterized by elegance and system unity. However, the rest of the world does not operate in this heroic mode and that is why we seen lots of mediocre software applications just limping along.

If all of us could operate in this fashion we would not require process models and technique notes. What we really want to do on average is to find out what the system or application is targeted at and define this in a very crisp and understandable manner that we can implement.

4.1.2. Analysis in Detail

Once more, referring to the real waterfall model which assumed feedback during the process and throughout an Agile project where incrementalism is built in, analysis is found in all phases of the lifecycle. Analysis is the task of understanding anything complex in order to understand its essential features. So if you are developing a system test plan, you are doing analysis. I am trying to understand the system I must test. In risk analysis I am trying to understand many complexities and how they interrelate which might potentially put our activities at risk.

We typically work top down incrementally and add more and more refinement to both our understanding and our solution in the face of a given problem. At every level of such problem solution analysis is called for. Traditionally, analysis is considered an up-front task (early in the life cycle). I do not see it that way - in practice people analyze problems throughout the lifecycle. The danger of course is that one may have committed to a solution prematurely and later analysis finds new details that reverse the solution's prescriptions. One can view this as normal evolution or it can be in actuality a fatal or costly blow to a project's progress.

Design is often considered a separate phase in the lifecycle. We are basically creating a plan for solving a real world problem for which we already have an analytical representation. The requirements analyst may provide the specification to an architect or may be the architect themselves. Architects normally build a scale model, artists create rough sketches for oil paintings, a model in clay is not done for software. For software prototypes provide a scaled down design solution for some analytical problem. Design, like any step in the development process should proceed a little at a time with feedback to prior or parallel activities

In illustrating the difference between analysis and design I used to tell the story of Frankenstein a la Mary Shelley. This is where Dr. Frankenstein analyzes the problem of creating human life to be the simple requirements of some spare body parts and a spark of lightning. What this analysis translates into as for design is a real monster. In software development most of us have seen such projects and predictably either tried to slay the monster or run the other way. As I write this chapter a project I am familiar with of nearly US $20 million is currently taking the shape of a monster which is more of the ilk of the emperor's new clothes. That is, everyone knows the project and system it is producing should be killed but no one has the bravery to stand up and fight it.

What does this tell us about requirements? The key lesson here is that if you cannot model it and cannot specify it you probably cannot build it either. Also, this shows that despite all the learned people and published best practices projects still become entangled in their own complexities, tradeoffs, and political unrealities. A key mission of the system engineer and requirements engineer is to cut through these difficulties and keep the focus on the essential, practical, and workable. As we introduced in Chapter 1, Gall states that any large complex working system started from a small simple working system. This is often forgotten at the peril of those that take another route.

Turning back to look at system analysis again we have many specific tasks to cover. First we have to understand the problem and then propose a solution. What we really must do is to communicate both the problem and the solution to all the project stakeholders. This does not mean that we will provide a complete solution to the problem since this will require additional increments of prototyping and learning about the solution's suitability. What is important is to use some kind of methodology that has proven its worth in communicating in standard design mediums and which help structure the problem solving effort. So for example the industry is replete with analysis methods such as "top-down", SASD (Structured Analysis and Structured Design), IE (Information Engineering), and of late OOA (Object Oriented Analysis) – see Fig. **4** below on the perpetually useful model types and their natural dimensional reinforcement of each other [4]. These all provide methods for solving problems and stating models of these solutions in standard ways as we have mentioned. Each varies in their syntax and approach but all aim at the same tasks of Analysis and Design. Keeping each one in the tool box is wise. A craftsman should acquire appropriate tools as needs call for them and not discard them from storage unless space is at a premium. Since these methods are all intellectual this should not be an issue. In my case I have kept reference materials for all the methods I have used or observed for future use.

Some of them have died out (like structured design notations which I was trained on at Bell Labs) and other have morphed from early methods (like Rumbaugh's OOA technics) into standard methods (like UML). Some of my books have more dust than others but it is the concepts that I reuse more than the strict methods.

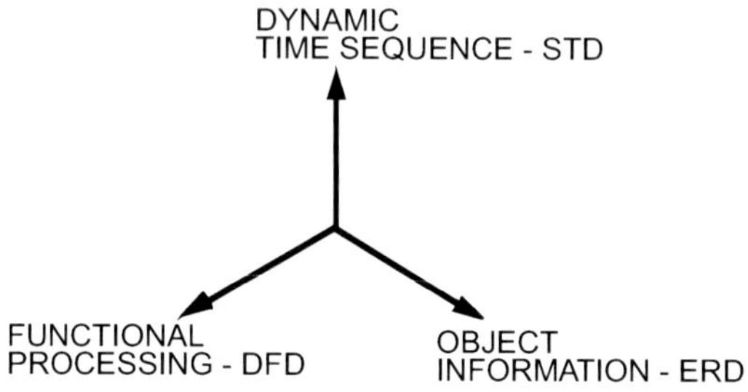

Figure 4: Three basic modeling tools that never go out of style – Time, Function, and Information (or Object) models. These can be called the STD (State Transition Diagram), DFD (Data Flow Diagram), and ERD (Entity Relationship Diagram) or any other name (see Shakespeare on a rose by any other name …). This representation comes from [5].

To deploy these methods against the analysis tasks requires tools including creativity and discipline. Sometimes you need to think out of the box to solve a problem. When a methodology gets in the way of this you cannot be a slave to the process but need to exercise your engineering judgment (see Chapter 1 for this tool's introduction) to make the method work the way you require. One problem is using the same solution for every problem regardless of its appropriateness (this can be called an anti-pattern) *e.g.*, everything is a state-event machine. A good designer with have experience on different types of systems, different application areas, different classes of machines, *etc.* You will be introduced to many different types of problems during your career which will assist in analysis down the line. Sometimes a hammer is what is needed.

References are important in analysis. This means both technical references and previously deployed software systems. Most likely in a software engineer's career one will not be developing systems which have not been developed before. Some may get into an area that has never been automated or may develop a completely novel application. However, if you are ever assigned to an inventory control system project you can be guaranteed that it has been done before and done very well also. Redoing all the analysis is wasteful. You need to find a source for an existing system and learn from its design. In today's world many of these systems fall into the category of ERP (Enterprise Resource Planning) packages or the more general COTS (Commercial Off The Shelf Software). These pre-developed solutions are excellent in terms of domain coverage, pre-built status, and customizability or extensibility but lack in terms of true uniqueness or business differentiation. If all your competitors are running the same ERP system how do you use IT as a strategic differentiator? This is one of the roles for the requirements engineer to solve. It is not only about the specific problem at hand but also how the needs will best be met for the organization or customer base.

Analysts tend to think in broad terms and in general concepts and allow designers and programmers to create the specifics for implementation. For many developers analysis techniques are rarely used. However, the output of analysis - data dictionaries, object models - are commonly used for their design efforts. Thus it is important for a programmer to understand the nomenclature of the analysts models. In an Agile mode, it may be that little formal modeling will be done or it may be deemed that an entire sprint would be dedicated to design modeling. The model is that flexible. What is important is to have the right people educated in these methods. Not everyone will be expert at analysis and modeling. Not everyone will be the best programmer. Sometimes this will be the same person and a small team will carry through the entire project oscillating between analysis, design, and implementation together tightly.

One interesting point for analysts to keep in mind is that you must reconsider all the underlying assumptions made in producing the environment or task that you are trying to automate. In one system I visited the user sites and found that they kept asking about "green tickets". They were very concerned that the new system should be able to support these "green tickets". I asked what they were and found that they were manual log forms formatted in a word processor and printed on green paper. When the current system failed to complete a specific transaction (which was often) the agents filled out a green ticket to be processed in some other way. I could not get the users to understand that we would not need a green ticket for the new system because it would not fail in this manner.

Whenever the software changes there is an opportunity for a process redesign. This means that the current system requirements may not be the full requirements for the new target system. Typically new requirements will enter the process. Today in reengineering, software and IT itself are vital to instituting organizational changes. Software staff are often not very popular since the mapping of the real world processes to software is so difficult and the processes often must change to adapt to the software. It is very important to remember that in building software the analyst is deciding on how to impact a work process. It is critical to ask many questions - "why do you use green tickets", for example. In another example, while automating some company processes that would eliminate work steps that were manual, the unionized work force strongly objected to some design decisions that they felt would encroach on their workforce keeping their relevance. This kind of practical political issue is a real threat to a requirements engineer. The tools for managing conflict and resolving problems between groups now becomes much more important than any method, programming language, or technical framework. Such tools include active listening, focus groups, and diplomacy (which I sometimes am lacking in being from the go-go North East). One Japanese word I like to use in this context is *nema-washi*. This term has no direct English translation but can roughly be thought of as preparing the planting site and root ball of a tree for planting. You must dig carefully, try not to disturb existing plants, yet achieve the right balance of new soil set to the right angle. In practice this means many meetings and discussions and appropriate back and forth, give and take. When all parties have had a true say and consensus is truly built then the new system can easily be laid in.

Assuming that we have a project kick off already and a need has been identified for new or modified software to be developed and deployed the questions we need ask include: what is the problem we are trying to solve, how is it currently being solved, what information is available about the problem, also who are the domain experts we can interview. The first things to focus on are the key areas of the problem domain that will produce the most value to the customer. In the early stages you want to consider the perfect solution if there were no technical limitations. In essential systems design you can begin by assuming nearly everything and using only the preliminary facts to begin shaping a solution. The focus is on what would be the "prefect" scenario and ignoring any implementation specifics. Memory, disk space, and performance, are all assumed to be unlimited.

This is the intellectual framework which applies to the kickoff of your analysis. You can then create models to represent to both the problem space and the solution as described above. Eventually, you will have to tailor your ideas to fit onto actual computing space. Finally, you will arrive at a model that is far from the initial concept and close to an implementation detail. In terms of actual development activities it is common to move continuously between analysis and design. We first explore the problem and attempt a partial solution, peeling the onion as it is sometime called. Then we return to the analysis work and slice off a bit more of the problem, and so on.

As we continue with analysis and design we are always moving back and forth from the essential aspects of the problem space to the more reality grounded projection into an implementation. Depending on where we are in this process, models help us to communicate with each other, from customer to engineers or from engineers to implementers. Models help us verify our thoughts and help us to transfer knowledge from one individual to another or one group to another. They also help us to understand how close we are to solving a problem.

To accomplish this modeling and requirements specification certain skills are required. Skills for an analyst starts with a wide background. Analysts typically have lots of experience. However, with the right skills somewhat inexperienced "systems" thinkers can succeed. Analysts think in terms of systems - at a higher level - not at the level of bit masks. That kind of thinking is good for implementation. A systems perspective is required for analysis. Defining problems, representing information, stating things clearly are the goals of the analyst. An analyst needs to understand how to collect and understand data. They also need software systems as well as business knowledge - domain expertise. Aside from models, analysts tend to be called on to communicate often in documents, email, and presentations. In addition, they have to be able to ask questions politely yet in an exploratory sense to uncover facts. They also need to be able to present complex information to a wide variety of people. In thinking about our tool box once again communication comes to the fore but here it is very specialized and targeted at the acquisition of information, data, and knowledge for systems elucidation. Other skills our analyst must have includes business process modeling the basis of which we covered in Chapter **2**. In addition to the flow charting and analysis modeling described above the process modeling of Chapter 2 details the tasks, inputs, outputs, precursors, and post conditions required to demonstrate the end to end flow of a business activity. Understanding the vocabulary and context of the target business is essential to building an appropriate solution to any systems problem. Finally, analysts need current knowledge of computing environments, equipment, capabilities, and even office equipment as devices such as scanners, hand-helds, and specialty input or display devices are embedded in business workflows.

4.1.3. Object-Oriented Analysis and Design

With these definitions and tools in mind it is worthwhile to look at the most popular concepts in systems design – OOA. Some basic tools that are needed are the CRC card, Use Cases, and Object Models. The CRC is the Class-Responsibility-Collaborators index card introduced by Hansen [6]. We used this method in the early 1990s to great success and for beginners in OOA I recommend looking into this method. It is simple and effective. Essentially, for every noun in the requirement space or domain space a card is created. The noun is tested for class stability – that is – does it stick, does it make sense as a class. What is a class? Let us explore.

A class is a generic representation of an real world object. So dog may be a class which your pet named Fido will belong to. For each class there can be zero, one, or many objects of that type. For example an eagle is of the class bird. We can also introduce the characteristics or attributes of this class. Eagles are predators and have sharp beaks. If you see an object of type eagle and you are of type mouse you should hope to have the responsibility of “run for your life”.

More formally, according to Booch [7] a class is a description of one or more objects with a uniform set of attributes and services including how to create new objects in the class itself. An Object on the other hand is an abstraction from the problem domain which reflects system capabilities and information and encapsulates attributes and services of the class which defines it.

We can find lots of objects - events, roles, places, organizations. Often it is hard for beginners to find objects but then they find too many. To know when to keep them in the design you need some criteria. Information over time, such as an order which retains information over time. Needed services, take the order, process, fill, ship, bill, purge, the order. Should have many attributes, date, item number, quantity, price, *etc.* Common operations are considered when generalizing or used by many other objects. These are the essential considerations for the system.

With generalization we take an attribute and abstract it as a generalization about all animals - taking an attribute we have observed in both cats and birds and we are abstracting that out of the classes that describe those to objects and moving it into a superclass in a generalization step. Thus any animal has the attribute of being alive or dead. This is how a class hierarchy is built. This type of thinking is ideal to model the real world. This is how we as humans image the world and classify the things we observe from the time that we are toddlers all the way through life. We are always building abstractions and classifications both to our advantage and disadvantage. Using this approach in designing software brings the power of our natural thinking to bear on analysis needs.

When we abstract we are saying that instead of implementing a specific instance of something let us consider how that might lie in the problem domain naturally and describe that in a general sense and then create from that instances of that type.

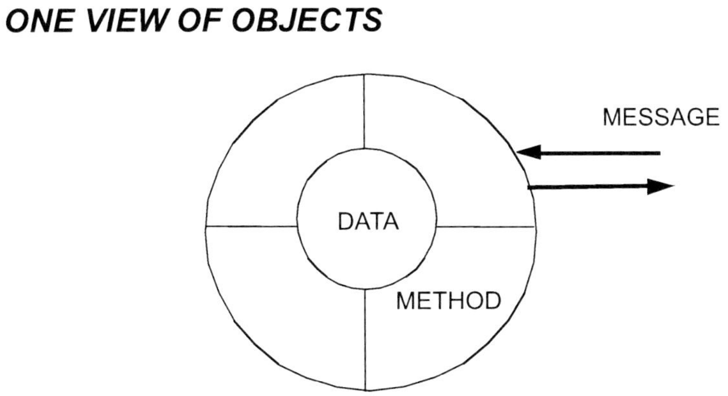

Figure 5: One of the most powerful tools in my toolbox – the understanding of what an object is *versus* a class and how to wrap/encapsulate attributes in associated methods.

If we have an instantiation of a bird and cat what might be a message that a cat might send to a bird? Perhaps 'I'm going to eat you'. The response from the bird will depend on its type - a sparrow might fly away with all haste while a bluejay might swoop in to threaten the cat. These are signals that objects send each other and behaviors that are invoked. In many OO languages this comes down to method invocation which is essentially a function call. If this is implemented as a function and another class sends a message to toggle the isAlive attribute then the cat object will die. In the most general sense we can visualize an object as in Fig. **5**.

As an example lets take a traffic monitoring system. Today many roadways have electronic sensors embedded in the asphalt so that traffic conditions can be monitored. That is, how many cars pass by at each time of day. If we put our analysts hats on for a minute we might brainstorm what a system like this might look like and what it would be capable of. From an OOA perspective we could easily come up with the sensor object itself and some core data attributes and methods on the class. The layout of this basic object and what it would possess in terms of attributes and methods it might look something like the following diagram:

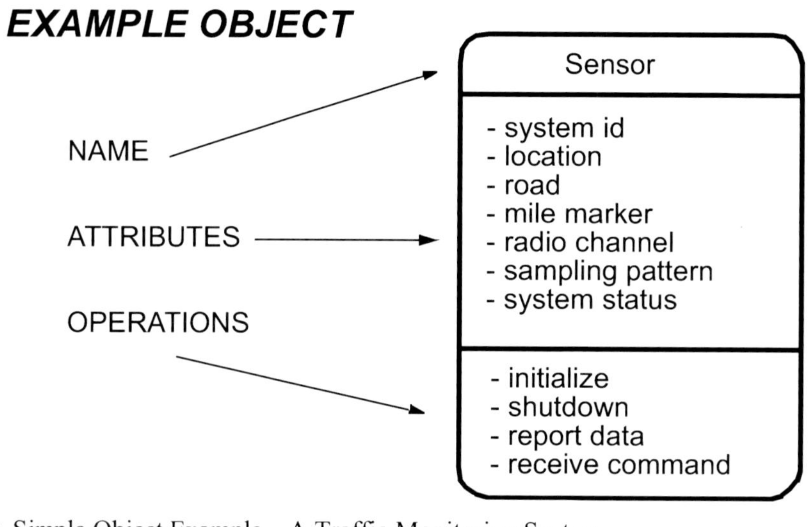

Figure 6: A Simple Object Example – A Traffic Monitoring System.

Lets take a look at what a basic class definition would look like in C++. Here is a class definition of the sensor object, just the bare bones with a few minor enhancements to the design above.

```
class Sensor {
private:
  int SystemID;
  int location; // requires expansion to GPS coordinates
  int road;
  int mile marker;
  long RadioChannel;
  char SamplingPattern[10];
  int SystemStatus;
public:
  int initialize(int restart);
  int sleep(int interval);
  int ProvideReport(char type);
  int DownloadNewCommands(int offset);
}
```

The beauty of object oriented analysis is that one can move from real world observation or needs to abstraction to computing model and implementation very rapidly. The code fragment here that allows for the class of *Sensor* to be defined would easily lend itself to further analysis, design, and rapid build out of a prototype. One might have the first version running in a matter of hours if you knew the programming interface to the road sensor device itself. The point here is that as a tool OOA and OOD as well as OOP (Object Oriented Programming) provide a strong trifecta in moving from essential abstractions as introduced at the beginning of this chapter to running code. We can see from this code snippet that the private members of the class are the encapsulated data fields and the public methods are the means to which external parties can access these fields. This type of construct if understood by the analyst is very powerful.

Analysts have long known that it is necessary to have an information model that can represent the way in which a problem is going to be solved. What was new with OO is that we add a few new elements to the analysis output. We build on ER diagrams and traditional systems analysis. The new things are the class hierarchies and the methods bound to data attributes.

There are many advanced and even arcane design possibilities within a language like C++. For the requirements analyst these will not be of importance. However, the important point is that there is a continuum of design capability and this is not fully an OO issue but when used in an OO environment helps in flexibility and evolvability of systems. Thus, if the original domain hierarchy is laid down correctly in the initial systems design then its eventual perfection can be well assumed. In one project I worked on the team got to the dozen core objects or classes in the course of a few months and then built out the remaining system in the course of about two years. Once that was done the foundation was so solid that it has never required revisiting to this day nearly 15 years later. Even though the system is still in operation and needs some updates it does not require design changes to its core processing engine since the analysis pegged the problem domain squarely and allowed for graceful evolution.

The new things are the class hierarchies and the methods bound to data attributes. Today these have become routine but they were new at one time. Modeling these system attributes is still as time consuming as in structured analysis. Thus, working at the problem recursively or incrementally as in Agile methods makes sense.

All of the industry leaders in analysis and design methodology have swung over to the object world. This is a trend to take notice of. There are no new publications on SASD past 1990. We started by talking about SASD and now we see that the people who created those techniques are no longer working on them. They and the techniques have generally migrated and evolved to OO. However, the scars won in the fight for these methods prompted the rise in OO methods and eventually in the modern lightweight solutioning using frameworks.

4.1.4. Use Cases

In our discussion so far we have avoided one core concept: use cases. Jacobson introduced this concept early in the OOA movement [8]. Use case modeling is a scenario modeling approach popular for documenting scenarios and driving the implementation. Key components are actors and use cases and relationships. As a classic example take Jacobson's recycling machine using the basic notation of use cases (actors, use cases, interactions).

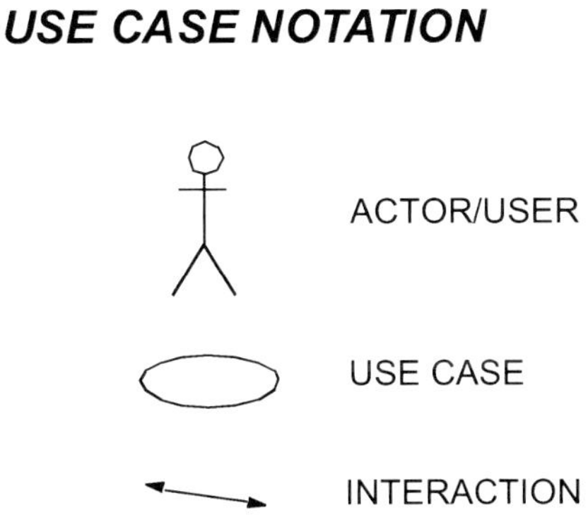

Figure 7: Use Case Notation.

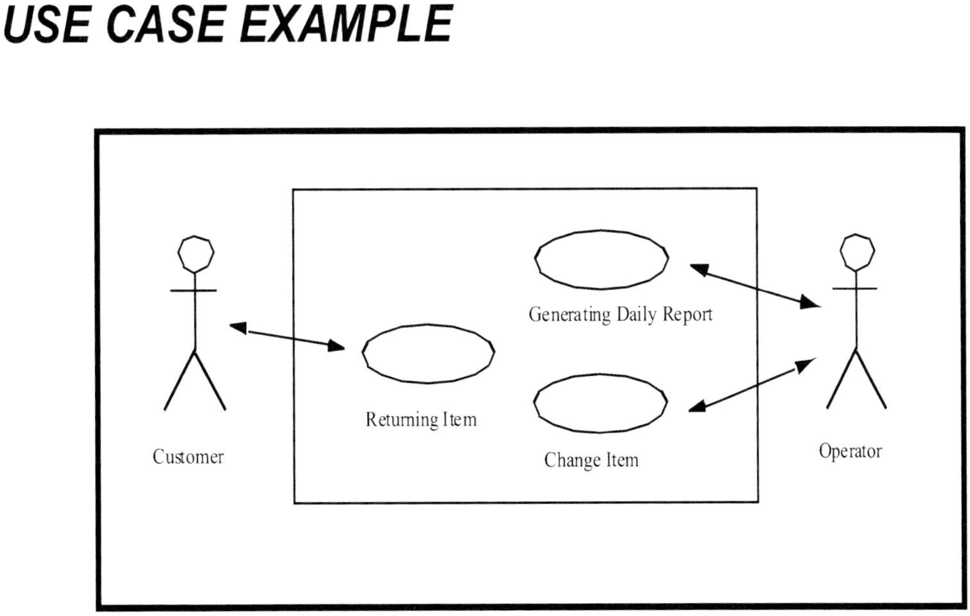

Figure 8: Use Case Example – Jacobson 's classic recycling machine example.

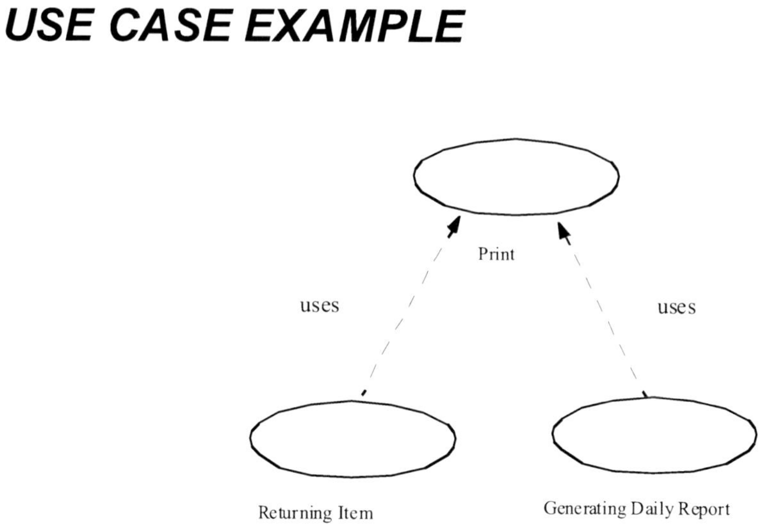

Figure 9: Use Case Example – Jacobson 's classic recycling machine example.

Scenarios have been used in software analysis for decades but Jacobson 's major progress point was to standardize the notation and process of doing user modeling. In many ways this modeling approach has been supplanted by the user stories of the Agile methods. This notation eventually was subsumed by UML but the basics are still here. Using these simple notational objects we can describe the input/transform/output process we introduced in Chapters 1 and 2 (see Figs. **7** and **8**). An example of using these notations for a Use Case is presented in Fig. **9**.

In the analyst's tool kit, the scenario, whether a use case or another type, is one of the most important tools. It is perhaps more apropos to discuss it at the beginning of the analysis story instead of the middle. It is through understanding user scenarios or user stories (the Agile methods term for the same thing) that requirements can be understood and that object nouns can be discovered in the domain space. If we go back to the beginning of the chapter and look again at the essential systems analysis method we discussed it is through use cases that we can be guided in the spiral from the unspecific to the specific. User interface design is a topic on its own. When using scenario driven design you will have to tackle the user interface also. This can be done with layout techniques on paper or in software. The relationship between the requirements and the user interface solution can be tightly coupled. I have always preferred working prototypes to paper requirements. In today's world often the design style of the solution will be driven by choice of toolkits. That is, once you buy into a particular programmatic environment you solution will trend towards the design metaphor embedded within that environment (say Windows). However, from a requirements stand point it is important to focus on the essence of the problem domain first and not to be dragged into the solution technology to early or if at all as those environments come and go.

4.1.5. Definitions & Roles

One classic approach to requirements analysis is to define the system "shalls". This is the classic format of a functionality specification. This might be a bullet list or a spread sheet or the dreaded Victorian novel format. Hopefully, with the tools defined above – Use Cases and OOA – this will not be the case. The requirements will be represented as rich models or at minimum the "shall" list will be supplemented by a required design model or prototype. We need a communication vehicle of some kind, I am not a stickler for the type as long as it gets the job done – captures the needs, allows for reliable and incremental decomposition of the problem, and faithfully matches the problem domain with a solution architecture.

Thus when we communicate from the client perspective to the implementation process - if the client does not really know what they want or what they want the system to accomplish we are able to help them discover that. As such we must capture information for others to understand. Clients tend to know what they want but do not know how to state it in systems engineering terms. They can state their problem in business terms. For example, they might say "we are spending too much money collecting our bills. Can you help us?" This can often mean that they are focused on cost reduction. For the analyst this means you need to study their current operations - is it manual, redundant, outdated? If so there may be an opportunity to make a quick hit by automating some new aspect of their process or streamlining current computer based processes.

It is not good enough for you to understand it and walk away – as we have stated, you must capture information, and format the problem for a ready solution. The requirements artifacts are also crucial for quality control. You need something to review in order to make sure the right things will be built. This is also a major input to downstream process activities as we shall see in subsequent chapters.

Once the specifications begin to be translated into software often the communications become more difficult and the reaction speed slower. The first few iterations build up considerable assumption layers and design choices. In an Agile mode you will even be committing your analysis to working and perhaps implemented system code. The mapping of the specifications into software puts distance between the client and the implementation. Prototyping can help this since most business people have at least moderate exposure to computers. Showing the client a scaled down solution (or clickable prototype) for their bill collection process on a PC will help them to help you conclude the specifications.

If you pursue a functional requirements process but intend to use object based technologies for analysis and design of the software there may be a disjoint. The issue is the difference between functional decomposition and object oriented analysis. Systems need to deliver functionality to the user. That is what is preeminent - the user facing functionality. The representation of the problem for solution, for example, using object models, is not as important. This is irrelevant to the customer. They want to know if the software will carry out it functions. The mapping back to objects or other design constructs is not important to them. However, objects are a closer fit to the real world constructs. This is where use cases or user stories come into their own. Most users can understand these models very easily as they speak to their standard problem domain quite clearly.

4.1.6. Review of Requirements Tasks & Techniques

Regardless of the method used, some basic requirements steps need to be covered. A generalized process might look like this:

1. Discover and state the problem.

2. Define a solution for the problem.

3. Document the nature of the proposed system or system enhancements, its purpose, users, benefits, and costs.

4. Develop or modify the system architecture: what are the parts of the system and how are they related.

5. Develop a processing model or use case scenario model for the system.

6. Develop an information model for the system: what data, terms, objects, and content, are either consumed, produced by, or comprise the system.

7. Model or prototype these system characteristics and review with client and technical experts.

Success in Software Engineering requires taking a task, breaking it down into its composite steps, and organizing for it as a process to achieve the results you are looking for. For requirements definition the issue is how does this fit into the sequence of tasks that produce the deliverable of interest. If your process calls for a specification document (some Agile methods will not) an example software requirements specification template may look like the following:

CONCLUSIONS

In exploring the requirements step we have encountered the natural heartbeat of a project – evolution. Projects do not move forward in defined phases of understanding but in a spiral from essential analysis to implementation. The methods of early software engineering, functional decomposition, flow charting, and structured analysis can still play a role but object methods have become the most dominant. Within my toolbox all of these tools still have a place and are used when they are needed.

REFERENCES

[1] Stevens, W., **Software Design Concepts & Methods**, Prentice Hall, 1991.

[2] Rumbaugh, J., *et al.*, **Object-Oriented Modeling and Design,** Prentice Hall, Englewood Cliffs, 1991.

[3] Wetherbe, James C., **Cases in Systems Design,** West Publishing Company, 1979.

[4] Cusick, J., **Software Engineering Student Guide**, Editions 1 & 2, Columbia University Division of Special Programs, New York City, September, 1994 & September 1995.

[5] Rumbaugh, J., *et al.*, **Object-Oriented Modeling and Design,** Prentice Hall, Englewood Cliffs, 1991.

[6] Hansen, Tony, "*One Team's Experiences Using CRC Cards*", **C++ /Object-Oriented Technology Day**, Software Technology Center, AT&T Bell Labs, Murray Hill, NJ, 1993.

[7] Booch, G., **Object-Oriented Analysis and Design with Applications**, 2nd Edition, Benjamin/Cummings, Redwood City, CA,1994

[8] Jacobsen, I., *et al.*, **Object-Oriented Software Engineering: A Use Case Driven Approach**, Addison-Wesley., Wokingham, England, 1992.

Send Orders of Reprints at bspsaif@emirates.net.ae
Durable Ideas in Software Engineering, 2013, 129-166

CHAPTER 5

Architecture & Design

Abstract: Defining architecture and its relationship to requirements implementation and the design process. Introduction of architecture styles, architecture patterns, design patterns and discussion of their relationship to the development process. Review of tiered architectures, Client/Server principles, distributed architectures, and related topics. Introduction and discussion of many Internet implementation architectures including Web based static architectures, CGI, SAPI, .Net, and mobile architectures like iPad environments.

Keywords: Software architecture, architecture styles, architecture patterns, design patterns, multi-tier architectures, Internet architectures, protocols, reference architectures, hybrid architectures, mobile architectures.

5.1. INTRODUCTION

Regardless of the approach followed to build software, whether small team or large, an architecture of some kind will be required for success. Architecture, defined as the "art or science of building" [1], is an often overused term in software. Architecture at its simplest refers to a high-level design which defines the major components of a software system and how they interrelate. The practice of software architecture runs the gamut from an "arts & charts" approach of drawing with unstructured semantics to rigorously defined architectures using formal languages. Within my virtual toolbox are several tried and true methods, reference patterns, and techniques that assist in building or evolving an architecture. We will explore these in detail in this chapter.

In discussing architecture it helps to start by defining the tasks required of this phase:

1. Defining the problem at hand.
2. Providing a solution.
3. Preserving and implementing a clear vision of the solution.

In practice, by defining requirements (see Chapter 4) the first task is often accomplished. However, there is an iterative flow to architecture development. As

James J. Cusick

requirements are developed a solution architecture often comes into focus. The relationship with requirements extends to the final piece of this as well. It is often the architecture picture that project members keep posted on the wall for reference and it is these pictures that create the shared view of what is being built. The requirements often cannot be coalesced into a single picture.

There are many flavors of "architecture" which people talk about: system, computer, hardware, software, physical, processing, functional, data, object architecture, and so on. We will focus mainly on: 1) systems architecture; 2) software architecture; and 3) architecture styles and patterns. System Architecture embodies the entire scope of the apparatus deployed to solve an engineering problem. Software Architecture is the composition of the processing and computational structure of the solution. Information Architecture is the analytic representation of the domain constructs upon which the software will operate. Thus the Information Architecture is manipulated by the Software Architecture and the whole is given life by the underlying computing environment as defined by the System Architecture.

In this chapter we will consider first what architecture is, then what types of architectures exist for computing systems, and then we will discuss the current styles and patterns of architecture, and finally look at some implementation architectures for Internet based systems.

5.1.1. Requirements to Architecture

Just as physical structures such as buildings or homes should fit an environment or terrain, software architectures must suit a given problem domain. As system requirements are developed the nature of the architecture which meets these requirements begins to take shape. If the requirements call for intensive data entry then the designer will consider an OLTP (On-line Transaction Processing) architecture. If the customer needs thousands of records processed we may consider a batch orientation. However, to start with the engineer must first be familiar with the standard architectures of software and software based systems in order to choose the right kind.

As we define how a system will be comprised to meet the specifications an architecture emerges. Using Architecture as a bridge from requirements to implementation servers to preserve the vision of the solution. Typically, once we understand the features requested of the system we begin developing a high level concept of the architecture. Often times the architecture or part of it are dictated to us in advance. The customer may have a certain kind of computing infrastructure and we have to deploy new software in that existing environment. This determines certain things that can and cannot be done (for example, platform and Operating System may be predefined). Some of the architectural issues fall by the wayside. We do not have to define the computing environment because it is already defined. If we are building a new system then we may have to do considerable work on processing platforms, networking, and data storage design. Today, most systems are at least considered for Internet deployment. Such a requirement goes a long way to defining the communications, performance, and functional characteristics of any system.

In considering architecture, we should start with an understanding of the relationship of an architecture to requirements and implementation. In Fig. **1** we see the benefits of the abstraction layer of architecture residing between the requirements space and the concrete implementation. Understanding this value add is important for the designer. Without this abstraction layer true spaghetti implementations can emerge.

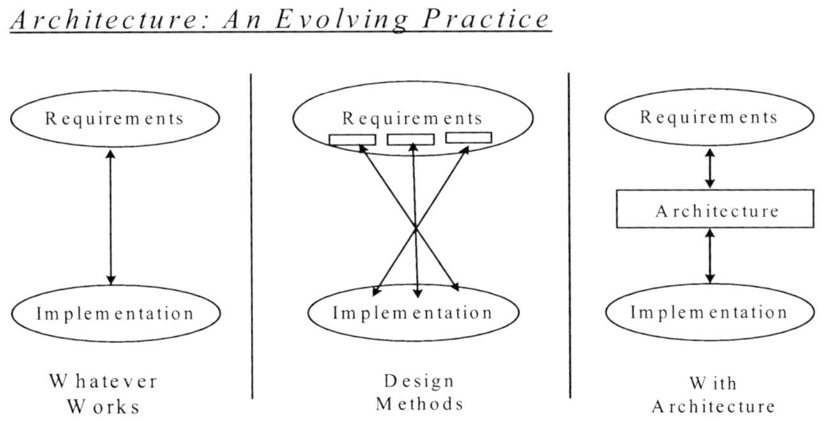

Figure 1: Requirements and Architecture as Related to Implementation [2].

One thing that is normally done is to provide a general procedural structure for the system. Old or new we will have to translate the feature functionality requested by the user into a processing architecture. This includes data, performance, and the allocation of functionality to specific parts of the architecture. We move from the problem space that defines how the business is working to some kind of specification and architecture. These two design artifacts are not always clearly separated. Requirements tend to be in the form of documents listing what the system should do while the architecture is often dominated by diagrammatic representations of the system modified by supporting characteristics.

5.1.2. Introducing Architecture

Clearly, requirements help shape architecture. But what do we mean by architecture? One description of architecture takes the following form [3]:

$$\textit{Software Architecture} = \{\ \textit{elements, form, rationale}\ \} \qquad \textbf{(7)}$$

- Elements: processing, data, connecting.
- Form: properties, relationships.
- Rationale: motivation for style.

This view affords a clean model for discussing the nature of architecture in software, helps guide the visualization of specific architectures, and underlines the implications of design choices.

Another valuable definition is that architecture is [4]:

$$\textit{Architecture} = \textit{Components} + \textit{Connectors} + \textit{Constraints} \qquad \textbf{(8)}$$

Peeling the onion reveals that below this elemental view of software architecture there are a variety of specific concerns which require attention in developing architectures including the following:

- Goals of the system: performance, reliability, scalability, low cost.
- Design criteria: users to support, transaction rates, data volume, response time, reliability, performance, security, procedures, maintenance.

- File placement: centralized, replicated, partitioned, hybrid.
- Replication strategies: chain letter, broadcast, peer-to-peer, propagation.

Regardless of the model used to define or describe architecture or the detailed design criteria required, architecture provides us with several important benefits. Through architecture we can hope to achieve some level of reuse and we can better plan the evolution of an application. Architecture supports analysis by providing a model that can be reviewed for its ability to support the implementation of requirements. Finally, architecture also supports the management of development efforts by providing a high level view of the work being carried out.

In the 3 C's model it is worth pointing out that the connections piece is well described in the recent literature and technology base around SOA (Service Oriented Architecture). SOA contains a forest of acronyms which are best found defined elsewhere [5]. SOA relies on web services and other technologies to realize a loosely coupled macro architecture between or within systems. In my first programming assignments in the telecommunications field this was achieved by proprietary messaging formats or APIs (Application Programming Interfaces). These often enabled complex inter machine coordination of functionality. In discussing architecture tiering below this messaging structure should be kept in mind. The SOA solution to this classical problem is perhaps one of the most useful modern developments in software architecture since the advent of the World Wide Web (along with XML) and is definitely a tool in my architect's toolbox.

Perhaps most important use of all for software engineers, however, is the utility of software architecture in providing a comparative framework with which to judge one's own design decisions. When enough architectures are available in the public domain, a developer can pursue the extent to which their problem matches another and if their solution can be enhanced by an existing solution (see Booch Architecture Collection online [6]). This is where Architecture Styles, generic descriptions of successful architectures, begins to have an influence.

5.1.3. Patterns

Of all the tools that have emerged in the past 20 years of my practicing software development, patterns are clearly one of the most powerful. The early work on design idioms by Jim Coplien [7] led to the development of early Pattern Languages as described by Erich Gamma [8] and company and inspired by Alexander's "Timeless way of Building" [9]. There is a rich and extensive literature in this area so I will not attempt to replicate this or extend it but I think it is worth explaining how I use patterns and which types of patterns I have found useful within my toolbox.

First of all let's review the definition of a Patterns:

> *Predefined design structures that can be used as building blocks to compose the architecture of a software system.*

Properties of patterns include:

- Scheme for implementation.
- Well proven design.
- Abstract above level of class & instance.
- Provides common design vocabulary.
- Provides reusable building blocks.
- Domain dependent or domain independent.

Patterns are communicated in a "Pattern Language" which takes the form of a template which will include at minimum the following:

- Name.
- Intent.
- Context.

- Problem.
- Solution.
- Applicability.
- Diagram.
- Implementation.
- Examples.
- See Also.

Where I have found patterns useful is in helping me to navigate from the general to the specific. As we discussed in Chapter 4, essential systems analysis will take us from the architecture to the implementation in ever evolving spirals. With patterns we can get assistance in doing this. The primary classification of this leveling of patterns are:

1. Architectural Frameworks.
2. Design Patterns.
3. Idioms.

This concept is shown in Fig. **2**. If we work our way down the hierarchy, Architecture patterns start us off at the global or enterprise level. From system to application to framework we are in the realm of the design pattern and implementation brings us to the idiom. One of the most useful tools in my toolbox has been the concept of the architecture style. The architecture style we introduced above. These include OLTP, Decision Support Systems, and more.

5.1.4. Architecture Styles

There is an old saying that there was only one original program ever written and everything else has been copied from there. In architecture we are now approaching a time when much the same can be said. Thus, as a basic tool in my architecture toolbox are the architecture patterns published by others. Through an active community of architects and developers who have codified and published their designs in a shareable format called a "design pattern" there are now hundreds of successful architectures and designs to copy from when building a new system. Designers can now reflect on their requirements and in responding to the domain needs of the problem, author a resultant flavor of processing emerges as a specific architecture.

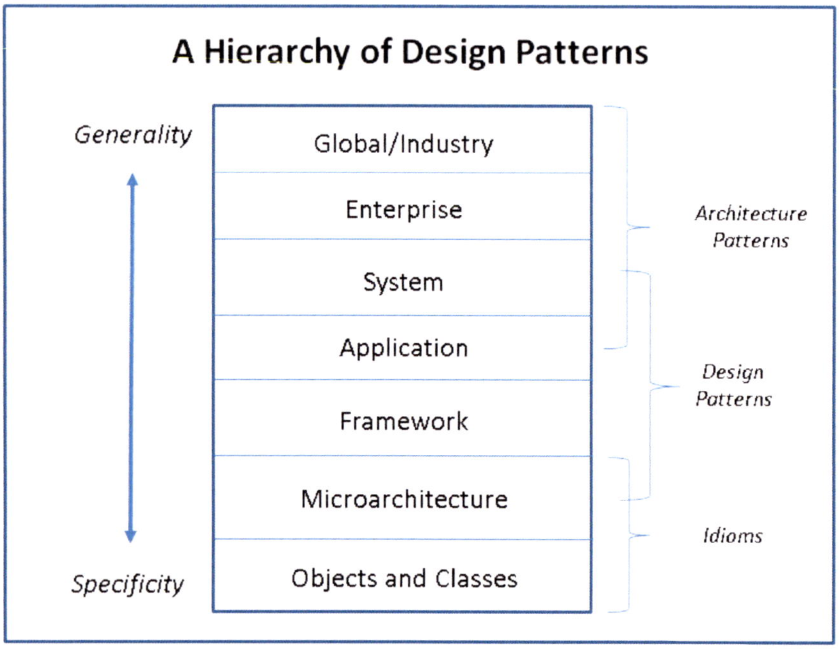

Figure 2: A Hierarchy of Design Patterns.

Architecture Styles provide specific approach to categorization. Bellanger [10] defines Architecture Styles as:

> *A set of operational characteristics common to a family of a software architecture and sufficient to identify that family.*

Furthering these ideas have been the development of Pattern Languages for software. A Pattern Language codifies "well-proven design experience and provides a common vocabulary" for software design [11]. The relationship between Architecture Styles and Patterns was demonstrated by Tepfenhart [12].

To be more specific, Architecture Styles describe families of related systems providing:

- A vocabulary of design elements.
- Design rules and constraints.
- Semantic interpretation governing construction from base elements.
- Analyses of validity per family.

Typically we pull from existing styles such as the following:

- Command & Control.
- Data Store.
- Data Streaming.
- Data/Object Abstraction.
- Decision Support.
- Distributed Processes.
- Domain Specific Architecture.
- Event Based Implicit Invocation.
- Hybrid (Heterogeneous Architectures).
- Layered Systems.
- Main & Subroutine Organization.
- OLTP.
- Pipes & Filters.

- Process Control Systems.
- Real-Time.
- Repositories.
- State Transition Systems.
- Table Driven Interpreters.

5.1.4.1. Architecture Styles Discussed

Once we understand the requirements, we can define a physical architecture initially, and then a processing architecture that helps determine the software architecture we use. The requirements should flow from the type of system we are trying to build. If we are building a checking account managing system we are not going to look at real-time for the architecture or inter-processor intensive. (Inter-processor deals with file transfers, event updates, etc). Just as the saying goes "there is nothing new under the sun", in software architecture, most approaches have been tried and documented already. It only makes sense to select a proven design.

Batch – in the early days of computing batch style architectures dominated. Batch architectures spool information to be processed or manipulated in runs. These runs are done without human interaction and can be scheduled in advance. Today finance applications still rely on batch depreciation runs, for example. Batch runs may activate every month on accounting systems to do closings that include depreciation or other calculation. Batch style architectures are at the core of many large scale applications even though they may be wrapped by interactive shells.

OLTP – On-line Transaction Processing architectures dominate most interactive systems today such as airlines reservation systems. In these systems data entry results are visible immediately to all agents in the world using the system. Add, change, delete capability is typically provided to a range of transaction types from account creation, purchases, and modifications. Large scale OLTP architectures typically support hundreds or thousands of simultaneous users.

Real-Time - devices working with discrete time budgets responding in human perceptible time use real-time architectures. There is a range of real-time systems from hard real-time to soft real-time. Hard real-time systems typically involve the control of physical devices such as control surfaces on airliners (known as fly-by-wire) while soft real-time systems often must respond in defined time budgets but may not control real world devices (for example some telecommunications software). Real-time systems require additional modeling and design steps in order to define actions within time budgets as opposed to the best effort level of response in say an OLTP system.

Data Streaming – another major architecture style is that of data streaming which typically receives data feeds from multiple "upstream" systems, processes or manipulates the data it receives and passes the data on to one or more "downstream" systems. In many cases this type of architecture can utilize a batch style architecture as a base but also requires the communications interfaces of a distributed system. This type of architecture may also support some inquiry capability.

C/S (and web) – most systems today are developed in a Client/Server model. C/S systems are distinguished from monolithic systems by their multi-tier segregation of functionality from client device and server layer. In this model a client requests a service of a server application. Today most internet systems are implemented using C/S architectures. At face value, any implementation type, say a checking application, can be done with C/S that will be both data entry and batch – and may even include communications to other machines also seen as clients or servers.

Decision Support - data entry and reporting or modeling, often used for combat decision support, data warehouse applications. These applications may be part data streaming and implemented on a C/S model. They typically collect business or operational data and allow for inquiry on the data to support decision making. A good example might be customer churn monitoring applications in web or telecommunications networks which look for predictor behavior in customer data and then suggest actions, such as discounts, to attempt to retain the customer who appears likely to drop a service.

Hybrid – few modern systems rely on only one of these models exclusively. In many cases a system is fed by upstream systems and feeds other systems, data streaming, but to do so utilizes C/S computing and is also used as a decision making platform.

Deciding on an architectural style, or combination of styles, the goals of the system must be kept in mind. What is the best system type to meet the needs. Further, what are we trying to maximize? Is performance the most important or legacy support? If performance is the goal we might specify high-end processors throughout the architecture. If we are looking for a low cost solution then perhaps a terminal-host configuration would be best. Just one mini-computer and a bunch of dumb-terminals (say in a POS (Point of Sale) application) might do better. This will be cheaper than several servers, networking, and many PCs. But this may not suit the customers overall needs. If the customer needs to do some graphics and they want to use 3rd-party spreadsheet tools, then perhaps they cannot use a terminal host architecture. However, this might be solved by giving them a set of PCs for managerial use but terminal interfaces for the remainder. Of course in today's economy PCs tend to be the cheapest initial cost but with Net PCs on the horizon this scenario has come back as an additional issue for the architect and system engineer. Another tradeoff area is communication speeds and cost. Moving bits around may seem free but the costs are a part of the architectural solution space. These are the types of considerations that come into play with processing architectures and application styles.

Solidifying the architecture by working through these types of issues which an experienced architect knows to ask about happens in tandem with further discussions with the customer where requirements are firmed up. As the major requirements settle the architecture that will suit them should come bubbling up to the surface. Often their needs will fall into one of these broad style categories. If the customer is building a spacecraft chances are you will be building a real-time system. If they want to keep track of accounting records it will be a data-store system. Once you understand the significant families of architectural styles your requirements discovery process will lead you to a standard and proven processing model. This is part of the art of building software applications, knowing from the problem domain and the problem to be solved what application types are applicable to the solution space.

5.1.5. Multi-Tier Architectures

From the beginning of computing mainframes dominated. These were considered single tier architectures. Eventually, multitier architectures appeared and today dominate the computing landscape. In many environments it is hard to discern how many computing tiers there are – a front end tier (both fixed and mobile clients), an application tier, a business rules tier, a database tier, a storage tier and so on.

Mainframe technologies, however, remain in use and due to the scale and proven capabilities still receive consideration. These platforms have received a lot of investment and are well proven. However, C/S at first with "fat client" applications and today with web client applications are both popular and cheap. Windows PC architectures remain dominant and popular as a platform for development of either C/S applications, shrink-wrapped applications, or SaaS (Software as a Service) and web applications. In any of these configurations the architect must make a choice on functionality distribution. On the client side you have user presentation and sometimes limited business rules. On the servers you have business rules, file services, fax services, print services, email host, and Internet host.

This physical separation also carries with it functional associations, separations, and allocations. Often we have a separation into three distinct areas in software architecture: presentation, logic (application or business rules), and data storage. For example, on the PC client the user may see an order entry form. A query may be submitted by them with "part 300" requested. The middle tier logic may trap that and suggest that you also need to install part 301 since they go together. This may be presented back to the user and then the modified request committed to the data tier on the backend. This physical and logical layering of an architecture is a key tool in my virtual toolbox when it comes to design.

The use of a 2 tier C/S architecture has mostly been bypassed in recent years. As a best practice, even if the architecture is a physical 2 tier it is recommended to design in a 3 tier fashion. One reason the "fat client" style has gone out of favor is that you need to maintain version compatibility on all the clients. Often on boot up of the client the server refreshes anything that may be out of date. This can be rather complex. Queries in any model often go against stored procedures installed on the database layer. These have to be coded to the specific database vendor software so that they are typically proprietary and may cause portability problems to some extent. Scalability is more of a problem based on the server choice. Nevertheless, the 2 tier is good for masking heterogeneous databases

With 3 tier architectures we have presentation and logic on the client but almost all the business rules move off to the application server at tier 2. This new server acts as a buffer or proxy for the database. The advantage here is that the rules are moved off the client and we also have more specialization of processors in the architecture to aid in performance and scalability. Thus, we see the use of multiple machines each with a role for print services or mail services off-loading the work of the application request routers. Adding more 2 tier application servers is a performance gain. These concepts are important enough to require some additional detailed discussion and the introduction of some reference diagrams as well.

5.1.5.1. Tiered Architectures

Current trends in architecture use the concept of tiers to clarify physical, network, and application concerns in system design. Just as in a wedding cake, modern systems are built in a pyramidal shape, each level connected to the one above and below. These levels are called tiers. Using the architecture styles described above we begin to partition the application across one, two, three, or n-deep, architectures.

5.1.5.1.1. Single Tier Architectures

The terminal-host style of computing (Fig. **3**) has a long and successful history as mentioned. All early time-sharing systems were of this kind. Most ground-breaking applications in Banking, Telecommunications, Air Traffic Control, and more used this style. Today, many of these systems continue to operate. However, most new applications have migrated to other architectures using multiple tiers for additional flexibility. Such Mainframe platforms have been invested in over several decades and are well proven.

5.1.5.1.2. Two-Tier Architectures

The two-tier architecture (Fig. **4**) popularized the client/server model of computing. While C/S designs predate the PC and the typical PC-LAN configurations of the late 1980s, it was the applications using this topology that brought PC computing to the forefront of modern application development especially in the early 1990s. On the client side you have user presentation and sometimes limited business rules. On the servers you have business rules, file services, fax services, print services, email host, and Internet host.

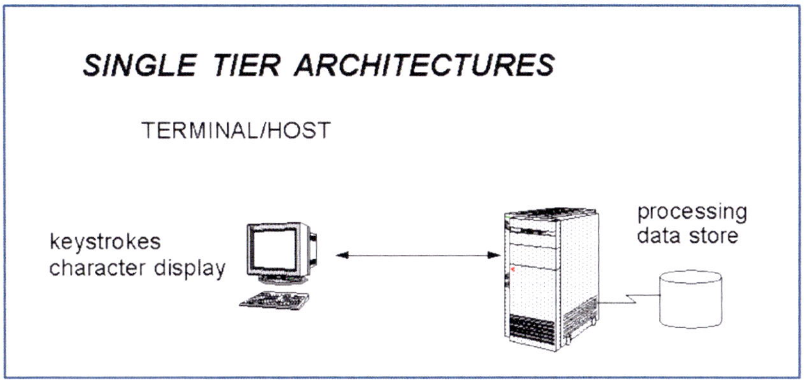

Figure 3: A Single Tier Architecture.

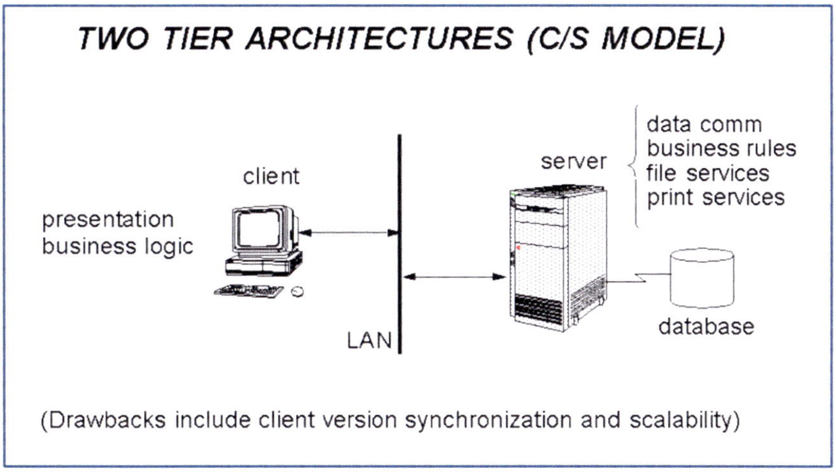

Figure 4: Two Tier Architecture.

What really lies behind this architecture is a simple yet powerful distributed computing approach. In Fig. **5** the fundamental aspects of the C/S model is depicted in the call and return relationship. This can be within a program, between two programs, or across a network. C/S is quite simple in concept, much like the relationship between customer, waitress, and cook. Servers have processes which are always running and waiting for requests. Clients may or may not run. They make a request and complete or loop for the next request. Many of these applications rely on multi-threaded solutions to implement.

With the 2-tier platform, powerful desktop PCs could perform many complex user interactions such as GUI display, data preparation, and so on, freeing up the server platforms for other work. Open communications and networking standards allowed for any client (tier 1) to talk to any server (tier 2), at least in theory. This platform style remains popular for low-end departmental applications or for the access path to more sophisticated 3-tier platforms. Within modern C/S applications over the web the SOA (Service Oriented Architecture) nomenclature has become dominant. SOA takes the idea of C/S and abstracts the interfaces into callable methods across the network. Instead of an RPC call you might implement with a SOAP (Services OAP) call.

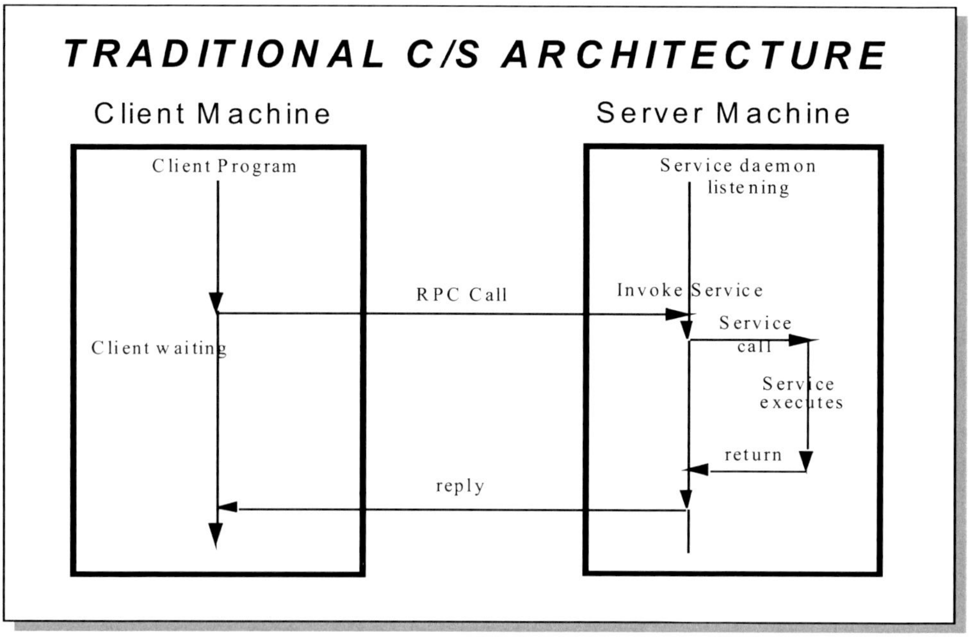

Figure 5: Client/Server in its Most Fundamental Form.

5.1.5.1.3. Three-Tier Architectures

Three-Tier applications grew from the merger of high-end application servers with 2-tier user based LANs. Providing single source data repositories, shared transaction clusters, and pooled application resources, the 3-tier architecture is highly flexible. In this model clients access a tier-2 intermediate application router which brokers access to tier-3 resources. In this way optimizations can be made for large user pools.

While this model of computing is still popular it has evolved to an n-tier model or Intranet/Internet model. The n-tiers allows for a variety of higher tiers to be designed where multiple network hops might be required to complete a transaction. In many cases servers act as clients in contacting other servers on behalf of a client request.

With 3-tier architectures (Fig. **6**) we have presentation and logic on client but almost all the business rules move off to the application server at tier 2. This new server acts as a buffer or proxy for the database. The advantage here is that the rules are moved off the client to allow for a common distribution point within the architecture and we also have more specialization of processors in the architecture to aid in performance and scalability. Thus, we see the use of multiple machines each with a role for print services or mail services off-loading the work of the application request routers. Adding more 2nd tier application servers is typically a performance gain.

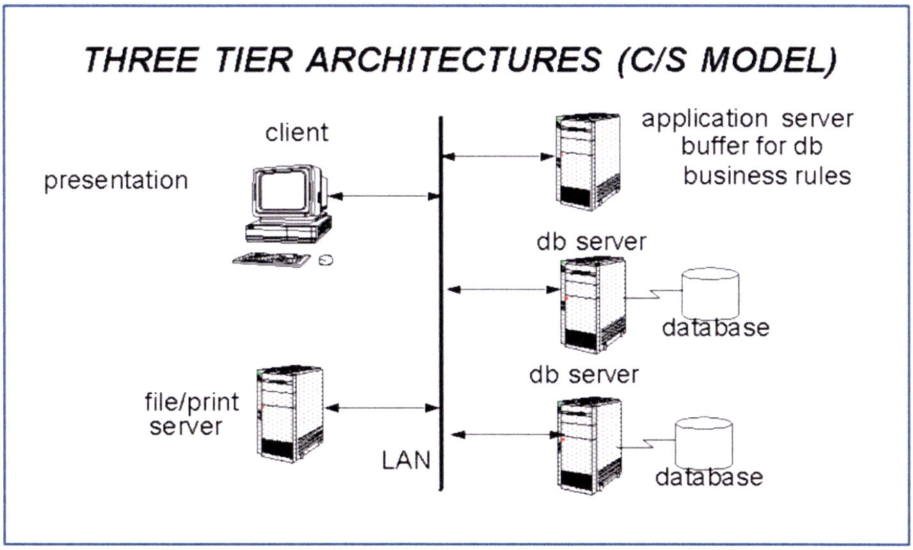

Figure 6: A Simplified 3-Tier Architecture.

5.1.5.1.4. N-Tier Architectures

Using the processing topologies of all its predecessors, N-Tier Architectures (Fig. **7**) are now providing massively scalable and flexible computing solutions. The distinction between client and server and between tier-x and tier-y is not as crucial. Instead, services themselves (SOA) are the relevant architectural backbone of large-scale computing solutions. Internet browsers make universal application access simple in this environment. Seamless blending of private network resources and public information sites opens an entirely different set of opportunities for the system architect.

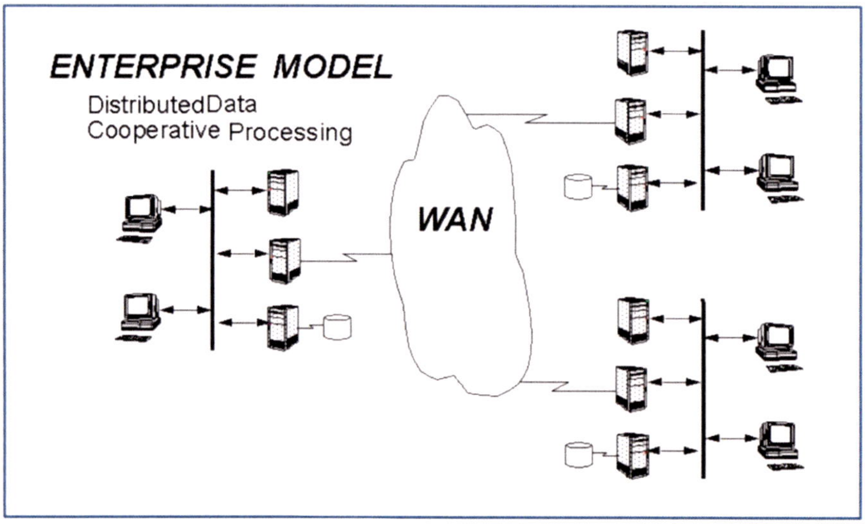

Figure 7: An Enterprise Systems View.

These types of tiered architectures can also be reflected in a pattern. Regardless of the tier-ing used, a design pattern to support our implementation of these applications can be derived (see Fig. **8**). Using a client/server agent architecture, an application will spawn any number of search agents to find the best possible contract price in a broker application for example. The trader will then be able to choose the one that is most preferable to the client. The point here is that the architecture pattern in use is abstracted above the implementation level.

A conclusion from looking over the tiered architecture space is that there is flexibility in each. In today's environment with web applications dominating the multiple tier architecture is most common. Mobile device development is also bursting on the scene today. Development for the iPhone, iPad, and Android platform have increased dramatically since the introduction of these client devices. Now the architect has more devices to work with but the backend platforms remain similar to traditional solutions. Providing scalable solutions for millions of handheld devices poses a new challenge but many tried and true tools can help solve these problems which we can discuss now.

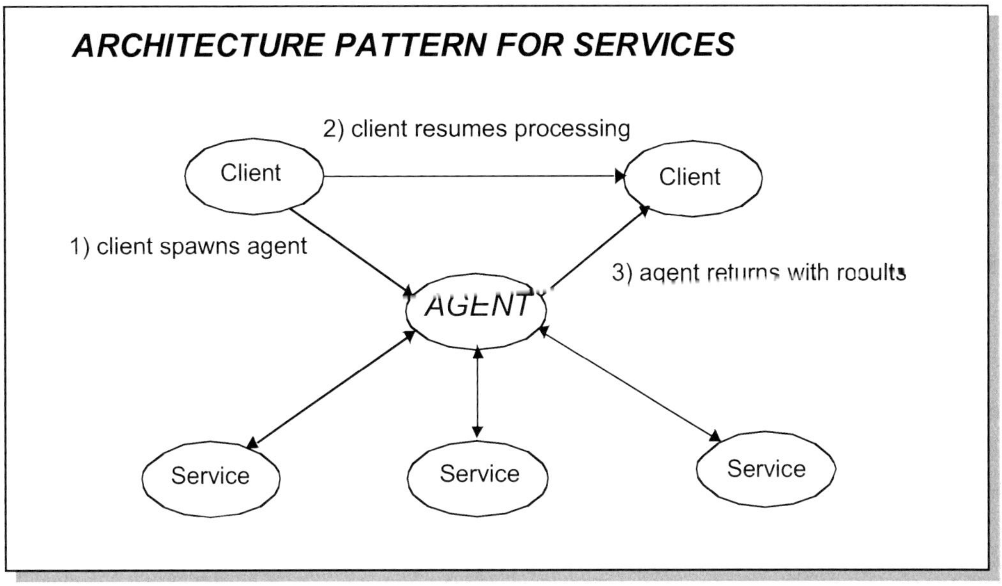

Figure 8: A Services Pattern.

5.1.6. Web Architectures

The growth of the Internet called on the architecture styles and multi-tier C/S processing models to culminate in a variety of specific architectures to support the needs of on-line applications. This includes mobile and touch screen devices. The nature of the Internet, its history and enabling technologies, have generated a significant interest in building applications to take advantage of its widespread influence and capabilities. For the purposes of software development the Internet can be viewed as at least three high-level segments. These segments have been called the Internet, the Extranet, and the Intranet [13]. Each of these spheres as shown in Fig. **9** are relative to one another. Keeping these different views in mind allows for many subsequent architectures to emerge. This enriches my toolbox of software architectures and are worth exploring in detail before looking into the patterns for many of the overlaying designs.

Each internet architecture zone is based on the same fundamental computing constructs and standards (*e.g.*, HTTP, TCP/IP), however, each sphere is accessible to a different audience and is driven by a different purpose. Applications can vary from region to region and each can be segregated from the other. At the innermost level the Intranet represents the World Wide Web (Web) based applications running inside an organization's firewall. Users of these applications are typically employees or contractors given access to internal computing resources. Applications are instantly deployable and can be reached by nearly anyone with a workstation and a network hookup.

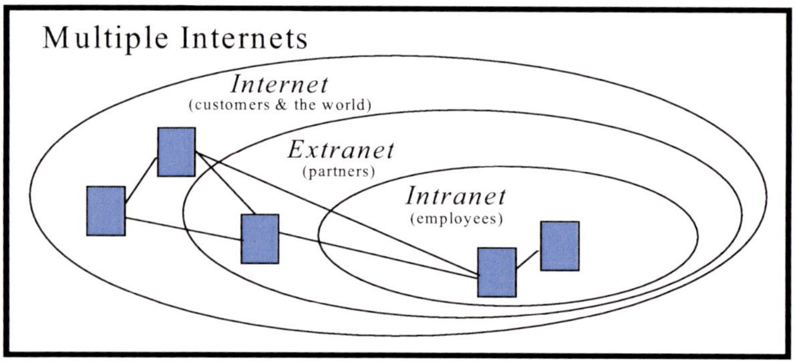

Figure 9: Multiple Internet Environments.

The next level out is the Extranet which is comprised of trusted customers or franchise owners (say private insurance agents of an insurance company). Applications are run in this zone for the same reasons as Intranet applications but they are now exported to trusted business partners or customers. This zone holds promise for businesses since it builds on past electronic interfaces like EDI. Nearly all major corporations run Intranets today. Finally, there is the Internet at large. The Internet is the unrestricted globally distributed cooperative computer network. On this level, applications are visible to anyone having access to the network infrastructure.

5.1.6.1. The Internet (s) and the Developer

The application developer wishing to take advantage of Internet based technologies will first need to consider which portion of the Internet world they will develop for. Each development effort or system must understand if its audience is "internal", "trusted external", or "consumer". These different types are often called B2B (Business to Business) and B2C (Business to Consumer). The tools needed to develop for each class of user will be nearly identical except in perhaps two key areas:

Performance: Intranet and Internet applications may demonstrate different levels of performance even if the application is the same. The architecture of the Intranet benefits from relatively fast LANs and well-engineered WANs under the management of the organization's personnel. The Internet in comparison is much harder to predict in terms of performance. Access to Internet resources is through proxy servers and firewalls. Overall, the impact on application performance will be negative. Designers should keep this limitation in mind.

Security: Intranet applications may not require the same level of security that Extranet and Internet applications will require. Extranets may necessitate cloning entire Web facilities outside the firewall or in a "sandbox" within the firewall that will not be fully accessible to the public as are Internet applications or to use password schemes. This may require additional design and security steps (such as SSL, encryption, authorization, SSO (Single Sign On), and authentication).

Image: Internet and even Extranet applications pull developers closer to the needs of graphic design and rapidly changing multimedia content creation than Intranet applications. The Internet culture is one of polished images, quickly evolving sites, and non-traditionalist design. Specifically, multimedia authoring kits, image editing, 3-D application kits, live data feed subscriptions, and more, will all need to be considered to keep a site fashionable within the Web universe. Naturally, image and multi-media will also be important on the Intranet as requirements emerge to use these techniques to increase work tasks and collaboration.

5.1.6.2. Application Types for the Internet

A variety of popular application types or architectures can be ported to the Internet environment. Many applications found within the corporate portfolio could be built or redeployed on the Intranet. Further, new types of applications can be deployed quickly that might work with hypermedia or rely on rich content types like multimedia. Applications currently running on the many corporate Intranets include employee time reporting, the employee directory, divisional and departmental information sites, software distribution, software component catalogues, document publication and archiving, project management, personal and project calendars, news services, library access, and more.

Many application developers have added a Web interface to permit access to existing large scale applications without a complete rewrite. Corporations and organizations of all kinds have also deployed thousands of public Internet sites for commerce, research, or communication purposes. At this point in the evolution of the Internet countless applications have also been written ground up for Internet deployment.

Obviously, all of these applications reflect very different customer requirements and technical architectures. The GartnerGroup [14] provides a slightly different model for application types which both overlaps with and enhances the Anderson model. The addition of a Hybrid type of application is especially valid in viewing the variety of features observed in today's Internet applications:

- Information Access.
- Entertainment.
- Collaboration (Social Networking and Web 2.0).
- Transaction Processing.
- Hybrid.

These application types call for differing types of architectural solutions and understanding their nature is important to having them used properly form our toolbox. Outlining these application types helps to define the approaches and tools required to build them. An understanding of how each significant type of application is built in terms of its computing constructs will serve our purposes better. Several key designs supporting these application types are briefly introduced below and then more fully explained.

5.1.6.2.1. Information Access

These applications are supported by Static Hypertext, Dynamic Hypertext, Query Architectures, and Hybrid approaches.

Static Hypertext: These applications post HTML documents on the Web with static indexing and are well suited to on-line books, project documentation repositories, and news archives. Such applications are built using simple HTML tags in a set of index pages organized by subject or date that reference document files that may be in HTML or native format (*e.g.*, PDF, MS Word).

Dynamic Hypertext: Similar to Static Hypertext, applications of this type generate customized content "on-the-fly" in response to user selections or queries. Typical of this type of application is an HTML template that is filled out with data after a user input. Data may be pulled from another file(s) or from a database.

Query Oriented: Applications of this type are constructed in much the same manner as the Transaction systems but the end goal is normally to provide the user with a desired set of data. Such applications could either provide responses from a file based repository, a database, or a combination of remote data stores. A related type is the search engine of which there are two types: the restricted search of the local server or a broad search of the Internet /Intranet. Many search engines exist that provide this facility on the Internet.

Collaboration Applications: These applications are supported by Conferencing, White-Board, Virtual Reality, and Discussion Group applications. There are many technologies supporting these applications.

5.1.6.2.2. Transaction Processing/IT Applications

These applications are supported mostly by Transaction Oriented technologies and Query and Reporting technologies.

Transaction Oriented: Some Web applications are transaction based. In this type of application the user is typically presented with a form or a set of forms to fill out. Once the data entry task is complete the user submits the data and moves on. In this type of system the user must be authenticated (often with a password) and a session may need to be simulated with the user. The transactions are often fired from a CGI (Common Gateway Interface) program or other backend service models like SOA that will then interface with the database managing the user accounts.

Query and Reporting: These applications provide management decision support roles. Many applications have already been developed of this type. Technologies can be purchased to report on data resident within standard databases. Also, many development technologies are being released with web based interfaces such as defect tracking tools for software development.

5.1.6.2.3. Entertainment Applications

The applications within this domain are virtually unlimited and rely heavily on the techniques of Multimedia, VRML (Virtual Reality Markup Language), and on-line chat sessions. On-line virtual reality communal game rooms are a good example. For business applications it is more likely that the component technologies (such as video, animated graphics, and audio capabilities) will be incorporated into systems that deliver data or other business value.

5.1.6.2.4. Hybrid Applications

Naturally, most applications pull elements from many design types. It is quite common for applications to have both static Web pages and dynamic Web pages. Transaction Oriented systems often offer searching, retrieval, and query capabilities. To combine these various design approaches requires the type of planning and rigor in development that is normally seen in large-scale distributed systems projects.

5.1.6.3. Limits (Oh my!) to the Web

Obviously the domains of interest that can be ported to the Web are quite extensive. However, not every domain can be served by a hypertext browser interface. Applications requiring real-time or near real-time functionality cannot as of now be built using the Internet due to the absence of scheduling services and task preemption. Here we consider some of these issues:

Today there is no reliable way to predict end-to-end performance levels for an Internet/Intranet application. In traditional applications we deliver quantifiable performance in the mili-second, sub-second, or multiple-second response ranges. On the Internet or Intranet it remains virtually impossible to predict such performance levels. On some applications QoS (Quality of Service) is provided through defined network traffic prioritization schemes guaranteeing some performance level.

There also remains no existing end-to-end transaction control over the Internet due to its stateless environment. Several techniques are available to provide transaction simulation (*e.g.*, the "cookie" client side session hold, hidden frames, or HTML hidden fields). Most major database and tool vendors now promise transaction integrity each using a different proprietary approach.

One can build relatively serious applications on the Internet platform but in terms of expected application reliability information remains limited.

5.1.6.4. A Development Reference Architecture

In order to discuss the design and development of custom applications on top of this standard infrastructure, we need a more abstract view of essentially the same architecture where certain aspects of the service environment are assumed. Fig. **10** indicates this abstract Internet Application Reference Architecture [15].

Large Internet sites may have 100,000 pages of content or more, and receive millions of hits per day on multiple servers and databases. This Application Reference Architecture is designed to reflect this type of application demand to support this. Such an architecture assumes dynamic routing of service requests to a variety of supporting systems and applications. This enables the construction of complex multi-tier applications accessed both by Web connections and traditional C/S or distributed computing mechanisms.

Briefly, the components of this architecture include:

Browsers: Application developers cannot normally specify the browsers that access their designs or the workstations they are run on. Naturally, Intranet applications can assume more homogeneity in browser types but should not build-in exclusivity to their applications.

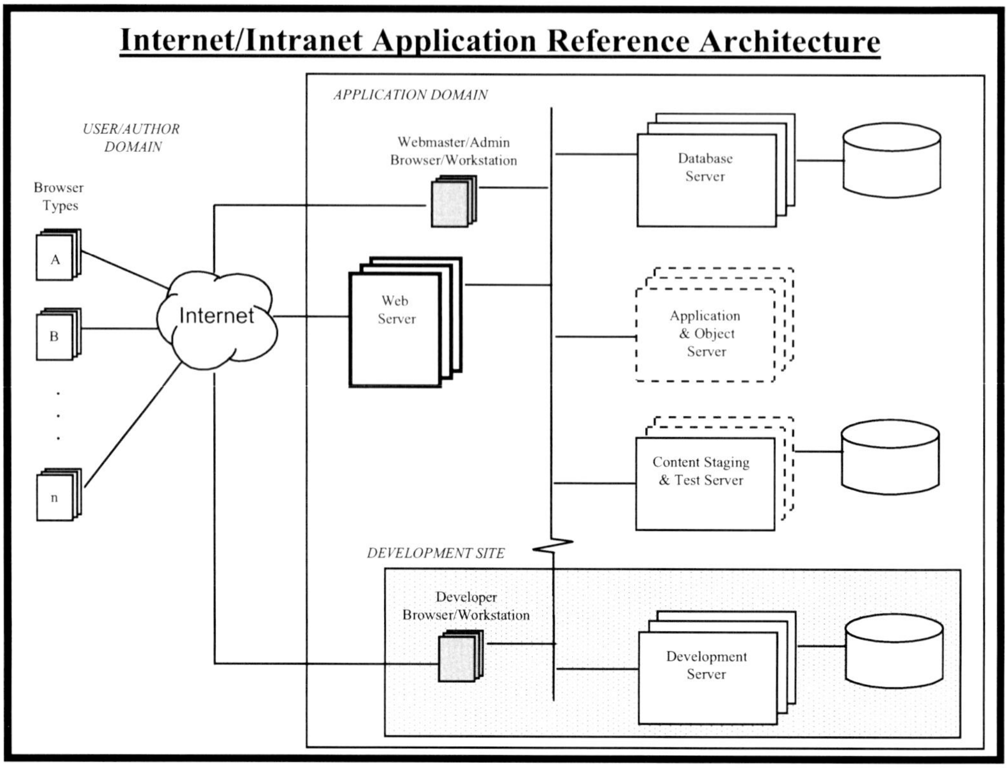

Figure 10: Internet Application Reference Architecture.

Internet: Many of the infrastructure components in the Internet computing environment may not be modified by an application. Firewalls, gateways, domain servers, and so on, will be deployed and supported in nearly all cases by a central authority which is typically not the developer themselves. Thus, application developers may not find a need or the freedom to reconfigure such devices. This may put some limits on the architecture of an application.

Web Servers: Within the site domain we find web servers offering HTTP services, hosting content, and bridging application services. Site aspects such as scale, redundancy, and functional specialization, may vary from server to server. Web Servers will normally be in the reach of developers to modify or customize. This is true of common servers such as IIS and Apache.

DB/Application Servers: In support of the Web Servers are the database and application servers. Relying on gateway products or custom interfaces, applications on these machines will be triggered by the Web Servers (several of these approaches will be presented below). Architecting these configurations require the same skills used in developing traditional distributed systems.

Staging & Test Servers: Many sites will have the need to stage content publication due to the complexity and large data volumes involved. Test environments can piggyback off such content staging servers. These servers have evolved to include Content Management software.

Development Environment: In order to safely develop and deploy applications the familiar model of separate Development, Test, and Production environments may need to be maintained. This may include Development databases, web servers isolated from the Internet/Intranet, and sample data or test scripts. Many development tools now offer personal web servers to facilitate this need.

5.1.6.5. Development Options and Technical Choices

The Internet presents many choices for developers. Building applications for the Internet environment described above brings up many questions:

- Which languages and tools should I use to build my application?
- Which APIs will be most resilient to rapidly changing technology ?
- What are the preferred file formats for document storage?
- How do I provide session control and end-to-end transactions?
- What is the best method of database access?
- How do I develop applications that deliver predictable performance?

Such questions require familiarity with the implementation options available for building Internet applications. One of the primary concerns while looking at Web development issues relates to the difficulty of betting on emerging technologies. There are several major options for implementation each of which is discussed below.

- Static HTML.
- Common Gateway Interface.
- Scripting & Extended HTML.
- Server API.
- Server Side Scripting.
- Web Enabled Client/Server.
- Adjunct Application Servers.
- Database Generated Applications.
- Java Development.
- .Net development (replaced the earlier ActiveX Development (with ASP)).
- IIOP and the Object Web.
- Other (Groupware, proprietary platforms, *etc.*).
- Hybird Environments.

5.1.6.5.1. Static HTML

Static HTML applications represent the first generation of Internet applications. Pages of HTML are served to the requesting browser from files on the local disk where the Web Server resides. These pages may be complex being composed of text, graphics, audio, and video clips. These implementations require updating of each file when changes are needed and can cause maintenance problems.

5.1.6.5.2. Common Gateway Interface

Common Gateway Interface (CGI) is still a mainstay of many Internet applications. CGI Scripting is often done in the PERL language. This is a flexible but interpreted language. PERL has relatively poor performance but it is moderate in programming difficulty. Overhead is added by the fact the each time a CGI script is invoked it must be loaded, run, and unloaded. Services are not available continuously but only on an as needed basis (**see** Fig. **11**). Database connections cannot be sustained between requests so this adds to the performance problems. For these applications one of the most important tools is a good text editor.

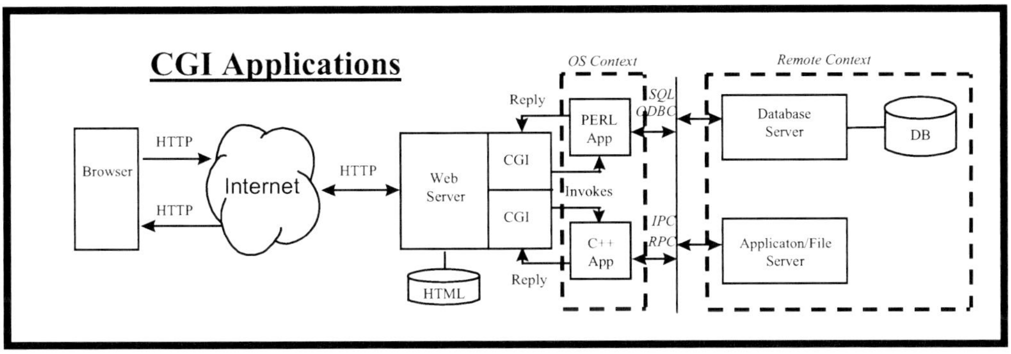

Figure 11: CGI Applications.

CGI programs can also be developed in C/C++ quite easily. Performance is a major advantage to this approach as well as the ability to accommodate legacy hooks. C/C++ may have some database connectivity issues but these can be worked around.

Aside from PERL and C++ many other languages can be selected for scripting and development. Common choices include Python, Visual Basic, Tcl, VB Script, JavaScript and ksh. In fact there is no real barrier to using any language for building CGI based applications and in fact vendors of programming tools are continually releasing new tools to the market. The real differentiators in selecting a language will be familiarity, performance, integration capabilities, and tool availability.

5.1.6.5.3. Scripting & Extended HTML

Another implementation option is to use HTML extensions or embedded scripts in client-side HTML. These techniques embed 4GL constructs into HTML content pages which are then executed by an application engine somewhere on the back-end. Alternatively, HTML tags that are not part of the HTML standard are sometimes used to provide additional functionality. Scripting language commands are also supported by some browsers allowing for pre-processing of data input and other routine tasks. Embedded 4GL is not a preferred option due to vendor lock-in, poor maintainability, and reportedly difficult debugging. Similarly, extended HTML is not recommended due to the proprietary nature of the extended commands. However, embedded scripting languages are powerful, simple, and effective and are widely used. JavaScript is one of the most popular of these languages and is highly flexible.

Server API

Web server applications can be built using the SAPI (Server Application Programming Interface) offered by each particular vendor. These proprietary APIs are helpful in deploying functionality in the short term but will tend to bind developers to a particular server as other vendors will vary their offerings to capture market share. This will severely limit portability and application consistency. However, using SAPI has the advantage that programs can be triggered by the server and run as part of its process space thus using less physical resources and providing better performance (see Fig. **12**). The other difficulty is that SAPI was not designed to access databases and some limitations need to be worked around. SAPI applications can be developed in most languages discussed in the CGI section above. Nevertheless, many applications may find the performance benefits worth the limitations. Also, many tools will support the use of a SAPI interface. There are a wide variety of tools which follow this pattern including Ruby on Rails and many others.

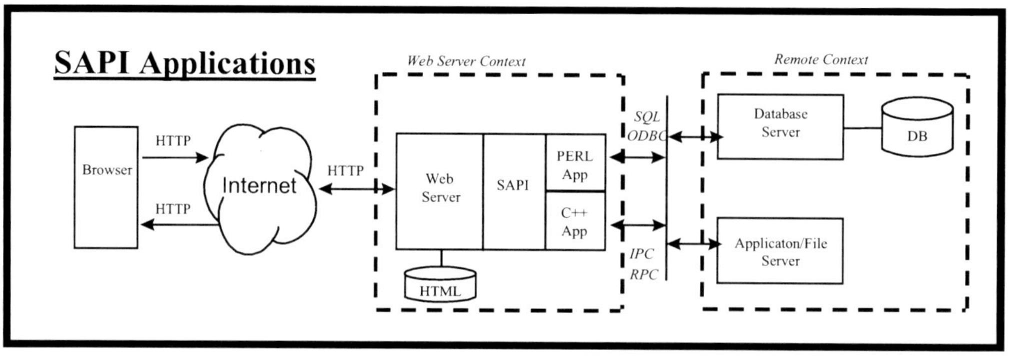

Figure 12: SAPI Applications.

5.1.6.5.4. Server Side Scripting

Web Servers have introduced additional ways to execute scripts or other programs on the web server. Basically, this model replaces the CGI or SAPI interfaces to server side logic with natively integrated script execution capabilities. A good example of this approach is the Active Server Pages or.Net interfaces from Microsoft which is explained in more detail below.

5.1.6.5.5. Adjunct Application Servers (The Brokered Transaction Model)

There are many tools that allow developers to augment both the facilities of the web server and the database server by adding a yaas (yet-another-application-server). In this class of application an additional server is placed in the architecture which manages many facilities that the programmer working in PERL and CGI would normally need to develop by hand. Facilities for session management, database access, and user control are typically part of the application adjunct server (see Fig. **13**). Such tools as NetDynamics and MS InterDev were early examples of these types of products. Some vendors are also offering alternative methods to return results directly to the browser bypassing the web server altogether and speeding up performance. This model resembles a 3-tier C/S model. However, in this case a runtime server is in place onto which the middle tier application logic is added.

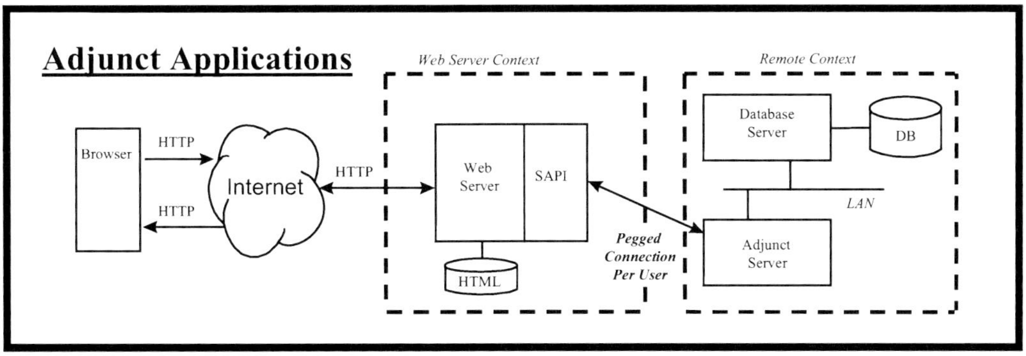

Figure 13: Brokered Transactions.

5.1.6.5.6. Database Generated Applications

A variant on the Adjunct Server is the Database Generated Application model of implementation. In this pattern the database vendor provides capabilities native to the database engine that can results in a dynamically generated page from content stored in a (typically) relational database. In this implementation a URL is translated on-the-fly into a query against a database that contains content matching the query. The reply to the browser comes *via* HTTP directly from the database and bypasses the web server for better performance. Significantly, there is no adjunct server involved and the programmer does not need to maintain the site in HTML but instead manages the content in a relational schema. Obviously, this is self-defeating for applications where a relational model is not suitable, but is promising for transaction oriented systems.

5.1.6.5.7. Java Development

Naturally, Java is being used as both a platform (JavaOS) and as a development language for standard applications as well as Internet applications. Java was the only language choice which is truly platform independent although C# has followed in its footsteps. Java is based on C++ and Smalltalk but does not contain pointers or multiple inheritance. Java is a partially compiled language that is interpreted at runtime by the Java Virtual Machine which delivers the platform independence to the language (as long as the client has the Vitual Machine installed). Java also provides simple database connectivity with JDBC (Java Data Base Connectivity) as explained below. Java applications can be sent to the client side or configured to run on the server itself (see Fig. **14**).

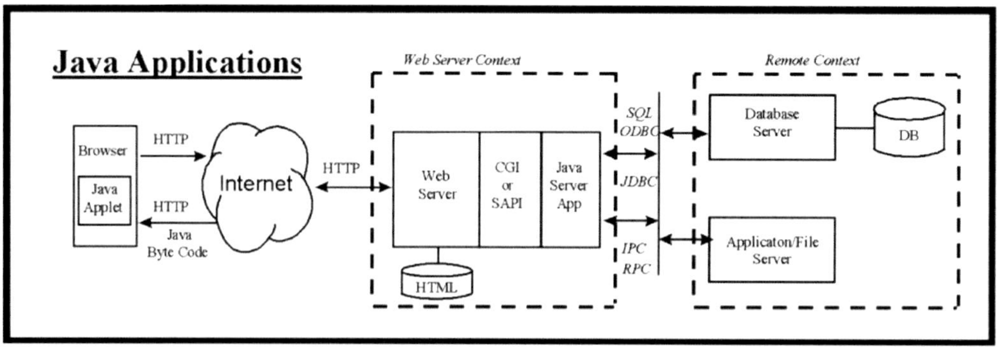

Figure 14: Java Applications.

The flexibility of the Java architecture adds to its portability and platform independence to make it one of the most popular choices for application development for the Internet platform. Understanding these common base architectures provides a key set of tools in the architect's toolbox. Knowing which approach to follow given a certain set of requirements is the challenge. It may not always be possible to choose the optimal architecture from your toolbox due to practical considerations or legacy requirements. Nevertheless, understanding the scope of available architectures plays a significant role in the act of architecture.

JDBC (Java Data Base Connectivity) is the Java API for executing SQL statements. It is a set of Java classes and interfaces that allow a developer to create database applications using a pure Java API. There are generally two JDBC Models for database access: 1) Two-tier Model - in this model the Java application or applet talks directly to the database, and 2) Three-tier Model - in this model SQL statements are sent to a "middle tier" server which interacts with the database and sends the results back to the Java application or applet.

5.1.6.5.8. Net Development

A replacement technology for Microsoft's early web platform technologies including Active X is.Net. While there are still a variety of tools that allow for the development of Internet applications with vendor specific technologies like.Net, this technology has carved out a large market. ActiveX from Microsoft was a refit of OLE and OCX controls for Internet applications. Limits and technical obsolescence of ActiveX led to the rise of.Net and ASP as the dominant Microsoft offering for web development..Net is a powerful toolset that allows developers with large prior investments in Microsoft code to immediately use that functionality on the Web. Unfortunately, Microsoft tends to expand its offerings into proprietary areas and does not always adopt open standards (Silverlight is a good example of this). Thus, some parts of the Microsoft tool suite may not be supported by all browsers or platforms nor is it recommended for heterogeneous environments.

5.1.6.5.9. iPad and Mobile Architectures

There has been a boom in development for smart phones and other mobile clients like the iPad and various tablet computers in the last few years. The iPad essentially created this market on a sustaining and growth trajectory where many such technologies had failed in the past. While many of the technologies involved in these applications are beyond the scope of this book, like RF technology, stylus operations, touch screens, and more, we will just touch on what is behind the scenes on the platform or to introduce a common buzz word – what is inside the cloud.

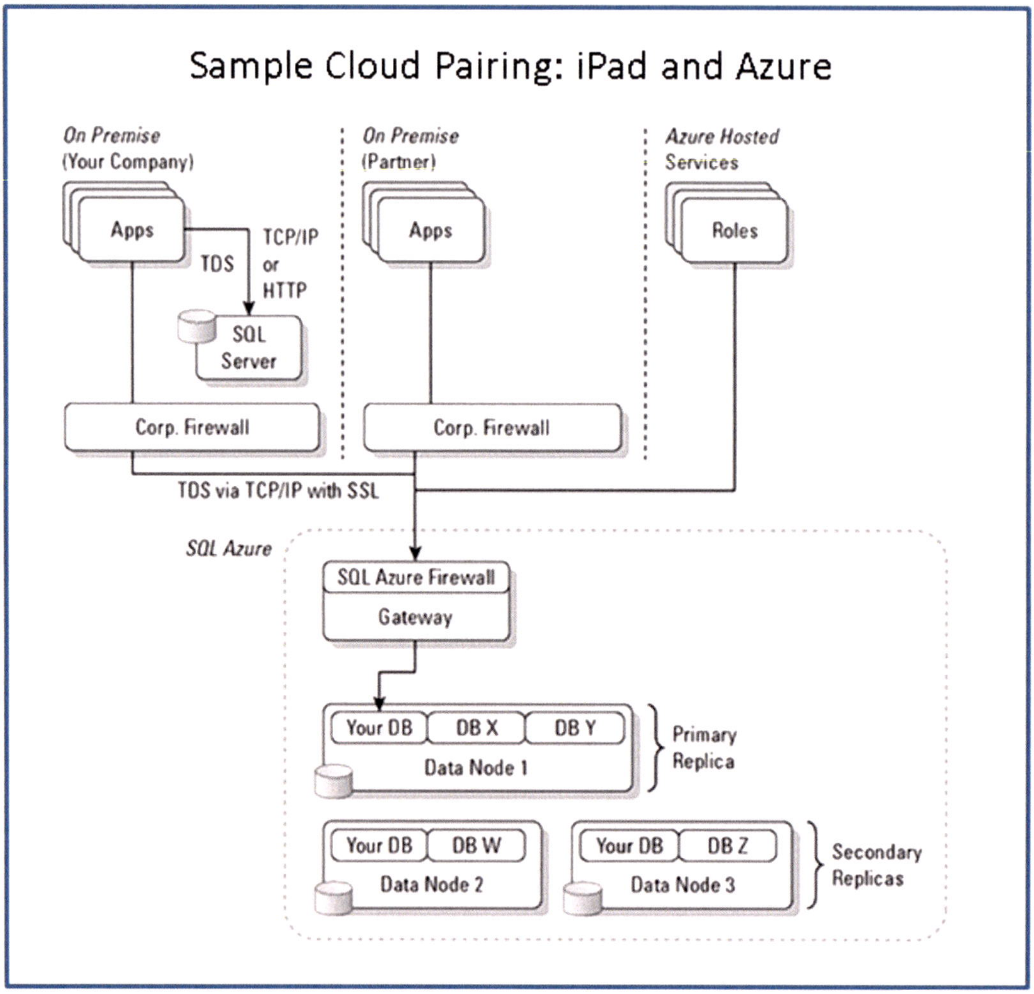

Figure 15: iPad application integration with backend Microsoft Azure – Note the same architecture pattern used in these mobile applications – the front end client is irrelevant to the backend API [16].

In actual fact, cloud computing is a mirror of the technical patterns we have been discussing in this chapter. Tiered architectures, remote invocations, separation of concerns, and loose coupling all play a critical role in could technology. What is new with mobile development today is its ubiquity, flexibility, feature expanse, and future dynamism. Mobile applications combined with cloud computing lead us to a new generation of scalable utility architectures. A good way to explore this is to look at recent integrations of new mobile APIs with existing backend technologies. As an example we can look at Microsoft's Azure cloud offering which is a traditional enterprise scale hosting service for various software capabilities. This platform can be the backend for any end point device including an iPad and its thousands of applications. What is interesting is the similarity of this integration (shown in Fig. **15**) with the standard tiered architectures we have been discussing and the web architectures detailed above. Thus, our toolbox has proven more helpful than ever as with a small incremental stretch of the integration of a new API an entirely new style of end user computing device can be brought into our platform (or cloud).

5.1.6.6. An Example of a Hybrid Architecture

To conclude our look at architecture, let's consider the fact that most large scale commercial enterprises require a variety of computer based software systems in order to function. These may range from Point of Sale to manufacturing process control applications. Typically these systems cooperate and interface with one another to form a wide scale network of application logic reliant upon a robust and distributed physical infrastructure.

Software developers must be able to build applications that appear to be stand-alone to their users but may in fact be intertwined with several other large applications. In Telecommunications environments, orders are taken by one system, facilities are provisioned by another, those facilities are operated and maintained by still more systems, and finally bills are generated after data is feed all the way through the chain.

In many business fields this level of interdependence is common. This has been called a "system of systems". Each system has its own architecture suited to its mission in the organization. Bills are generated by traditional batch processing, marketing analysis is accomplished with data warehousing and ad hoc reporting, manufacturing is supported through real-time applications. When all of these applications are combined through negotiated interface agreements the sum of the whole is greater than the parts. Fig. **16** indicates what such a system of systems might look like from an abstracted architectural viewpoint. This view applies several architecture patterns to comprise a suite of systems operating together to support a broad range of functionality for an enterprise.

The system of system model shown in Fig. **16** uses standard architecture patterns to describe a typical commercial enterprise. Notice that there are four architectures within this model:

- Shared Repository.
- Database Intensive Decision Support.
- Legacy Wrapper OLTP.
- Pipeline.

These are some of the most common architectures found in commercial applications. Consider the business functionality which these architectures might support for a clothing manufacturer.

Design: The shared repository model will support a CAD based clothing design team. Using a common repository of shapes, textiles, measurements, and colors, new items can be designed and modeled.

Sales: The legacy OLTP system can support sales orders and reporting.

Marketing: Using a database decision support model trends in sales and regional variations can be observed and adjustments in advertising strategy can be made.

Coordination: The pipeline architecture connects all the other systems and may be considered as a part of each system or a system of its own. The pipeline takes new product codes from design to sales and customer demographics from on-line order entry to market research. The pipeline ties the whole enterprise together.

The next step on this application would be to investigate how the complete data models, object models, and code, support its operation.

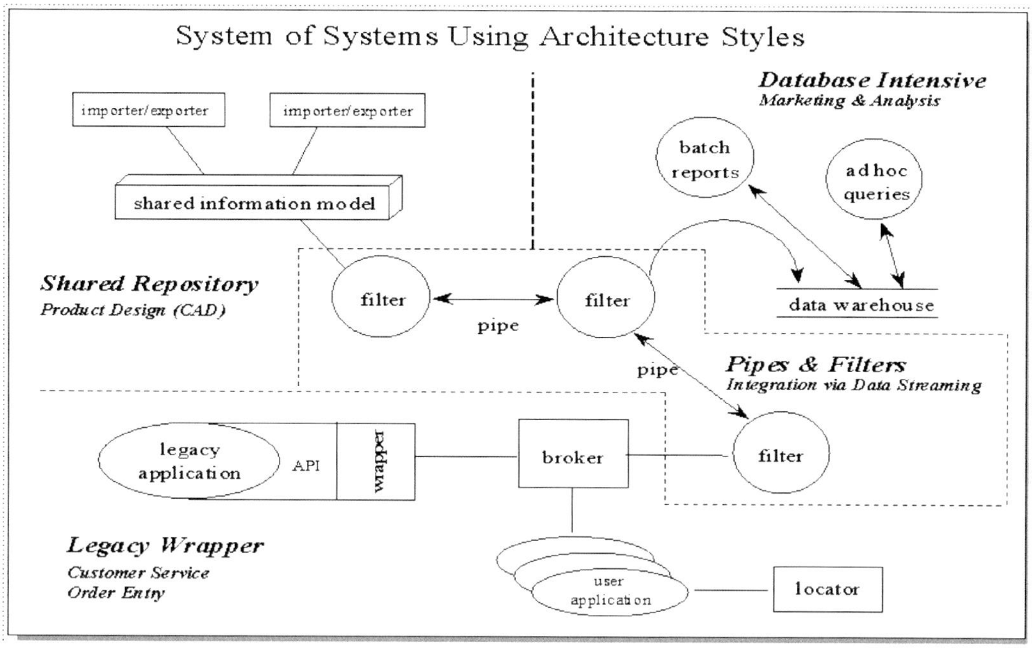

Figure 16: A System of Systems Based on Standard Architecture Patterns.

CONCLUSIONS

As we have seen, architecture provides the key map from requirements to implementation. Further, there have been great strides made in the last 20 years around the definition of patterns and especially architecture patterns. In the context of web architectures there are numerous implementation technologies but we can overlay the more abstract application architecture patterns on top of them. In the end we have seen that there are numerous factors that will lead us to architecting in one style or another including technical and feature requirements, available technology, legacy mandates, and more. The knowledge and awareness of architecture styles have been critical in my own work in software evaluation, design, and quality reviews. These considerations keep architecture and architecture styles at the handiest spot in my toolbox. The specific tools of relevance are 1) an intervention layer of architecture to map requirements to design; 2) architecture concepts (like the 3 C's); 3) tiered architectures; and 4) architecture styles and patterns. These various tools provide a very powerful means to turn any set of requirements into functioning implementation that are well structured and understandable by others.

REFERENCES

[1] **The American Heritage Dictionary**, Second College Edition, Houghton Mifflin Company, Boston, 1982.

[2] *Software Architecture,* **Communications of the ACM**, June, 1995.

[3] Perry, D., & Wolf., A., "*Foundations for the Study of Software Architecture* ", **Software Engineering Notes**, ACM Sigsoft, vol 17, no 4, October 1992.

[4] M. Shaw, R. DeLine, D. V. Klein, T. L. Ross, D. M. Young, and G. Zelesnick. "*Abstractions for software architecture and tools to support them*", **IEEE Transactions on Software Engineering,** 21(4), Apr. 1995, pp. 314-335.

[5] Erl, Thomas, **Service Oriented Architectures: A Field Guide to Integrating XML and Web Services**, Prentice Hall, 2004.

[6] Booch, G., *Handbook of Software Architecture,* viewed December 10, 2011, http://www.handbookofsoftwarearchitecture.com/index.jsp?page=Main.

[7] Coplien, J., **Advanced C++ Programming Styles and Idioms**, Addison-Wesley Professional, September 9, 1991.

[8] Gamma E., *et al.*, **Design Patterns -Microarchitectures for Reusable Object-Oriented Software**, Addison-Wesley, Reading, Mass., 1994.

[9] Alexander, C., **The Timeless Way of Building**, Oxford University Press, 1979.

[10] Belanger, D., *et al.*, "*Architecture Styles and Services: An Experiment on SOP-P*", **AT&T Technical Journal**, Jan/Feb, 1996, pp54-63.

[11] Coplien, J., ed., **Pattern Languages of Program Design,** Addison-Wesley Professional; 1 edition, May 12, 1995.

[12] Tepfenhart, W., & Cusick, J., "*A Unified Object Topology*", **IEEE Software**, Jan-Feb 1997, vol. 14, no. 1, pp. 31-35.

[13] Zwicker, D., "*Web Applications: From Presentation to Real Functionality*", **Proceedings of Web Interactive 1996**, Mecklermedia, NYC, 7/31-8/2, 1996.

[14] Gartner Group, **Proceedings of Client Server meets the Internet,** San Diego, CA, March 12-14, 1997.

[15] Bickel, B., "*Database & Application Development for the Internet & Intranet*", **Proceedings of Web Interactive 1996**, Mecklermedia, NYC, 7/31-8/2.

[16] *CodeGuru, http://www.codeguru.com/, viewed 8/16/2012.*

Send Orders of Reprints at bspsaif@emirates.net.ae
Durable Ideas in Software Engineering, 2013, 167-194

CHAPTER 6

Implementation

Abstract: Exploration of multiple types of implementation work in the software industry including writing, programming, process development, and management. Description of useful technical document templates and approaches, programming methods and considerations, programming environments, languages, and related topics. Discussion of process engineering methods, challenges, models, and techniques. Reflections on proven management experience in staffing, organizing, recruiting, and staff development.

Keywords: Technical writing, research, programming, programming languages, design implementation, process engineering, management, recruiting, staffing, organization, staff development.

6.1. INTRODUCTION

In my career I have been a technical writer, programmer, enterprise technologist, process engineering consultant, project manager, and support director (as well as a few other roles). In each of these roles implementation is a key activity. This is where ideas become reality. Where architectures become code, where feature requirements become documents, and where plans become actualized. In each activity there is a flavor of authorship and craftsmanship. The writer works in words, sentences, and paragraphs. The programmer works in control blocks, functions, and classes. The manager works in tasks, timelines, and assignments.

This chapter will touch on some of the aspects of implementation in these roles. This chapter is not meant to be a programming guide, a writer's tutorial, or a manager's bible. Instead it is a rough catalog of the common tools I have used and have seen others use to be successful in the transition from plan to working system. Let us take writing first, then programming, then process, and finally management.

6.1.1. Writing

In nearly all technical projects writing is a required step. It may be simple emails, or it may be full blown user manuals. In either case a document must be planned, crafted, edited, and finalized. Many engineers have trouble writing and still more are not native speakers of English and often times deliver repeated errors in their

James J. Cusick

works. My first job in technology involved technical writing of user manuals, proposals, and other software documents. Since then I have always been required to write internal memos, plans, reports, and analysis. Once started on publishing results from my applied research in software engineering I continued at a fairly steady pace of about two external publications per year. This has continued for about 25 years up until now resulting in nearly 50 papers and talks. Keeping in mind that the audience must be reached *via* the medium in the author's triangle is a key concept in being a successful writer (see Fig. **1**).

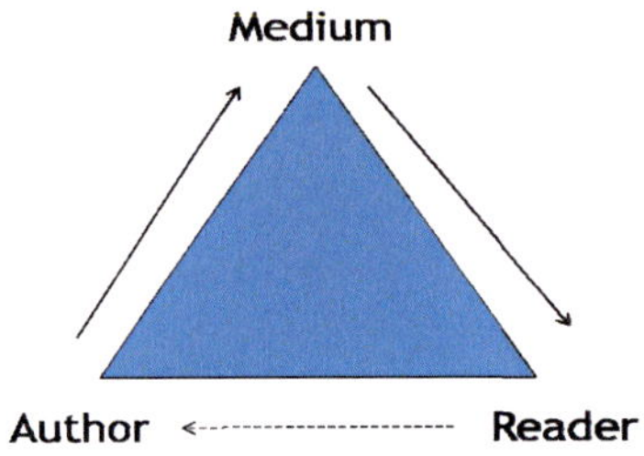

Figure 1: The Author's Triangle.

From the Greeks to the Renaissance to the massive steps of the 19th and 20th century, the written word from the Scientific community has had deep and far flung impacts on philosophy, society, and technology. The works of Plato and Aristotle and of the entire "Greek miracle" which formulated not only ideas but methods to discover still further ideas set a foundation for Western Science. Prolific thinkers and writers in China and India independently developed both concepts and technologies which built up human understanding and capabilities [1]. Later Arabic scholars translated, preserved, and improved on both the Asian and Greek thinking in their own language and in countless books and articles. Eventually this written material was translated back into Latin for its reintroduction to Europe in the late Middle Ages primarily in Moorish Spain.

The revolutionary impact of one specific single Scientific writing cannot be over-emphasized and its significance is generally difficult to imagine today. By putting the Earth into motion, Copernicus threw out eons of belief in the centrality and divine supremacy of humans. All of Church doctrine had to be reconsidered and rethought. This has been the pattern of the impact of Scientific writing since this time. From Kepler to Newton to Darwin to Einstein modern humans have had their centrality, stability, and ascendancy in Nature's world continually attacked, reordered, and often psychologically diminished or at least fully restacked. Science writing can have colossal impacts.

The writing we do for software development may not be as earth shattering as the work of Copernicus or Newton but one can never tell. In general there is formal and informal writing and internal and external writing. I typically write dozens of emails every day. These are informal in 95% of the cases. They may be a quick reply to a question or a directive to my team. The few formal emails are typically where significant decisions are involved or reports to senior executives are called for. In the case of these more formal emails I will read over them carefully sometimes 3 or 4 times and edit them very carefully looking for mistakes of fact, typos, or potential misunderstandings in the presentation of information.

When it comes to internal memos and external publications quite a different process is followed.

I am often charged with a task or an initiative. One of the first things I do is perform some level of background research on the topic and start developing a guiding document. This document will include a definition of the problem space, goals of the initiative, and an approach. This document will be for internal usage thus it will be formal but not overly formal. The amount of effort expended on its language will be limited. Only when the document is going to be widely distributed or if it becomes of broad interest will I spend significant time on its further improvement.

It is with external documents that more care is taken. Typically, I have published most of my work as applied research and especially as experience reports. These are useful internally but especially to the industry as there tends to be a paucity of good reports on actual technology usage (*i.e.*, reports from users as opposed to vendors or academic researchers). A sample structure of such a technical report might follow the approachh below:

1. Introduction.

2. Background.

3. Related Research.
4. Approach & Goals.
5. Tools & Environment.
6. Results.
7. Discussion.
8. Conclusion.
9. Acknowledgements.
10. References.

An introduction will start the piece. Some creativity is required in order to make dense technical material readable. In my case an introduction typically uses a theme of some imagery such as a popular movie or a familiar object. Once a link or metaphor is established it is easier for the reader to follow the sometimes abstract concepts of the paper.

Next the author must place observations in context of prior research. This means at minimum 6-12 references will be cited helping the reader understand what prior work has been done and how the new work contributes to the story. Naturally, the content must be compelling to the reader. If for example the reader has no interest in inspections themselves, they are unlikely to read the paper even if it is an excellent one. At the same time, the author must have useful information to share. Further the required data must be presented well both in textual form and in any graphics or tables. The author must maintain logical consistency and be persuasive. The paper is after all attempting to convince the reader of the author's point of view, theory, experimental results, or new concept. If the author does not write convincingly the reader will not take it seriously. Finally, clear conclusions should be drawn and the author should always discuss new directions following from the presented facts.

As for style itself engineering publications tend to be factual but they need not be dry. Unfortunately, a complex vocabulary may be required which may be specific to the domain. It is a good idea to state the precise technical term and define it or use an analogy. Thus, one might write something about "multiple-inheritance" which might not be widely understood outside a narrow technical community or having a prior meaning in lay man's words. As a result the author can provide an alternate description or definition like "a software object which takes attributes from more than one parent object". This explanation should be understandable by any reader within the context of the paper.

The writing process has been described by many. For myself I need a concept, some basic input, and ample time to craft the document. Over the years I have fallen into a certain pattern of writing and as long as there is adequate structure each sentence can flow out. It is part motivation, part inspiration, and part drudgery. In terms of construction, the word is the basic building block, the sentence the key structure, the paragraph the fundamental package, and the outline the organizing construct. For each building block some expertise is required. One needs sufficient vocabulary to select the right word and use it properly. Sentence construction should be both efficient and readable while also providing the desired meaning. Personally I have always written in passive voice while all my editors have struggled to convert my work into active voice. Finally, a good paragraph has a topic sentence, a body, and a concluding sentence. With such detail the paper should come out well.

6.1.2. Programming

> *"We should recognize the closed subroutine as one of the greatest software inventions; it has survived three generations of computers and it will survive a few more because it caters to the implementation of one of our basic patterns of abstraction". Djikstra, 1972 [2]*

One of the first questions to ask in writing programs is what language to use. Naturally, this will be based on the design approach you select. It is with this programming language that you will author your working solution. Some say that "the code is the spec". Gall [3] says that any large complex working system started as a small simple working system. Thus the true task in programming is to find a language to express your architectural design, solve the remaining design issues, and iteratively build out the solution with stages of testing built in. By using an Operational Profile (described in Chapter 7) I have often prioritized this coding. Starting with the operations that are predicted to be more commonly used and working down to the least popular functionalities you can quickly get to a baseline working system and then to a completed working system as shown in Fig. **2** (as introduced in Chapter 2). Note that the octagon represents that system architectures and the cubes represent the increments of development. It is these cubes that need to be brought to life by your programming. So for implementation, incrementalism utilizing componentry is the starting assumption in my toolbox.

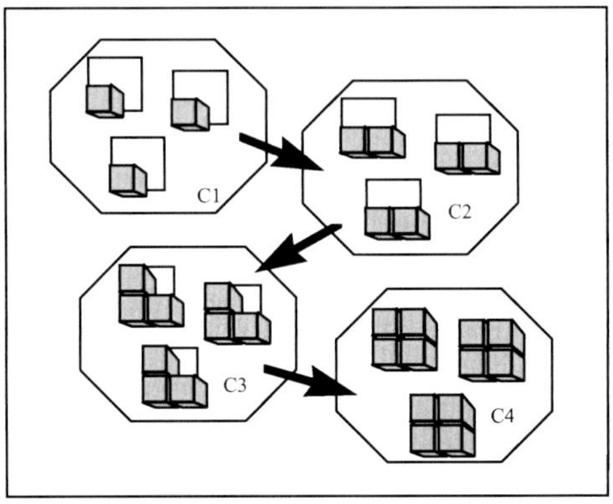

Figure 2: Incremental Development Driven by Operational Profile: In this diagram the octagons represent the entire system at different stages of completion (C1, C2, C3, C4).

We are always moving from the essential systems perspective to the implementation. From architecture to design to implementation requires several design steps to be solved either between the architecture and implementation phase or during it. Design quality comes from: efficient organization, modular partitioning, data and procedure distinct, independent modules, interfaces which minimize complexity, derived from requirements in a repeatable manner. Design also calls for an understanding of the user: users change their minds, users make mistakes, users are impatient, preferences are transient, - designs should be: useful and powerful, simple and straightforward, learnable, understandable, dependable, fun. Moving from requirements and analysis into design requires the further mapping of abstract feature descriptions into design constructs of data and function. In data design must consider: required data, data outputs of system, data transformations, method of data movement to, from, and within the system.

The kinds of design principles that will be covered to manage all these complexities might include:

- Modularity.
- Span of control.
- Data structures.
- Information hiding.
- Cohesion.
- Coupling.
- Algorithm Selection (sorting, searching, string processing, graphics, mathematical).

Each of these classical design problems will need to be addressed to realize your architecture once you have selected your working medium, your implementation language. For most web applications these days HTML will be a given. To do some client-side pre-processing you might at JavaScript, PERL, Ruby, and VBScript. To do some CGI or SAPI programming look at PERL, C/C++, Java, C#, or VB. For hardcore backend application development go with what you know. Use C++ or Java for higher performance and complex processing needs. Obviously, SQL will play a role to get to your database. For all your choices balance staff skills, tool availability, and performance requirements.

Once a language is selected (let's go with C++ as we have already introduced that in earlier chapters) packaging of classes is the first step. Depending on the platform and tools in use you will create a project and assign families of classes to libraries. You will then need to create a build script for complex applications. In doing so you are transforming your conceptual architecture to a concrete architecture. One of my favorite tools for understanding this path is a topology model I helped develop some years ago [4]. In the topology which reflects two dimensions, abstractness of implementation and application domain (See Fig. **3**).

In this model of development coding is guided from the architecture *via* design patterns and finally through the use of APIs and frameworks to a concrete instance of a program. While this explanation is a 10,000 foot view of the art of programming it can inform us of many important aspects of development.

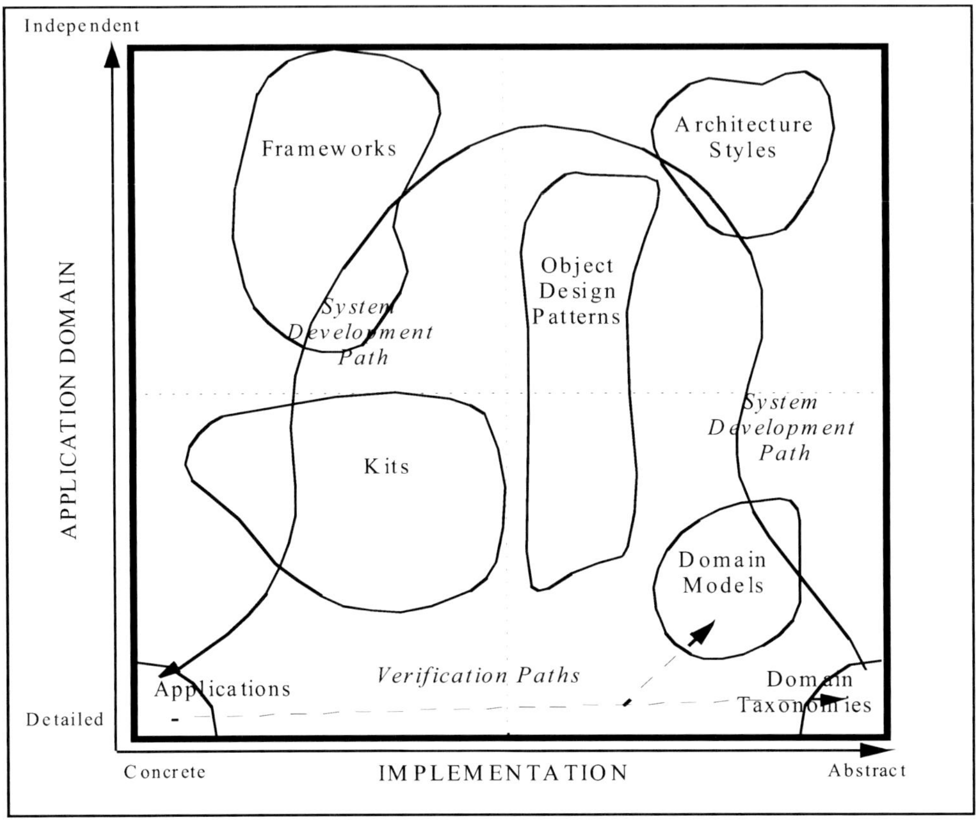

Figure 3: The Implementation Path of the Object Topology.

The Object Topology also addressed the resilience of APIs in the public domain and how to keep a handle on which will be most resilient to change. Vendors have launched lots of proprietary protocols to get around the limitations of HTTP and to add native support for advanced features. Use caution in betting on these technologies especially when they are proprietary especially on web projects.

As with any application a database is an architectural choice which is often required. For Internet based applications the goals of the site must be considered along with the scale. For larger scale applications that are primarily transaction based consider the database vendor's solutions and the adjunct architectures. For specialized or custom approaches CGI or SAPI interfaces will provide the most flexibility as discussed in Chapter 5. In either case SQL will be the language of choice for interacting with the database whether using stored procedures, real-time queries, or embedded queries.

So with these technologies as a given and the overall implementation flow determined where do we start (once our package architecture is decided). First we begin by building out the classes and their methods both public and private. Below is the class definition presented earlier in Chapter 4. We might start our implementation by writing the constructor or singleton class to create a sensor object. We could then continue by developing each method.

```
class Sensor {
private:
  int SystemID;
  int location; // GPS coordinate (needs expansion)
  int road;
  int mile marker;
  long RadioChannel;
  char SamplingPattern[10];
  int SystemStatus;
public:
  int initialize(int restart);
  int sleep(int interval);
  int ProvideReport(char type);
  int DownloadNewCommands(int offset);
}
```

We might find that some data types are not what we need. Thus we might modify the design at this point. For example, we might realize that the *char* parameter type declaration for the reporting function needs to be a character array. It may also need an identifier passed in for the *system_id* in order to select the proper sensor to report on.

```
int ProvideReport(int SystemID, static char type[150]);
```

For each method an algorithm or set of processing steps would have to be created and written. For the reporting function this might look like the following:

```
int ProvideReport(int SystemID, static char type[150])
{
  if(SystemID == 1)
  {
        // set report type to success
        type = "success";
              return SystemID;
  }
  else if(SystemID == 2) {
        // set report type to failure
        type = "failure";
              return SystemID;
  }
  else
        // this means the type is unknown
return 0;

} // end of method
```

Thus, in an iterative manner the class would be built out and tested. For each class a full implementation would eventually be realized through this authorship. During implementation the essential systems analysis, high level design, class diagrams and state diagrams now become code in class declarations and method creation. The tools of choice here are a good IDE (Integrated Development Environment). These tools have all the relevant and necessary tools including advanced editors, debuggers, and profilers. Probably one of the most important tools is patience along with language familiarity. Knowing the target language, its syntax, and semantics along with patience in employing the language is essential to success.

At this stage, build and deployment become critical aspects of implementation. With ever larger applications, libraries, and components, configuration management including build management and deployment strategies take on a key role. For relatively small programs this may be a trivial aspect but with larger applications with multiple developers (or especially with dozens of developers) working on a single code base a division of responsibility from development to deployment is essential for smooth operations and accountability. The techniques for configuration management go beyond the bounds of this eBook but are certainly within the scope of implementation concerns. There are many published best practices in this area and we will touch on some of these in Chapter 8 when we discuss support functions. A simple tool that I use from my toolbox is to keep a build and a development hive of files. Using one of many configuration management tools you can enable check in and check out capabilities against the development path. When changes are ready for group use they can be checked into the build path. Those new versions will generate a deployment package. In recent years I have managed my own web site using a similar pattern. This web site contains HTML, Javascript, and various content including dozens of PDF and image files including drafts of this eBook. I maintain a backed up version of this source branch which is an exact copy of the "production" version running on my hosting service's Linux server and accessible to the public Internet. When I want to modify the site I can create offline versions of the new content, test it locally, and then when satisfied publish to the web. This represents in microcosm the same versioned and multi-path development needed in a large development program. Such a configuration managed approach (supported by a tool like SVN) is absolutely a requirement in my toolbox especially for any professional level work.

As for performance quantification of your program most performance tools on the market currently focus on network utilization monitoring. For application developers on the Internet platform there is no substitute for modeling, benchmarks, design, and testing. Up front modeling can predict overall application performance in a controlled network environment. In the Internet environment the predictability of network utilization is hard to factor, however, the rest of the components of the system (browser, server, and database) can all be modeled adequately. Usage data may also be hard to determine but will be required to do such modeling. Benchmarks will be helpful in selecting products. Ask the vendors what transaction rate or number of simultaneous users they can support. Design will be a key aspect of building an application that meets user's expectations (remember users are impatient). Select compiled languages over interpreted languages where it makes sense in order to gain a performance edge. Focus on modularity and precise data modeling (all the good things you would do on any software effort). Also, consider using smaller graphics or less animation. Finally, performance testing should be a standard activity performed at each step of development not done at the end of the process only.

Most implementation decisions will be heavily influenced by the programming language or languages used. Often the language is dictated up front by issues such as runtime environment, staff skills, and tool choices. But if we were to look at programming languages first with our requirements in mind we might first ask what types of languages there are and what are they used for.

6.1.2.1. Language Types

Several major computer programming language paradigms exist:

- Procedural.
- Declarative.
- Object-oriented.
- Functional.
- Hybrid or mulit-pardigm languages.

Added to this is the distinction between compiled and interpreted languages. All languages have a syntax (form of expression) and a semantics (meaning of expression). Languages are comprised of lexical tokens or words which are parsed in a lexical analysis step where strings of words are broken down into decipherable tokens. Typically tokens are based on column settings, commas, or other methods. A language will consist of names, symbols, numerical literals, and character literals. These characteristics are common in most languages. What differs is their features, capabilities, and the architectures they lend to applications written in each. The programmer will need to keep all these aspects in mind but once the first language is learned it is typically easier to learn additional languages except when crossing over from one paradigm to another. In that case entirely new programming ideas may be necessary to learn.

In designing a language certain tradeoffs will always be made. Typical areas of optimization or design focus might be on utility, convenience, efficiency, portability, readability, modeling ability, simplicity, or semantic clarity. Other goals may also drive the design of the language. The result will be a language that may be perfectly suited to the engineering problem at hand or one that is ill-suited to the task but madly popular in the industry. The software engineer must choose carefully.

The task of the developer moving from design to implementation is to translate the higher level abstractions of requirements, architecture, and information models, into concrete machine executable instructions. Often there will be a gap between the two. If a language was not selected early on now is the time to make that decision. The following discussion will also help if one is in the architecture stage and considering how the system might eventually be implemented.

The critical aspects of a programming language for a development project include:

- Ease of use.
- Compiler efficiency.
- Source code portability.

- Availability of development tools.
- Maintainability.

The minimal selection criteria should include:

- Target Application Domain.
- Computing Environment of Application.
- Performance Characteristics.
- Data Structure Support.
- Algorithmic & Computational Complexity.
- Staff Knowledge.
- Availability of Tools.

There over 1400 programming languages according to one study. Choosing the right one for any given application might seem to be a daunting task. However, there are several languages that are the most widely used. These often meet the bulk of the above criteria and have proven track records.

For myself, I learned the following programming languages in this order:

- Fortran.
- BASIC.
- Pascal.
- C.
- 8086 Assembler.
- MUMPS.

- DOS Batch Scripting.
- UNIX Shell.
- SQL.
- C++.
- HTML.
- Java.
- Prolog.
- C#.

At this point in my career as a manager I do little programming but I still do HTML coding and I review C# programs from time to time and I may write a script also. But the programming I have done in each of these languages varies. With some languages I have only used them as a student (Fortran). Other I have used professionally to build large scale systems in a hands-on manner (C/C++ /SQL). This leads us to a key distinction or concept: programming in the small *vs.* programming in the large. Writing programs in one of these languages may not be that challenging until we try to apply the large scale architecture and performance requirements we discussed earlier. In that case we might need to develop tens of thousands of lines of code each working well as a whole.

Furthermore, large systems need more testing and testing of more sophisticated types which we will discuss in detail in the next chapter. For the programmer, they need to unit/component test each deliverable. In general this testing is conducted by the developer themself.

The developer needs to understand glass box & black box testing. Glass box is testing with knowledge of internal structure; black box is testing where internal structure is ignored or unknown. It is during development or implementation that unit testing or glass box testing is conducted. We will discuss this in detail in Chapter 7.

A final note worth making is that there has been great progress in the area of languages, classes, and interface architectures over the last 20 years. In the first applications I worked on we built custom inter-process communications vehicles, GUIs, and more. We did this without object orientation. Today there are thousands of classes available and standard web service interface patterns to use to facilitate rapid development [5]. It bears being mentioned that while all the computing demands described above remain in effect it is much more efficient to solve for many of them today than in the past.

6.1.3. Process Engineering

In starting on a process assignment I always start by listening and reviewing the current process. The task at hand is to understand what gaps there are and what improvements can be made. I always take the approach of working upwards from a single concrete problem to a method and then to an overall process. Flowing out the process in diagram form often helps. Each bubble in a process diagram can then be broken out into discrete process steps. For most IT areas existing process frameworks already exist and it makes sense to tailor these frameworks to the problem area or the organization.

We have already discussed the fundamentals of process in Chapter 2. Here it is worthwhile touching on some of the related steps in realizing process.

Assessment: As mentioned, the starting point is to assess the current process if there is one. If there is no defined process you may have to document what is practiced. This is the same for software architecture discovery process. You have to ask questions, read related documents, understand the domain, and immerse yourself in the problem area. Only by understanding the function can you begin the analysis and design steps required.

Analysis: The baseline process is typically the current process as defined or as assessed. There also needs to be a needs analysis. This is often done by interviewing key domain specialists. Usually a small team will conduct this analysis and bullet out the process requirements. This is not unlike a software requirements analysis approach. The end product of this step will be the baseline process, the delta to bring it to the desired end state, and the requirements for the complete process.

Design: Using the by-products of the analysis step, process design can be conducted, typically in parallel to the analysis. In Chapter 2 we discussed the nature of process and how to build out a process. In terms of implementation, the design piece now falls to the focus on a creating a deployable process. This means that all the artifacts required of the process need to be in place: descriptions, process flows, instructions, scripts, tools, *etc.* Just like in the software lifecycle design means the creation of a solution here the same thing is found but with process artifacts which are typically non executable.

Education: With process education is a key piece to the puzzle. People need to be involved in the creation of process especially when it impacts their work flows but they also need education prior to deployment as there is often a gap between the input they provide during analysis and the actual deployment. Further, just prior to deployment the final kinks will need to be worked out and the question and answer flow of an education session will assist with this. Today, process education can be done remotely and in mass. The objective of the education aside from gaining valuable user feedback prior to deployment is to make the deployment step itself more successful.

Deployment: Naturally, this phase is where the rubber meets the road just as in software construction and deployment. Typically, process deployment will be done in phases for any but the most trivial processes. The deployment may be done by function, region, or division, for example. Adequate support must be provided especially in the early days of process usage. A sample approach within software engineering using the Capability Maturity Model is to use a Software Engineering Process Group to provide this support for changes and evolution of the process as well as end to end measurement of the success of the process.

Re-Assessment: Finally, once the process is deployed a re-assessment will be required. Success cannot be assumed. You will have to measure the progress both quantitatively and qualitatively. You may use in process metrics or questionnaires or interviews or other means. Should issues be found then adjustments will need to be made and once again an incremental approach makes the most sense for this.

Some challenges in implementing process include:

1. ***Approaching Change*** – there is an old joke – how many psychologists are required to change a light bulb? None as long as the light bulb *wants* to change. The point is that people tend not to actively welcome change. In today's workplace change is everywhere and all the time. But people have not fundamentally changed for thousands of years. They are still creatures of habit by and large. Thus when changing processes (often supported by new tools) it is important to inform people what is changing and why as well as when and how they can be a part of the change either by providing input or by helping lead the change.

2. ***Overcoming Inertia*** – for most professionals they have seen an uncountable number of process initiatives both large and small. A challenge sometimes in developing and deploying a process successfully is getting a positive energy behind the effort. This requires lobbying and broad coalition building at times. Most of the time it also will require strong top down support not just in words but in a charter, town halls, reminders, and rewards.

3. ***Resistance*** - Once the process train is moving sometimes it will hit roadblocks down the line. There could be "pocket vetoes" or outright refusal to cooperate. In these cases some conflict may be unavoidable. People are being asked to change and they may not want to or may not see the new process as beneficial or correct. This may point to a failure in the earlier analysis and design stages where input was solicited. Or it may be a power struggle. In any case, for the new process to succeed this resistance must be overcome or undercut. Sometimes this can be done softly and with negotiation, other times through the use of present authority. The tool from my toolkit here is courage in the face of blatant "insubordination" when a process is formally chartered and all inputs were available during its creation. Progress must go on.

4. ***Backsliding*** – Once the process is deployed there may be a tendency to backslide. The tool to use here is reinforcement. This comes in the form of education, positive reward structures, and management focus on progressive groups adopting the new process.

5. ***Process Overkill*** – One danger is that to a process engineer everything looks like a nail – that is with only one tool (process creation) tons of process will be created thereby suffocating the organization. In this case there will be a rebellion either tacit or open. People will follow the process only on paper to the extent that they are forced to and will look for ways to work around it. These are the times when alternate processes start to pop up and the "process police" start to lose authority. My strongest tool to avoid this is to work from real problems to point methods. Then the point methods can be assembled into working and realistic approaches that fit on a page or two (a simple procedural algorithm for solving a problem). Each method can then be stitched together to form a process but if the pieces are reasonable the overkill should be avoided.

A few tools not mentioned in Chapter 2 that come in handy for process deployment include the following:

- **Hamburger Charts**: A useful process tool not discussed in Chapter 2 is the "hamburger" chart often used in formal process diagramming. The basic hamburger chart is made of rounded boxes with three sections (process level, process name, and Activity Functional Domain (if required) as shown below.

The concept of process modeling in this manner is one of compartmentalization and divide and conquer. This is very similar to the concepts in structured design created in the 1970s and mentioned earlier. In those methods the closed subroutine is pictured in a box with arrows connecting it to its calling functions. In the process diagram the same kind of leveling is used. Here level zero is the highest level in the model and each hamburger can be exploded to more detail below it. An alternative method is to flow out the work steps in "swimlane " diagrams where the actors are lined up in horizontal paths and the steps are laid out in each lane in a sequential and undulating manner.

- **Procedure Descriptions**: Following the creation of the hamburger charts, process diagrams, or flow charts, the procedures need to be defined. Typically, this will follow an input, steps, output template of some kind. Going back to the beginning of this chapter where we discussed writing, procedure descriptions now call on the process engineer to write concisely, clearly, and to cover the topic at hand thoroughly at the same time.

- **CMMI:** The enduring tool from the CMMI world is the maturity ladder itself. Actually, a very similar pattern was developed for child development theory by Ericson and then many variants were developed for personality theory and even ethical maturity development [6]. However, Humphrey 's great contribution [7] was in marrying the prescribed best practices with a maturity model. This has now been copied by many other domains and process areas.

- **Agile as Everything**: During the 1990s Agile as a method solidified itself and become more and more popular. At the same time the CMMI model become heavier and heavier. In the ensuing years Agile has clearly eclipsed CMMI in popularity. Today it is almost career suicide to speak ill of Agile. In reading a recent eBook on the subject the author states that with Agile "quality is always improved" [8]. For anyone with any experience in software this is a red flag. Nothing in engineering is a "silver bullet" as first described by Brooks in "The Mythical Man Month" [9]. This is not to say that somehow Agile techniques are not valuable but simply that they should be used in relation to grounded expectations.

- **ITIL:** An area neither CMMI nor Agile treats is IT service operations. This is where ITIL (IT Infrastructure Library) comes in. As we will discuss in Chapter 8, ITIL provides a useful set of organizing principles and best practices for IT operations [10]. This includes such areas as incident management, change management, and release management. Early in my career I worked in support and then again recently. However, it is only with my recent experience that I have come to use the ITIL model and found it a useful tool.

- **Questionnaires and Interviews**: For process development a critical tool is the creation of questionnaires and the conducting of interviews. It is through these means that information is gathered directly from project staff. Creating good questions takes time and effort. Some assessment frameworks like CMMI 's SCAMPI will provide required questions. However, when entering an unstructured environment it will be necessary to create custom questionnaires.

These can prove to be valuable intellectual assets in the future. Using them requires some finesse. At times people will want to share a lot and at other times they will want to through you off the trail. Conducting multiple independent interviews is a key to getting to the truth. The main tool here is being open with people and explaining the purpose of the dialogue.

6.1.4. Management

The classic software management eBook "Peopleware" [11] adequately covers much of the management territory one would hope to discuss. It also was a eBook that helped shaped my own views on software management. After re-reading it (in the second version) for the preparation of this eBook I found there was not too much to argue with or to add. However, a brief discussion on actual management practices that I use fits well with the implementation discussion of this chapter and bolsters the earlier discussion in Chapter 3.

Aside from reading Peopleware there were many influences on my management style. First off, my Father was a salesman and then an entrepreneur. He started a company and I watched him manage people from my childhood through my teens. I also decided to follow into management but ended up studying Organizational Psychology with the idea of building a consulting career before turning to technology full time.

From these influences, my Father's approach to leadership, my formal training in organizational concepts ranging from team structure, motivation, communication, and more, as well as observing corporate leaders, I developed a basic point of view. My Father was very supportive of his employees and took a personal interest in them. He helped them when they needed help and was tough when he needed to be. He hired and fired as appropriate and explained to me his rationale at each step. We had long conversations about this commuting together to the company during my high school days when I spent a lot of time working there. We talked over stock issues, financing, marketing, sales, and the technology aspects of the business (a wholesale dental equipment supply house). I worked in the warehouse, went to a few trade shows, and visited customer locations sometimes. I later realized not all of his decisions were optimal but his willingness to be a responsible leader was a key influence on me.

From my formal training at the University of California I learned about Maslow 's hierarchy of needs, Herzberg 's motivation-hygiene theory, Theory X, Y, and Z, and other useful psychological and sociological models applicable to management such as Myers-Briggs personality styles and more [12]. I also took courses in computer programming and systems analysis at that time. I took multiple courses in statistics which proved highly valuable in management trending, reliability (as discussed in Chapter 7), and in performance engineering. My thesis work was on change management (not the software kind) which was a hot topic way back then. Of all the tools in my tool box it is amusing that this training has stayed with me and has not gone out of fashion. Every year or two there is a new fad in management or a new eBook which is very popular. Without fail, these fads rehash many of the tried and true concepts of prior theory and experimentation from social psychologists.

In my graduate work I focused only on computer science which led me to my position at AT&T Bell Laboratories. At AT&T (and later with other companies) I learned from the best managers (and one or two not so good ones) what "real" management was all about. I once again learned that a good leader took care of their people in good times and bad (whether jobs were being eliminated or people become ill). Management includes promoting diversity in the workforce as well as encouraging new leaders to bloom. A key learning was that as a leader it was the aggregate outcome from the team that defined my success as a manager and not my own individual output as an engineer that mattered anymore (although that individual contribution was still called on).

I became a technical team leader almost 20 years ago and a manager a few years later. In all the years since I have learned not to take myself too seriously as a manager. I have also tried hard to keep humbleness towards technology (there is always something new around the corner) and towards the teams I have led (they always know more than I do). As a person with a somewhat "breezy" personality (easy to laugh) I have found that I can put people at ease with a joke but I can also muster seriousness when the situation calls for it. I think with my training and experience and personal style I have been successful as a manager on balance. I also think there is no formula for this. Each of us has to find our own path.

There is a little black magic to management so let me expand on a few specific aspects of what I do. Once again, some tools that are in the toolbox include:

Recruitment: Hiring someone into the organization has long lasting effects and should be taken seriously. There is a saying: "hire slowly, fire quickly". I have had about a 50/50 success rate in hiring people I know, that is, people I have worked with before perhaps as peers and then brought into a new organization. This sometimes works but can also backfire. Hiring an unknown may work just as well or better. Casting a wide net is naturally preferable. In today's corporate environment managers usually do not have complete freedom over the recruitment process but will follow an HR procedure to some degree. The manager will define the requirements, set the interview approach, and make the final decision. My preferred interview approach is to have multiple people conduct 1-on-1 interviews and have a group lunch with the candidate. At the end of the day everyone casts a binary match or no match vote and then I make a decision to hire or not. This approach is efficient, quick, and gives immediate feedback to the candidate.

Role Definition: Once a team member is on board they need to have a clear set of responsibilities, proper authorities to carry them out, and accountability (and rewards). The roles need to be defined as part of the organizational structure. A project team may need a lead, several programmers, a DBA, a build engineer, and QA staffing. Each of these roles need to be clearly defined (if not formally). The job description used to hire these individuals may serve as the base for the role definition. Recently I have been working mostly with supervisory level staff reporting to me directly. In the past I have also managed engineers directly. The approach is similar with both groups but the level of specificity required varies. For the engineers there will be many detailed questions and they will want to know more precisely what they need to do. For the supervisors there will be less of a need for detail and they can run with a broad task assignment quite readily. For both types, clear authority must be provided so they can get their jobs done. This may require both verbal and written authorization that the individual can conduct a particular task or function. With authority comes responsibility and accountability. Each individual needs to understand this. A good practice is to meet 1-on-1 regularly with staff members to discuss their role, progress, and obstacles. Staff meetings are also required to coordinate across multiple towers of responsibility.

Team Member Selection: Finding people for a project from a pool of resources can be challenging. There are many constraints in most real world cases. As discussed above, recruiting will get you only so far. You may also need to work from a list of available resources and you may have to agitate to get the ones that will fit the role and tasks best. Beyond that you will need to look at the task profile, the skills base and potential of the individuals, the potential mix of team members, and (once again) availability constraints. While there is no guarantee of success the best tool I can recommend is experience both in the shoes of a manager and also with the individuals involved.

Task Assignment and Tracking: As mentioned, frequent meetings with staff are required to keep track of status especially in a large team environment. In Chapter 2 project management fundamentals were covered and are applicable here. However, style is important as well, not just technique or method. Technical workers have pride in what they do and experienced professionals do not want to be micro managed. Nevertheless, work has to get assigned. Often people back away from unpleasant or overloaded situations. In that case the manager must work around the issues to get tasks assigned. It may mean stretching out a deliverable or finding additional resources. Once each task is assigned, a gentle update session whether formal or informal is necessary. If things slip there are few options. Putting pressure on the team is not one of them. Instead, looking for creative ways to reorder the tasks can be pursued. A tool I commonly use is to put this task back on the team or individual. That way they have the responsibility and will typically rise to the challenge of sorting out a way around the road block. If they cannot the manager needs to relieve some constraints.

Appraisals: Providing sufficient and timely feedback is important for any manager. People need to know how they are doing. One way of doing this is to utilize the 1-on-1 meetings that happen regularly (in my case I meet with my key staff members weekly). Hallway discussions are good too, a quick "way to go" is always welcome. I have made the mistake of publicly chastising someone who goofed, which is not a mistake I plan on repeating. As for formal appraisals each company will have its method. Some are rather onerous and include stacks of paperwork. I comply with such procedures as they are HR required. However, I also try to boil down the message of where an employee is doing well and where they can improve onto a 3x5 post it note. This provides great clarity in the communication. This provides a set of talking points for me and a set of reminders for the employee who can receive a copy of these points. This is a method I learned from one of the managers I worked for and I think it works well. From an HR point of view the formal process is important for promotional evidence and for disciplinary evidence if that becomes required. For the employee it is a good chance to hear from the manager what an external observer perceives about their performance. One key thing I was trained to do at AT&T in these sessions was to listen, listen, listen. The idea is that the manager should be brief and clear in providing supporting and corrective feedback (and everyone has something to improve on) and then wait to hear from the employee what they have to say. This dialogue is critical for advancing understanding on for both parties. There are many related topics around appraisals such as rating and rankings, removal of the bottom 10%, and other such practices. Those would require a much lengthier discussion, however, it is worth pointing out that I do not subscribe to the bell curve approach personally while I am often asked to follow it to suit corporate needs. It is my belief that a good manager can foster a team of superstars that break the bell curve consistently.

Mentoring and Skill Development: Learning and growth for the manager themselves and for the team and its staff members is crucial to long term success. When a technical team stops striving for the next accomplishment and the intellectual investing that is required to achieve it stagnation and execution deterioration are likely to follow. Managers have a need for self- development and for this the first understanding they must come to is that they are no longer engineers and they have to think about management issues, be trained on them, and read about them. At the same time they have to keep their technical skills sharp. In a broader sense they also have responsibility for building the next generation of managers and leaders (there is a difference) for the organization. It is said that a sign of success for a manager is how many times his group is raided for the talent produced there. There are several broad categories to look at in skill development – technical, leadership, "soft" skills, and managerial. Each requires investment and a specific training plan. Some training can be face to face other training can be *via* webinars, readings, or other means. There are many useful sources for understanding these methods. What may not be as readily available is the approach to mentoring. Mentoring is different than training in that it is a relationship which the mentee seeks out and the mentor agrees to enter into. The subject of the mentoring might be around technical approach, communications, leadership, or navigating the corporate bureaucracy or politics. For myself, I have benefited from having several informal mentors who I have learned much from and remain in contact with. I have also acted as a mentor at key points in the careers of several people to assist them in moving forward. The relationship is one of trust and confidentiality along with a sharing of experience from one to another.

Recognition: People need recognition of different modalities in order to feel appreciated for their work. For some people this is all about financial rewards. But for others this is about a certificate or a thank you. If you reread Herzberg 's motivation-hygiene theory you will recall that for many professional workers like software engineers pay is a required element but not sufficient for satisfaction and self-actualization. One of the tools I have developed both for mentoring, communications skills development, and recognition is a public forum for technical presentations which I called the "Tech Forum". Here people share their work with the organization as a whole and can perfect their presentation skills. They can also prepare work for external publication. In doing so they are recognized by their peers for their accomplishments which is often more important than any other type of recognition.

Conflict Resolution: Within any life some rain will fall and with any team some disagreements will form. The classic means to conflict resolution are first to reduce the stress in the situation by speaking with all affected parties separately and understanding their points of view. Then depending on the situation a multipart discussion can be held to try to alleviate the differences and get people moving back on track. I have found that many of these situations have to do with turf and ego. This is true when I have ended up in a conflict scenario also. In most cases getting through non protracted conflicts can be tense but not too painful.

When long standing conflicts emerge especially among senior staffers then efficiency can be impacted. It is best to resolve these situations early.

When a Fit Disappears: The toughest job a manager faces is the decision to end the employment of a staff member. This may be due to a poor fit or a poor financial situation or a restructuring. In any case it is not easy. The communication is tough and the after taste is bitter. Anyone who enjoys this part of the job is lacking in some degree of humanity yet it is a function that you sign up for when taking on the role of a manager. Corporations have become very practiced in downsizing over the course of my career but it still has not taken the sting out of it for me. When the cause is performance related it is best to try to rehabilitate only for a short period and then move quickly for the good of the organization.

Budgeting and Adminitrivia: Finally, an important job of a technical manager is creating and managing budgets of all kinds and dealing with the endless paperwork of some organizations. Budgeting is a vital task that lays out estimated spend on software, capital, and human resources for projects and support engineering activities. When operating a cost center there will be pressure on reducing budgets at all times. When operating a profit center there will be pressure on both revenue and costs. As part of this, depending on the byzantine nature of the organization, managers can face endless paperwork, forms, approvals, and processes to get things done. This might include getting phones and computers for people or having time recorded. The best tool I have for this part of managing is "grin and bear it".

CONCLUSIONS

What Software Engineers think of as implementation is simply programming. As we have seen here this definition can be broader to include technical writing, process engineering, and management as well. Each implementation mode requires different skills and tools. For programming this means languages and coding idioms as well as conversion of design to executable code. For process this can also mean the use of languages in the form of frameworks or at the minimum procedures and diagrammatic representations. The tools of the manager range from straightforward work to the much more complex dimensions of human relations. In all cases specific tools can be identified. Blending these modes of implementation together is required for any complex software product to become a reality.

REFERENCES

[1] Cusick, J., *A research paper on non-European scientific concepts introduced through Islamic Science* , NYU Poly Tech History of Science Program, 2008.

[2] Djikstra, E., 1972, http://www.cs.utexas.edu/~EWD/

[3] Gall J., **SYSTEMANTICS: How Systems Work and Especially How They Fail**, Quadrangle, 1975.

[4] Tepfenhart, W., & Cusick, J., "*A Unified Object Topology*", **IEEE Software**, Vol. 14, No. 1, pp. 31-35, Jan-Feb 1997.

[5] Spinellis, Diomidis, "Agility Drivers", IEEE Software, July/August, 2011.

[6] Davis, D., & Clifton, A., *Psychosocial Theory: Erickson*, viewed 11/5/2011, http://www.haverford.edu/psych/ddavis/p109g/erikson.stages.html

[7] Humphrey, W., **A Discipline for Software Engineering,** Addison-Wesley, Reading, MA, 1995.

[8] Schiel, James, **Enterprise-Scale Agile Software Development**, CRC Press, 2010.

[9] Brooks, F., **The Mythical Man-Month: Essays on Software Engineering,** Addison-Wesley, Reading, MA, 1975.

[10] Cusick, J., & Ma, G., *"Creating an ITIL Inspired Incident Management Approach: Roots, Responses, and Results",* **IFIP/IEEE BDIM International Workshop on Business Driven IT Management,** Osaka, Japan, April 19, 2010.

[11] Lister & Demarco, Peopleware

[12] Korman, Abraham, Organizational Behavior, Prentice Hall, Englewood Cliffs, New Jersey, 1977.

Send Orders of Reprints at bspsaif@emirates.net.ae
Durable Ideas in Software Engineering, 2013, 195-232

CHAPTER 7

Testing & Reliability Engineering

Abstract: Full description of testing in the lifecycle of software development. Discussion of test phases, test planning, test design, and test types. Focus on test environments, conceptual model for test environments, and a generic test process. Test planning approaches are presents with a test plan example. Detailed discussion of test case development including test factor analysis, glass box testing, black box testing, and scenario based testing. Discussion of software reliability testing methods and test methods including test tracking, reporting, and metrics.

Keywords: Test lifecycle, test phases, test architecture, application under test, test process, test plan, test case, test factors, glass box testing, black box testing, flowgraph testing, software reliability testing, software metrics.

7.1. INTRODUCTION

In becoming a programmer by definition you become a tester. A software tester is someone who runs a piece of code to validate the code and to verify that it performs its intended function with no side effects. In some situations the programmer themselves will conduct 100% of this testing. In many environments independent testing or verification is done by dedicated test organizations. In either case there is a general division between unit and system test as we will explore in detail. I have found that testing typically consumes a large part of the effort of any project – some say up to 50% when taking into account all types and phases of testing. As a result this is an area where a few handy tools are called for. The major ones for me include testing models, glass box and white box testing, Operational Profiles, Cyclomatic Complexity (both mentioned earlier), test automation, and more.

7.1.1. Testing in the Lifecycle

As system engineering turns to system design and then to implementation there is a progression from high level concept formulation to concrete software construction. Each assumption, concept, representation, and implementation resident within the system must be examined for validity and correctness before it can become a product. Thus, the lifecycle can be seen as a "V" in Fig. **1**. The

James J. Cusick

downward slope is the process of elaboration and implementation where ideas are cut into operable software (once again, in an incremental manner being preferred). The upward slope is the confirmation that the design and construction are valid in the eyes of the customer or user. This must be done to the extent possible. As we will discuss, defect latency in shipped code is a given. The question is how many defects will be remaining after all design, implementation, and defect removal steps are taken.

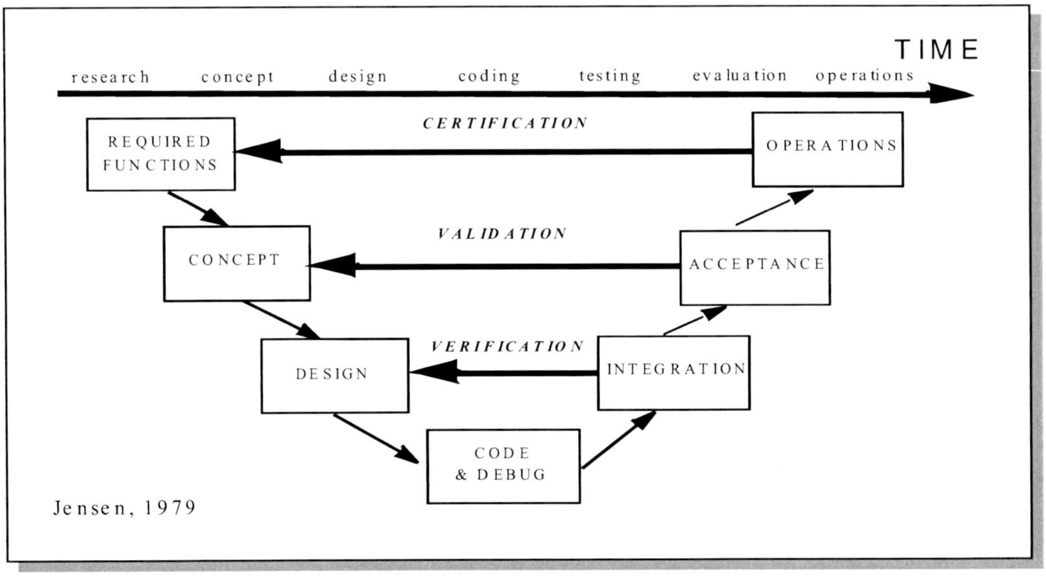

Figure 1: Testing in the Lifecyle [1].

Understanding of software testing was well accomplished during the 1970s. There have been advances over the years but fundamental definitions, concepts, and techniques have been long established and often repeated. One of them was Meyers [2] who stated that:

> *Testing is the process of systematically executing a program with the intent of finding errors.*

In testing it is helpful to have a plan (like we do for a project), often a test design, and always test cases. Again from Meyers, a good test case is one that has a high probability of detecting an as-yet undiscovered error. A successful test case is one that detects an as-yet undiscovered error.

Debugging is the activity of isolating and removing the cause of an error which was uncovered [during a test case].

Understanding the difference between testing and debugging is crucial. The code, try, debug cycle is often used by developers. The testing done here is glass box oriented in that the code structure is known and the developer is essentially experimenting with the design and its behavior which can be costly in terms of time. The alternative is Test Driven Development (TDD) where test cases are written in advance of any code (from the design). I recall my training in this technique upon being hired by AT&T Bell Labs years before it was given the acronym TDD. We were asked to write a test case for every line of code before we ran it. This included the segments of the code only reached upon failure by the operating system to allocate memory. In that case you had to enter the debugger, modify the return code, and then test the conditional reaction. I have seldom seen such rigor outside a classroom setting but the concept is important and has been an important tool in my testing toolbox in terms of thinking about the kind of test cases required.

7.1.1.1. Testing in Phases

Testing from the smallest unit to the largest unit of software is typical. When a developer tests a piece of the code they have written, as mentioned, this is known as "glass box " as they know the internal structure of the code. Glass Box testing proceeds based on the internal structural knowledge of the software. Black Box, on the other hand, is testing which covers feature capabilities delivered by many coordinated components and where the testers will not have internal knowledge of the implementation. Granular components tend to rely on Glass Box testing while large grain objects such as processes and systems tend to rely on Black Box testing. The range of testing techniques is show in Fig. **2**. For each method different techniques are required.

Integration testing is where we bring all the classes together for the first time to see how they operate. System testing is where software, hardware, documentation, and user substitutes, are brought together in the target environment for the first time. We test hardware, backup procedures, reconfiguration procedures, restarting the system, failure conditions on the hardware, and test how the software responds if the hardware becomes degraded or if power is shutdown unexpectedly. Releasing to the field then brings another level of complexity. Running software in the field on a weekend for example and not in the test lab, or an alpha/beta test with limited and trusted customers may be required before opening up the system to a general user population. Eventually GA (general availability) then follows or perhaps may have controlled/phased introduction.

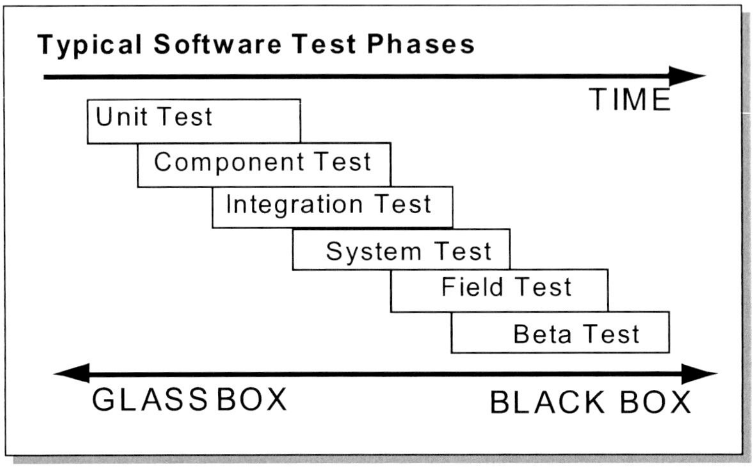

Figure 2: Testing Types and the Spread Between Glass Box and Black Box Testing.

7.1.1.2. Test Phases Defined

Unit Testing: Testing of smallest units of software: functions, files, programs, classes. Typically utilizing "line-at-a-time" testing and other White-box/Glass-box tests where internal structure of software is know and drives test design. Usually the responsibility of the unit author to conduct this level of testing (a.k.a., Component Testing).

Integration Testing: Testing of multiple units or components for interoperability. Often focused on data, messaging, interfaces, and timing especially in large or distributed systems.

System Testing: Testing of the entire system of which software is a part. This includes hardware, software, purchased components, user manuals, and other computing or communications devices. The purpose of this type of testing is to act as surrogate for end user or customer. Must simulate target operational environment to the greatest extent possible.

Field Testing: Following System Test, trials are often held in actual field sites, production environments, or customer sites (Alpha Test). Testing concentrates on interoperability with other equipment and actual customer usage demands.

Beta Testing: System made available to limited and trusted customer pool eager to apply soon to be available software. Focus is on customer feedback on final defect removal opportunity prior to unrestricted offering.

Other Test Types Include the following: Acceptance Testing, Configuration Testing, Load Testing, Volume Testing, Recovery Testing, Performance Testing, Security Testing, Operability Testing, Regression Testing, Equivalence Testing, Conversion Testing, Parallel Testing.

7.1.1.3. A Test Architecture Framework

Arranging testing to cover this wide spread of test requirements calls for an architecture for the test environment. Test environments today contain many components. In constructing a given Software Test Environment (STE) the ultimate measure of success is how well it supports the test requirements of the software under test. To achieve the highest level of test support for a given application the test engineer must understand both the application in question and the tools, techniques, and resources available for deployment in the test process. Typically these two task regions, understanding application architectures and developing test environments, are not always well integrated.

A model test environment is show in Fig. **3** grew from my work in testing large scale applications. This environment extends STEs described by Vogel [3] and Eickelmann [4] to include the concepts of patterns. In Fig. **3** a Test Management substrate supports the typical activities of repository management, configuration management, and template storage [5]. Test activities of design, development, execution, and measurement call upon these services. Adding to this environment the application specific test requirements as shown in the modules to the right completes the view. Using the concept of the test vector it is possible to determine the additional test resources or the nature of the test suites required by the inclusion of these architecture modules.

In Chapter 5 we discussed architecture styles and patterns in detail. While focus has usually been on the testability of design patterns themselves [6], some work has already been done to extend these concepts to the task of software testing. McGregor [7], for example, has developed a pattern language to support the testing of components in Object-Oriented (OO) software through the use of generic test harness classes.

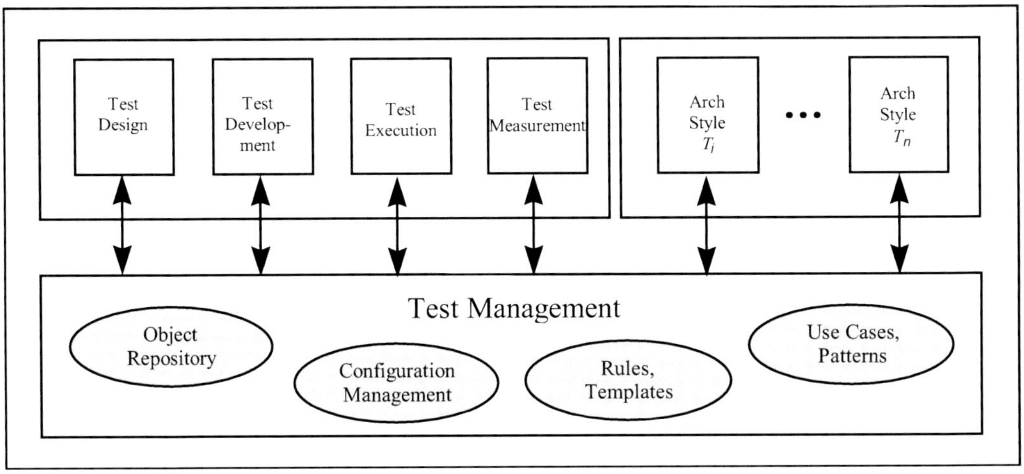

Figure 3: Test Architecture Framework with Architecture Styles. Underlying any STE are repositories of software, test scripts, and templates. These are used to develop test suites and to manage and evaluate results. In addition to these standard features of an STE each application under test brings with it a set of architecture specific test needs as shown to the right.

Here, this view is extended by introducing the concept of test architecture, implemented as a class. Once an application instance has been created of a given architecture style and through "design pattern" guidance, a test architecture must be built reflecting the application's style and construction. Using this concept one can derive multiple test instances for each software application under test (AUT) of a particular architecture family. More formally, test architecture is defined as:

> *The relationships and constraints between the platforms, components, and approaches, used in the design of a Software Test Environment to conduct the verification and validation of a software application.*

By knowing the Architecture Style of a given AUT a matching Test Architecture can specify the required STE. Applying the concept of an architecture style and the mechanism of inheritance closely links test environments to their target software applications. By doing so test environment design should be faster and reuse of test components will be facilitated. This model derives from conceptual work on test environments but proves to be very useful in practical means. As discussed below, each block in this STE has a defined and relevant role to play in test design, management, and execution. Thus, the STE is a core tool in my virtual testing tool box.

7.1.1.4. Test Management

Test Management provides the infrastructure to automate and document the entire application testing life-cycle. These methodologies and technologies manage software testing assets and can be either manual or mechanized. Project testing assets include the process and technology platforms, test targets, test data and the application tests. Test Process and Technology Platforms are the procedures and tools used for test organization, execution and analysis. Test Targets, sometimes referenced as Test-beds, are the fully integrated software and hardware components that represent the production environment. The Test Target includes the application defined Infrastructure configuration with the actual AUT, or Application Under Test. In Table **1** below we can see an example of how an STE facilitates the creation of a test approach. In this case there are intrinsic test needs and there are test needs derived from the architecture style itself.

Table 1: Data Streaming Test Environment Reference Vector

Sample Reference Test Vector Components: **Data Streaming Architecture Style**
Base Class Derived (Intrinsic) Test Needs
Process Derived Test Needs
operational profile(determines run characteristics)
test methods and procedures(specified)
test intervals(specified)
failure and fault intensity objectives(specified)
resource utilization validation(specified)
heuristics(local magic)

The Test Bus

test database(state maintainence)
sanity suites(checklists)
test results(recording, analysis)
test environment(construction, validation, calibration)
test-bed hardware/software preconditions(specified)

Architecture Class Derived (Specific) Test Needs

Data Reception Test Needs

test data generation type (ASCII, binary, relational bulk transfer)
test format protocol (negotiated, standard)
number of external system simulation or test-bed sources (specified)
test periodicity (continuous, hourly, daily, monthly)
test communications protocol (ftp, uucp, rcp)
test communications speed (specified)

Processing Test Needs

algorithmic functional validation criteria (alpha sort, reverse sort, etc)
algorithmic comparator (alpha sort, revese sort, etc)
algorithmic performance validation criteria (time budgets)
data intermediaries validation (file, memory, tape)

Data Transmission Test Needs

expected data type (ASCII, binary, relational bulk transfer)
expected format protocol (negotiated, standard)
interface verification of number of targets (specified)
expected periodicity (continuous, hourly, daily, monthly)
communications protocol verification (ftp, uucp, rcp)
communications speed verification (specified)
test output capture and comparison(ASCII, binary)
pass/fail output enumeration(specified)

Physical Test Suites are applied to the Test Target, populated with Test Data, to measure the intersection of System Objectives with actual Application Presentation and Behavior. Frequency, capacity, format and content are some of the parameters that are used to build expected and erroneous test data sets. This test data is generated for external interface verification and internal data source population. The application tests are the methods or programs employed to exercise the AUT, with respect to the system requirements and objectives. Tests have context that map to the objectives. These objectives can include application unit testing, regression testing, and load or performance testing requirements. The pass and fail criteria of application tests reflect the quantitative and qualitative measurement of the AUT implementation coverage of the respective system objectives. The following sections outline the components of a General Test Management Class.

Taking a closer look at the framework components we have:

Test Object Repository: The data store that houses information and assets, such as project, common, historical, current state, dependency and testcase data, is referenced as the Test Object Repository. Test Scripts: Test Scripts are the information, methods and programs required to determine specified pass and fail criteria.

Test Data: Test Data is composed of the static and dynamic information processed from internal or external sources that determines the AUT state.

Test Results: The current state and historical information, that specify the AUT quantitative and qualitative attainment of system requirements at a moment or in a period of time.

Configuration Management: Configuration Management is the process, technology and integration required to manage change to the Test Environment. Some of the attributes of the Configuration Management component include tracking deltas to any test object, maintaining change requests with associated states, version capabilities, build facilities and integration with the analogous processes in the Application Development Environment.

Rules & Templates: Rules and triggers provide the mechanism for configuration of application specific behavior of the Test Management component. This customization capability allows for definition of the test objects actions and appearance through a flexible interface. An example rule might include automated execution of test suites based on recognized application state change events. Templates are the skeletal outlines of test objects. Included in the templates are test attributes and default populated values, where assumptions are appropriate.

Use Cases & Patterns: Use Cases are the documented Application Operability and Usability requirements. These Use Cases are employed to design Test Objectives that will map into test pass and fail criteria.

In looking at the test functions in this framework we have:

Test Design: The process of planning application testing is referred to as Test Design. Some of the activities include determination of test objectives, performing application risk analysis, specification of entrance criteria, specification of exit criteria, calculation of required resources, identification of required test cases and test suites, preparation of test infrastructure and the formal description of the test methodology to be employed. This part of the environment would cover the following areas: Test Plans & Specifications, Test Generation, Software Reliability Engineered Testing (including Operational & Usage Profiling). Details of these practices are covered amply in other sources. For this discussion it is sufficient to mention that these process steps must be fulfilled.

Test Development: Test Development is typically the most resource intensive and complex phase of the application test cycle. The creative task of writing, organizing and verifying correctness of Test Cases can be as or more complicated and expensive than developing the AUT. The art of reducing the complexity and required resources weighs heavily on the insertion of proven automation technology and methodologies at appropriate intervals and for the most reusable test objectives. The Test Development process provides mechanisms and methodologies to create test cases and test suites. Test Cases are the smallest entities, or test objects, that are applied the AUT. Test Suites are logical or physical sets of test cases that are usually characterized by some common test objective or application component, that the Test Suite was designed to address. For example, Unit, Functional, Regression, Load, Stress and Performance are Test Suites that make up intersecting subsets of the universal set of test cases for an application. Each of these groupings is designed to address a specific test need and have an identifiable list of characteristics. There are tools and practices that are designed to meet the automation common needs of particular test case types. For example record and playback technologies are available to provide a test designer with an Integrated Test Development Environment to capture and program test methods, expected and actual application states.

Test Execution: The most simplistic explanation of Test Execution is the extraction and launching of test cases and test suites on a single or distributed set of test-beds in the static and run-time environments of the AUT.

Test Measurement: The collection and analysis of test results is commonly referred to as Test Measurement. Test Measurement must cover such aspects as Test Coverage, Defect Tracking, and Failure & Fault Intensity Objectives.

7.1.1.5. Understanding Testing

Moving beyond this discussion we can look at the particulars of testing. With software there is a fault stream. The testing phase is not where bugs come from - this is where they are found. Bugs come from errors in requirements, design, and coding. About half tend to be inserted during coding. Test code and test cases can also have errors but these artifacts are not shipped to or used by customers. It is only if a test is faulty and allows a defect to pass to production that a test case error can have consequences.

In manufacturing an inspector visually approves the products. Defects are often easy to detect and the product can be removed from delivery. In software defects in logic are difficult to detect and costly to fix. Some software is so bug riddled that the return on investment is too small and the system must be scrapped. A key point is that the cost of removing defects increases as the development process increases. Bugs found in testing will be X times more expensive than in the design phase (see Fig. **4**).

7.1.1.6. A Generic Test Process

1. **Understand the System**: Using the requirements document, design documentation, user manuals, and interaction with development staff and users, develop a complete understanding of the purpose and intended use of the system to be tested. This can represent up to 50% of the effort of testing.

2. **Conduct Test Planning:** Decide on a testing strategy. Consider traditional test approaches, automated testing, and innovative approaches. Balance testing needs with resource availability (mostly staffing) and technical limitations due to the system design. Most importantly, determine the exit criteria for the major test phases, especially the final test phase prior to customer handoff.

3. **Conduct Test Design:** Prepare test cases for both unit and system level tests. Reflect on the nature of the system and draw upon the test techniques which match it the best. Use a test case template to organize a test specification.

4. **Create Test Environment**: Based on the architecture of the system under test and the test approach selected an environment must be provided for running tests and capturing results. Typically, a dedicated system environment is used for testing in order to prevent performance and configuration conflicts.

5. **Execute Test Specification**: Case by case execution of the test specification requires careful attention to antecedent system status and results. Document each defect or anomaly and assign staff to resolve the root cause.

6. **Assess System Readiness**: Track test progress in terms of test cases run, defects uncovered, and other predetermined test metrics. A call must be made as to when the system has met shipping criteria.

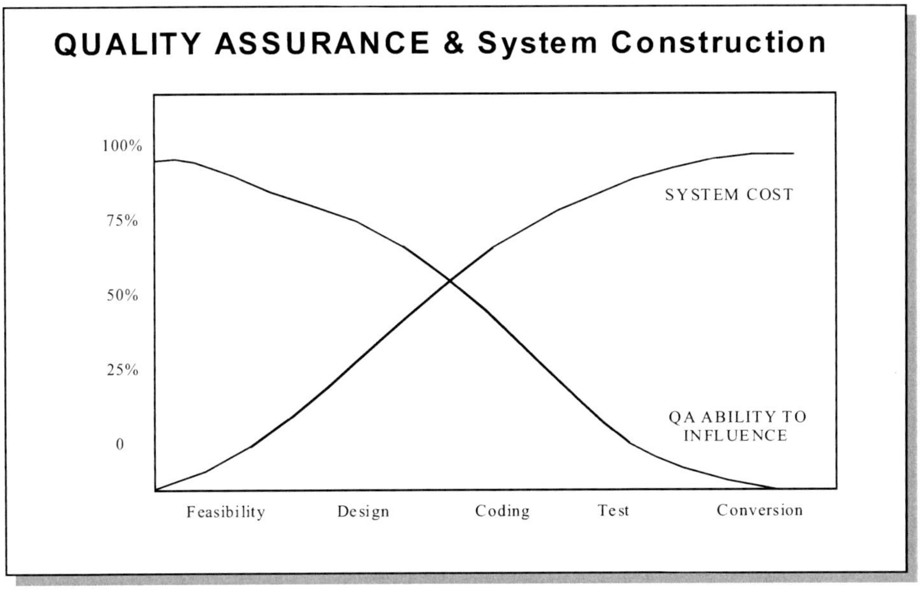

Figure 4: Quality Assurance activities are inversely proportional in impact in comparison to the system development lifecycle. The later a bug is found the more costly it will be to fix later.

There are a few *Testing Basics* that should be weaved into the approach above (from Meyers [8] and Biezer [9]):

- Know the expected results of your test.
- Don't test your own code.
- Test for valid and invalid inputs.
- Test that the program does what is expected AND that it does not do anything unexpected.
- Plan on your tests finding errors (leave time for debugging and recompilation, retesting).

Testing Success Factors:

- Focus on Bug Prevention from Start of Project (easier said than done).
- Find & Remove Bugs Early (reviews at each stage help).
- Users Involvement Helps (they may see things you don't).

When the inevitable happens - Debugging Approaches (from Meyers):

- Brute Force: storage dumps, print statements, debuggers.
- Induction: from clues to errors.
- Deduction: possibilities refined and canceled out.
- Backtracking.
- Testing.
- Debugging Guidance.
- Sleep on it.

- Describe the problem to someone.
- Avoid random experimentation.

Known Problems to Avoid:

- Fix the error not the symptom (trace to root cause).
- Be careful not to inject new errors while making fix.
- TEST the correction no matter how small.
- Check design - update specifications if required.
- Check process - how did the bug get into the system?

7.1.2. Test Planning

7.1.2.1. Testing Planning Overview

Early in your software development lifecycle, spend time on a test plan and/or a quality plan. This may be done in parallel to development activities. Test Planning resembles architecture and requirements development in that the needs of the customer must be considered and then represented in a concrete executable fashion - the test specification. Using the requirements, design documents, and standard test techniques a total approach to demonstrating software and/or system validity and quality is created.

Once requirements are reasonably well understood both the design and test paths can proceed in parallel (see Fig. **5**). It is vital that this be the case (when resources allow). One should not wait until the entire system is built to begin test planning. Instead, early decisions and trade-offs need to be made on the type of testing that can and cannot be conducted. Further, test case design can be difficult and time consuming. Work on test planning should be set to conclude at nearly the same time as the software implementation is complete. Test execution then commences and test results begin to kick error reports back for correction. Test execution is completed once the entire suite of pre-planned tests is completed, all bug-fixes have been tested, and the required level of product quality is achieved.

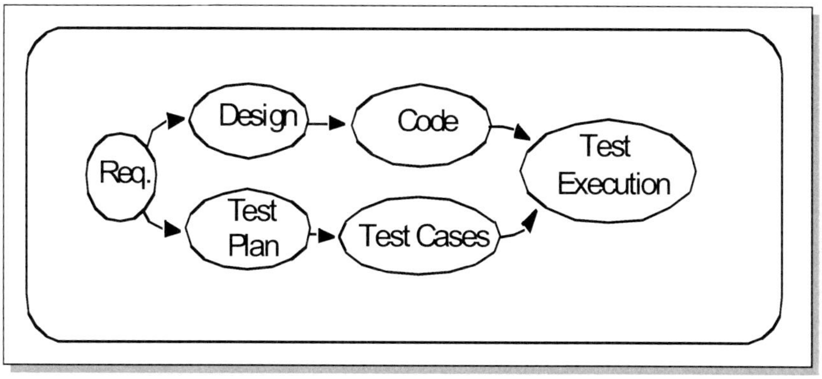

Figure 5: A Parallel Process for Test Planning.

7.1.2.2. Creating the Test Plan

Inputs: Requirements Document, Prototype, User Documentation, Test Plan Template, Test Case Template, Test Techniques

Outputs: Test Plan, Schedule, Test Specification, Test Data, Test Tools

7.1.2.3. Test Plan Template

Follow these steps to write the test plan:

1. Identify the specific requirements to be tested.
2. Associate each requirement with a software unit or process.
3. Establish a verification sequence (an order of demonstration of requirements compliance).
4. Identify the software groups needed to conduct each validation step.
5. Draw a diagram of the sequences of validation.
6. Estimate durations for each step and identify associated resources like tools or staff.
7. Review the plan and conduct additional planning iterations as necessary.

TEST PLAN TEMPLATE

INTRODUCTION

Objective
Revision History
Product Overview
(discuss nature of system to be tested)

GENERAL TEST APPROACH AND ASSUMPTIONS

General Test Assumptions
General Test Approach

MAJOR TEST RESPONSIBILITIES

Required Test Phases
Features to be Tested
Hardware Features
Software Features
Features Not to be Tested
Other Major Tasks
Beta Tests and Deployment
Test Deliverables

SYSTEM TEST ESTIMATES

Test Staff Estimates
(what is the required staff and staff hours to test the system)
Estimates of Defects
(what is the projected number of defects to be found)

EXTERNAL TEST RESPONSIBILITIES

Interactions with Other Organizations
(what are the roles and communication paths between groups)
Assumptions About Other Groups' Activities
(what activities are being relied upon from other groups that could impact test plans)

QUALITY CONTROLS

Standards
(what standards will be applied to the system or tested against)
Quality Improvement Plans (QIPs)
Entrance Criteria
(what criteria needs to be met by the system prior to testing)
Acceptance Test Evaluation Criteria
(what is the minimal level of performance required for the system to be tested)
Exit Criteria
(how will you know when to stop testing)

TEST ENVIRONMENT AND TOOLS

Hardware Requirements
Software Requirements

SYSTEM TEST TRACKING AND REPORTING

Tracking and Reporting Test Status
Fault Reporting
Other Test Metrics

SCHEDULES

CONCLUSIONS

REFERENCES

Figure 6: Test Plan Template.

7.1.2.4. Test Case Template

Once you have a test plan developed a task that you will need to tackle is to create test cases. You can use a tool for creating test cases or create a tool of your own. In either case you will need a simple set of meta data for each test case. I have found the following test case elements to be most necessary but there may be others:

- Test Case Number.
- Author.
- Date.
- Requirement or Function to Test.
- System & Version.
- Test Description.
- Test Pre-Conditions.
- Test Steps.
- Test Scripts.
- Test Data.
- Expected Results.
- Testing History.

Once the test cases are ready to run (and the environment is shaken out) you can start logging errors if your test cases are in fact successful and find problems. It is a good idea to log every event in the test environment whether successful or not. This will be critical in future debugging, reporting, and status determination. A simple problem record format follows in Table **2**. Such reporting is almost always done with a tool set (*i.e.*, BugZilla).

Table 2: A Problem Record Report Format

Test Tracking Log Sheet						
Date	**Time**	**Test Case Number**	**Pass/Fail**	**Defect Number**	**Severity**	**Notes**

One column in Table **2** depicts severity, it is worth pointing out that bugs will have different severities. Some will be severe and others will be minor. A reasonable scale which I use from my days at AT&T Bell Labs is as follows:

1. System is inoperable (entire system is down).
2. Major component or functionality degraded (no work around available).
3. Inconvenient functional impact.
4. Minor issue (spelling).

Such severity classes will be dependent upon the organization and some may not have a classification scheme. However, it is worth it set up something so as to get clarity around which bugs to prioritize. Just as defect discovery rates go up at each phase junction (that is when we move from life cycle phase to life cycle phase), we also see that even though we have progressed through 75% of the test interval, still we find that 40% of all defects may be of category 1 & 2 severity [10]. The point here is that we may be just about to release the software but we are still finding major bugs. One weapon here is to test with a Operational Profile (described in detail below) which prioritizes test scenarios around those that matter most and allows you to quantify probabilities of high impact errors. Nevertheless, you cannot let up your guard and you also cannot work under the assumption that just because you have reached the end of the planned test cycle that you have found all the defects.

7.1.3. Test Design Overview

Test Design is the task of creating tests for a software system. There are dozens of test design techniques just as there are dozens of software design techniques. There are also many kinds of tests. Generally speaking software test types and test design techniques can be broken down into two broad categories: Glass Box Testing and Black Box Testing.

Understanding the system is a bulk of the test effort (test planning) especially for Black Box Testing. We need to understand the design and create a test design that matches the system - the rest of the time you will execute tests and analyze results. Unit testing typically will be done by individual developer - thus they deliver a module design, manual page, test design, and the code. This will be a complete package. This might also include drivers and test data.

A test case is the fundamental component of testing. As we develop software each block of code will need to have test cases designed for it. In the best of all worlds requirements are traced through to the test cases. Thus we know which requirement is driving which modules and the associated test cases (aka, traceability matrix). Thus the test case will be documented with feature number, function number, or requirement number, which it is related to. If a feature is modified or removed this should trigger the associated test cases to be re-executed.

Test Design is difficult and time consuming. There are some basic concepts which underlie good test case design. These concepts and a basic example are included below.

7.1.3.1. Test Design Concepts

Test: A test is the planned execution of software in hopes of finding a defect.

Test Factor: A variable relevant to the target system that can be varied (changed or modified) during testing.

Test Factor Examples:

- Type of processor.
- Environmental conditions.
- Type of load.
- Command line arguments.
- Fields or field values on a screen.
- Order of operation.

Test Factor Level: A set of test factor values.

Good test case design starts with an analysis of the possible test factors and their levels. Complete test design may require using other techniques to find all the factors and levels for a system. These techniques are described under Glass Box and Black Box Testing.

7.1.3.2. An Example of Test Factors and Levels

As an example lest consider a test for a backup system. The tests for a file back-up system which can write to hard drive, tape, or network server, incremental or full backup need to be factors as follows:

Factor 1: File backup method

Levels: disk drive, tape drive, network disk

Factor 2: File backup mode

Levels: complete, incremental

Factor 3: Percent of changed files

Levels: 0%, <25%, 26-75%, 76-99%, 100%

Factor 4: Total size of file for backup

Levels: Small <100MB, Medium 100MG-1GB, Large 1GB+

As you can see with 4 factors and multiple parameters for each the number of test cases needed begins to expand quickly. In this case at least 13 test cases need to be designed just to cover the defined factors. However, the permutations when varying these factors against each other becomes much larger. In terms of a tool, the key take away here is understanding what factors you have, how many variances you will see, and what the scope of the testing needs to be. Understanding the scope of the testing required is of and by itself a critical tool in my virtual tool box. This cognizance will also be valuable in all additional testing methods we will discuss.

7.1.3.3. Glass Box Testing

Glass Box testing as mentioned takes advantage of the internal structure of software components to create tests. This type of testing is often typical of the Unit Test Phase.

Glass Box Testing includes the following key test design methods:

1. Flow Graph Testing and Complexity analysis based testing.
2. Boundary Value Analysis.
3. State-Event-Function Testing.

Several ad hoc but important approaches include the following advice:

- Test every line of code.
- Test every branch in logic.
- Test every program parameter.
- Test every interface (screen, field, dialog, or communications interface).
- Test every error condition.

Exhaustive testing is well known to be impossible due to the innumerous permutations involved in testing even simple software routines. However, these basic test requirements will go a long way in finding key issues in programs.

7.1.3.4. Flowgraph Testing with Complexity Analysis

The fundamental test design technique for unit testing or component testing is the flowgraph or complexity graph of a program. Since exhaustive testing (every possible path for every possible value) is mathematically impossible to achieve in discrete time we must make a compromise. Flowgraph testing is the basic test design technique used to find out how to test each statement and each branch in a program and to do so with the fewest tests.

7.1.3.4.1. Flowgraph Example

Consider this simple pseudo code fragment:

LOOP

DO get_use_rec

UNTIL stat is EOF

DO sel_rec

IF record selected

DO put_report

ELSE

ENDIF

ENDLOOP

If we use a simple acyclic directed graph we can visualize this logic in the diagram below (Fig. 7):

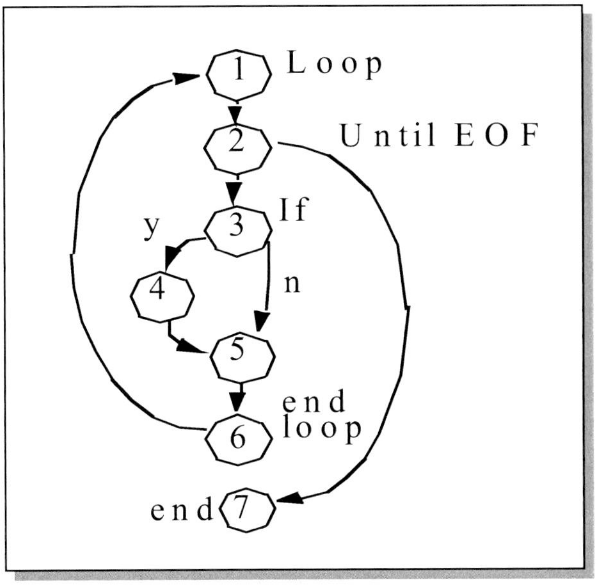

Figure 7: A Flowgraph to compute Cyclomatic Complexity.

7.1.3.5. Designing Test Cases

Using the diagram above we can design test cases based on the number of unique paths through the graph. For this example only three test cases are required:

P1 = 1-2-7

P2 = 1-2-3-5-6-1-2-7

P3 = 1-2-3-4-5-6-1-2-7

The number of test cases (3) is also the same number given to the code fragment for its "complexity". Thus by calculating complexity of a program we can find out how many test cases to write and if the complexity is greater than about 11 or 13 then it should become a candidate for simplification.

NOTE: There are automated tools for calculating complexity for most programming languages. For example, Microsoft Team Foundation Suite has built in support for multiple complexity metrics as do other tools.

7.1.3.5.1. BOUNDRY VALUE ANALYSIS

Many bugs are found when testing on or around the boundaries of a program's conditional statements. Always test the boundaries of each conditional statement as the example below shows.

7.1.3.5.2. Boundary Example

Using the simple technique of boundary value analysis many defects can be caught since programmers often set up conditional tests in the wrong direction or by assuming a different operator precedence than the compiler actually enforces. To avoid these types of errors always test as in the simple C example below for all relevant values of "a" and "b".

```
if(a == 1 && b == 100) {
do...
}
```

Required Test Cases Include [a=0, a =1, a = 2, a = -1, b = 99, b = 100, b = 101]

There are many good sources on Glass Box testing including Camer [11].

7.1.3.6. Black Box Testing

Black Box testing focuses on the functional capabilities of a software system. It tests the end-to-end architecture the software as a whole. This type of testing is often typical of the Integration and System Test Phases. Black Box Testing includes the following test design methods:

- Scenario Testing.
- Operational Profiles.
- Software Reliability Engineering.
- Robust Testing (Orthogonal Arrays).
- Load, Stress, and Performance Testing.

7.1.3.7. Scenario Testing

A scenario is an hypothesized chain of events. For Black Box and System Testing, scenarios are ideal mechanisms for driving typical usage profiles for the verification of a system's capabilities to meet customer requirements. A common scenario approach is the Use Case. Use cases were formalized by Jacobson [12] for Object-Oriented analysis. Eventually they became the standard artifact used by testers for scenario testing as they were (aside from requirements) the one user oriented specification document. From the use case, test cases can be developed (especially scenario based test cases).

Specifically, the test engineer models a scenario after expected software operations in the field often following a use case. An Operational Profile is an excellent way to help develop scenarios and *vice versa*. Use Case modeling also can generate scenarios and support the development of Operational Profiles which we will discuss next. More formally, a test scenario is defined as:

The sequence of actions and stimuli that are necessary to demonstrate correct software operation.

7.1.3.7.1. Test Scenario Example

Consider an air traffic control system as provided by Royer [13]. An aircraft will fly from London to Boston. There are several handoffs from local control stations to en-route control stations and airfield control towers. The scenario example traces such a flight and the support which the system must provide. It is written from the perspective of the user who is in this case an air traffic controller.

Here is the handoff sequence:

1. London ground control to London departure;
2. London departure to British en-route control;
3. At Shannon, Ireland transfer to transoceanic flight (no ground control);
4. Near Iceland contact made with Reykjavik;
5. Near Gander, American en-route establishes control;
6. Near Boston, Boston approach directs landing;
7. After touchdown the flight is guided to gate by Boston ground control.

Each of these handoffs must work flawlessly and under many circumstances. For example, they must work when there are multiple contacts being tracked, single contacts, delay conditions, and so on.

7.1.3.7.2. Creating a Test Scenario

To build a test scenarios for this or any situation follow these steps:

1. Write a detailed functionally oriented scenarios.
2. "Throw" requirements at the scenario. Good scenarios support more than one requirement.

3. For any remaining requirements where there are no scenarios fill in the gaps with new scenarios.

In writing scenarios concentrate on what the user must do with the system not what the system will be doing. There are several event types in a scenario:

- General Background Events.
- System External Events.
- System Internal Events.

Once the events are identified within a scenario set up a table of events and/or a time line to help plan test execution. Line up the events on a time line to make it easier to follow when you have to execute multiple event timelines in parallel.

7.1.4. Operational Profiles

An Operational Profile, mentioned previously, is a set of operations and their probabilities of occurrence. An operational profile can guide many development tasks including architecture, resource allocation, and testing. In the context of testing Operational Profiles can provide faster testing cycles that produce more reliable systems by aligning tests with actual customer software usage patterns. The Operational Profile was introduced by Musa in the 1970s [14] but formalized in 1993 [15]. This technique has its roots in the ideas of scenarios and their probabilities. We have mentioned the Operational Profile several times so far in preceding chapters but we need to spend some time defining it and providing an example.

Using an Operational Profile to guide system testing generates software usage patterns during testing in accordance with the probabilities that similar functional usage patterns will be followed in production. Basing your testing on an operational profile assures that the most heavily used functions have been adequately tested [16]. In Fig. **8** below we can see that as software execution proceeds (sometimes on multiple paths) certain events (failure events) may occur. The key question reliability engineering attempts to answer is how often will these failure events occur and it is the job of the Operational Profile to drive the software so that it exercises it properly into generating the failures that matter the most first so that the underlying causes (or faults) can be removed. If the Operational Profile or statistical behavior model is accurate enough the major faults will be found and the reliability realized by the system will grow to the target level. This is the essence of reliability engineering and how Operational Profiles fit in.

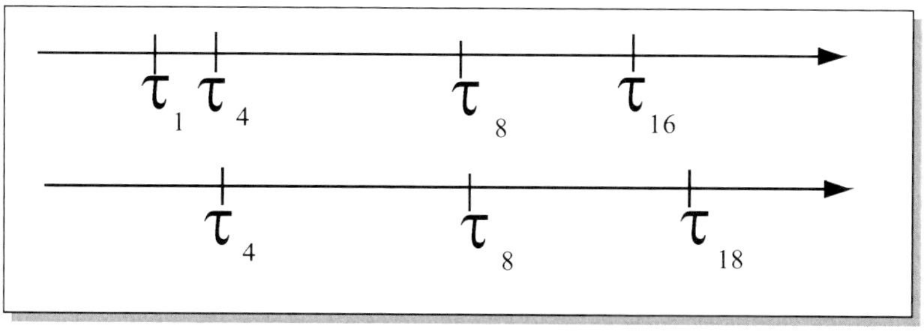

Figure 8: Events in a system time line. How can you predict them?

Key terms of the operational profile:

- Function - an externally initiated task performed by a system as seen by user.
- Operation - a task being accomplished by the system as viewed by the people who run the system. Often multiple operations make up a function.
- Mode - set of functions or operations grouped for the analysis of execution. A mode determines the types of functions used and their probabilities. Several modes may exist for a system and may run one at a time or side by side.

To creating a profile:

1. Determine the modes of operation (*e.g.*, normal, busy, daytime, evening).
2. Identify user types (*e.g.*, clerk, administrator, customer).

3. Develop functional profile (what are system functions and their probabilities).

4. Develop functional scenarios (what groups of functions make a scenario).

5. Map functions to operations (what set of functions relate to an operation).

6. Apply Profile (use in architecture planning, develop prioritization, and test case selection).

7.1.4.1. Sample Profile

Typical functional profiles resemble the one below from a telecommunications system. The diagram in Fig. **9** displays the list of the functions and their probabilities in a graphical representation of the profile. This model of system behavior is simple to understand if somewhat complex to build at times especially for a larger system or a system which is new and historical data is not available. Nevertheless, I use an Operational Profile on each system I work on and have employed it also for confirming porting of functionality and performance testing. In the example we can see that 80% of the system usage flows down the "standard" dialing path. After that 70% of the traffic is externally bound. Understanding the system structure and behavior in this manner is a key analysis tool in my tool box and yields a wide array of benefits. One type of testing it also supports is Black Box scenario testing leading to reliability calculation discussed next.

7.1.5. Software Reliability Engineering

Software Reliability Engineering (SRE) is primarily a Black Box System Testing technique. SRE provides a comprehensive philosophy towards testing software based systems. SRE also provides a user driven test profile (the Operational Profile as introduced above), quantitative measures for determining test progress, and finally it allows for the production of software with a known reliability level [17].

Key terms include the following:

- Reliability - the probability of failure free operation within a specified environment.
- Fault - a defect or error resident in an software system.
- Failure - an observed departure from system requirements or user specified behavior by the software or system.
- Failure Intensity - the rate at which failures are observed based on the execution time of the software.
- Operational Profile - the set of behaviors which the system performs and the probability of each one's occurrence.
- Execution Time – this is the time that the system is running, it may be calculated in CPU time or other units, I prefer to use a "heartbeat" measure like the number of orders in a time period.

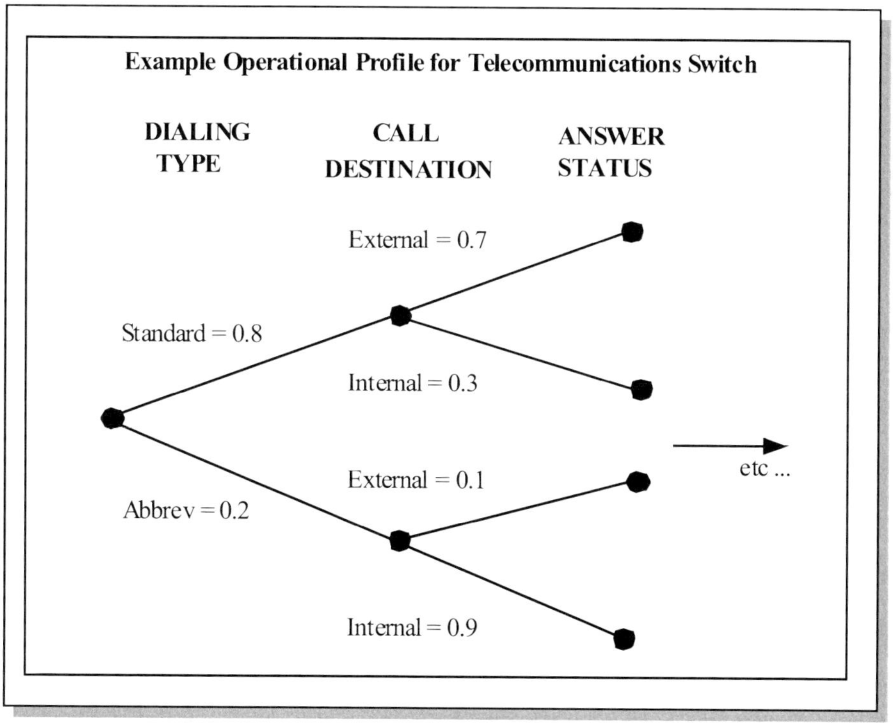

Figure 9: A Sample Operational Profile.

To use SRE to Conduct Testing follow these steps:

1. Define the Operational Profile of the system.
2. Define the failures possible for the system.
3. Set the failure intensity objective for the system.
4. Plan test selection using Operational Profile (assumes test design complete)
5. Execute tests specification with given probabilities
6. Count software execution time and failure occurrences
7. Make approximation of execution time if needed (transactions, wall clock)
8. Calculate failure intensity for system
9. Correct software faults and continue testing until objective is satisfied

7.1.5.1. Reliability Models

In order to know failure intensity or reliability we need a few models. One basic reliability model looks like the one in Fig. **10** (a and b). The first plots execution time and failure intensity. The second converts this to show failure intensity and calendar time. Using the following formula we can determine reliability:

$$R(\tau) = exp(-\lambda\tau) \qquad \textbf{(9)}$$

where

$R(\tau)$ = *reliability for time* τ

$exp = e^x$

λ = *failure intensity*

τ = *execution time*

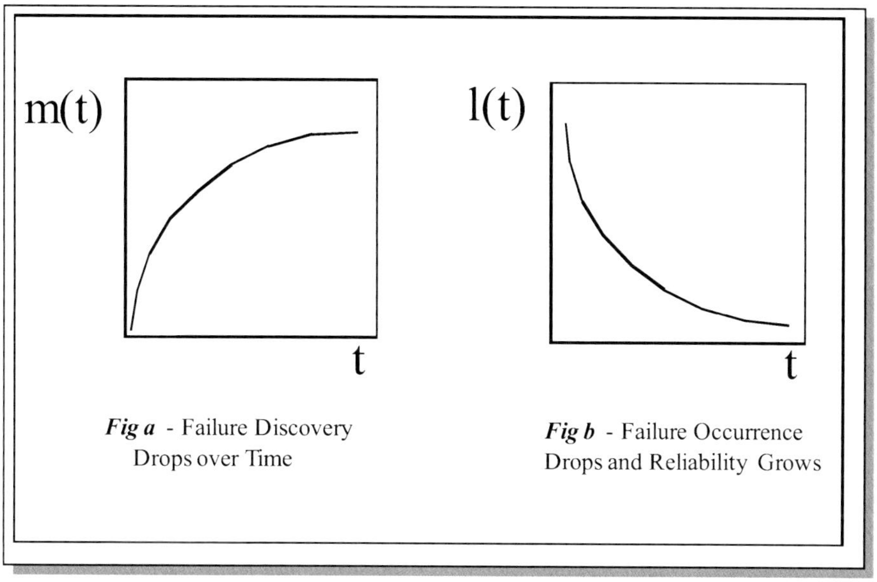

Figure 10: Figure a and b represents two sides of a coin. Fig. **a**) represents the rate of failures discovered and Fig. **b**) represents the growth in reliability as a consequence.

In order to derive a reliability measure for a system each of these variables must be supplied. SRE calls for the development of an Operational Profile, up-front failure classification, calibration of an execution time metric, and the collection and analysis of failure occurrences. With the appropriate attention to this pre-work when testing begins failures need to be logged against the execution time. If this is done the reliability level at any given time can be determined. I have used these methods on real systems and using small testing teams with mostly manual procedures and limited tool support. I believe the results which we achieved can be mimicked by other teams without significant overhead. Obviously for mission critical or life critical systems more investment may be necessary. However, for myself these tools are extremely handy.

7.1.6. Object Oriented Testing

It is worth pointing out that with the introduction of Object Technologies some new challenges found their way into the world of software testing. As we have seen, the classic test assumptions include the following:

1. Units of code are tested first using the white-box technique;
2. Units are assembled in integration groups and tested using the black-box technique.
3. The final system is assembled (then tested) and validated by end users.

However, Object Technology construction realities introduce new behaviors with the software:

- OO design is stimuli-(behavior) oriented.
- OO programming leads to fewer lines of code per method.
- OO units are classes and objects, not member functions.
- Programming of OO components is often evolutionary, class interfaces can be defined early without any functionality available.

Boisvert [18] conceptualized a way to handle some of these challenges. In an iterative approach with an inner loop and an outer loop as development progresses, testing also progresses utilizing basic testing of classes and methods, and later traditional integration, functional, and system test. Specifically, he proposed:

- Gray-Box Testing with emphasis on behavior.
- Source files as basic test items with message based testing.
- Basic Test Case Configuration.
- Test Automation (which has become more and more prevalent today).

Naturally, every technology brings new types of problems. With OO some of the related errors include: message errors, timing, states, garbage collection, concurrency, operation errors, inheritance violations, subclass violations of superclass. A conceptual way to manage this within unit testing (or Glass Box testing) is by creating a class tester (Fig. **11**). This is related to the Test Driven Development method mentioned earlier. By creating class drivers testing can be accomplished more readily.

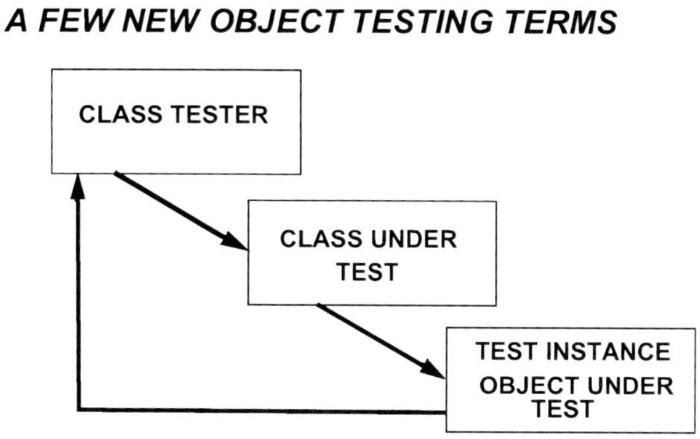

Figure 11: A view of Object Oriented Testing.

7.1.7. Testing Progress Measurements

As mentioned above, just because you have found a lot of defects does not mean you are through testing. Also, it does not follow that because your defect discovery rate has slowed that you are finished. There is a concept in testing that the software under test will "learn" how to defeat the test being thrown at it (aka, test suite immunity). Thus, measuring test progress can be challenging. The SRE techniques described above are the best ones I have seen used on real projects. They tell you what your end reliability will be with a high confidence factor. Other methods will not do so.

However, there are other useful measures. Defect prediction and DRE (Defect Removal Efficiency) are both useful. Defect prediction calls for some black magic of first understanding the number of lines of code in the application (KLOC or thousand lines of code) and also understanding (or guessing) at the defect rate per line of code. This can be expressed as: *Inherent Faults = (Faults per KLOC) * KLOC*. Based on this and the bug reports you can tell what progress you are making. If you predicted 10 defects per KLOC that means if you have a 100,000 KLOC application you would expect 1,000 defects to be found. If you have found less you may want to keep testing.

The other method which is useful is DRE. Here you look at the defect removal quotient per phase. So, in unit testing (assuming the errors found are logged) you compare with integration testing, system testing, beta testing, and so on. In this case, using the same numbers as above, if 500 defects were found in unit testing (of the presumed 1,000) then the DRE would be 50%. This can be stated as: *DRE = (Defects found in current phase)/(All defects detected in all phases)*. This can only be confirmed when all phases of testing are done, and unfortunately, when production experience is also calculated. Ideally, we would see a DRE in the high 90s by the end of all defect removal activities. This provides additional confidence that the software has been shaken out properly.

$$DRE = n/(n + S) \qquad \textbf{(10)}$$

where

DRE = effectiveness of activity to remove defects

n = number of faults (defects) found by activity

S = number of faults (defects) found by subsequent activities

I advise using multiple means of quality understanding. Thus, number of defects found, defects found *vs.* predicted defects, failure intensity, reliability, and DRE can combine to provide a robust decision making array of data points. I have also used the "pocket planner" provided by Jones [19] to predict defects. As long as you have access to the KLOC value you can "backfire" into Function Points and get an estimate of defects for the size application you are working on (as discussed in Chapter 2). In the end releasing software also involves a gut check. But with these tools from my tool box I suggest that gut check will be well supported.

7.1.8. Other Factors Contributing to Software Quality

To achieve high quality in software products designers must consider the following factors and strive towards the optimization of their products in each category:

- Correctness
- Reliability
- Efficiency
- Integrity
- Usability
- Testability
- Portability
- Reusability
- Interoperability
- Flexibility
- Maintainability

These factors are often referred to as the "ilities" as there is a long list of potential quality impacting yet "non-functional" requirements for any system including the above list. Keeping these requirements in mind during development is challenging but critical to long term systems success.

7.1.8.1. Reviews Introduced

One of the most effective means of preventing costly errors and defects in the development of software products are reviews [20]. Reviews can be held on any design artifact in software development and at any time in the lifecycle. Also known as Walkthroughs and Inspections, reviews bring a technical team together to carefully examine a document, design, program, or plan.

7.1.8.2. Review Particulars

Participants of a review will vary based on the task. However, reviews are not meant to evaluate the individuals who produced the artifact under consideration.

Thus, the individual's management is not normally present. Otherwise the review can bring together from 4 to 6 people of the following roles:

- An experienced moderator.
- The author, designer, or programmer of the review material.
- One or more technical experts in the subject matter.
- One or more testing or quality experts.

Executing the Review [21]:

1. Schedule the review for no more than 2 hours.
2. Narrate code or step through design in detail.
3. Look for problems and take careful notes - do not solve problems in real-time.
4. Expect the author/designer to find as many defects as the experts.
5. Use a checklist of common design or programming problems.
6. Use an applicable standards list to monitor compliance with agreed upon practice.
7. Moderator must maintain focus of review on technical issues and keep review moving forward to prevent morphing into design session.
8. Author/Programmer leaves with list of modifications to make, follow-up review is discretionary based on severity of problems.

CONCLUSIONS

In this chapter we took a whirlwind tour of the world of testing (and quality). There is much more to be said on this topic than can fit into one chapter. There is also a lot of sweat that needs to be put into testing to carry it out. With the coverage of the techniques above it is hoped that the reader will take away the basic principles of testing and what I have found to work the best. Also, it is expected that in order to implement many of these techniques further reading and training may be required. Regardless of the need for further elaboration this chapter servers as a backbone of testing methods found in my virtual tool box. I could not deliver systems without these testing methods.

REFERENCES

[1] Jensen, R., **Software Engineering,** Prentice Hall, Engelwood Cliffs, NJ, 1979.

[2] Meyers, G., **The Art of Software Testing**, John-Wiley & Sons, 1979.

[3] Vogel, P., "*An Integrated General Purpose Automated Test Environment*", **Proceedings of the 1993 International Symposium on Software Testing and Analysis**, pp. 61-69, Cambridge, MA, June 1993.

[4] Eickelmann, N., & Richardson, D., "*An Evaluation of Software Test Environment Architectures*", **Proceedings of ICSE-18**, Berlin, IEEE Press, 1996.

[5] Cusick, J., "*Deriving Software Test Environments from Architecture Styles*", **Proceedings of the 1999 AT&T Software Testing Symposium**, Middletown, NJ, June, 1999.

[6] Buschmann, F., *et al.*, **Pattern-Oriented Software Architecture: A System of Patterns,** John-Wiley & Sons, NY, 1996.

[7] McGregor, J., & Kare, A., "*Testing Object-Oriented Components*", **Proceedings of the 17th International Conference on Testing Computer Software**, June, 1996.

[8] Meyers, G., **The Art of Software Testing**, John-Wiley & Sons, 1979.

[9] Beizer, B., **Software Testing Techniques**, 2nd Edition, Van Nostrand Reinhold, New York, 1990.

[10] Mirsa, P. N., "*Software Reliability Analysis*", **IBM Systems Journal**, vol. 22(3), pp. 262-270.

[11] Kaner, C., *et al.*, **Testing Computer Software**, Wiley, 1999.

[12] Jacobsen, I., *et al.*, **Object-Oriented Software Engineering: A Use Case Driven Approach**, Addison-Wesley., Wokingham, England, 1992.

[13] Royer, T. C., **Software Testing Management: Life on the Critical Path**, Prentice Hall, Englewood Cliffs, 1993.

[14] Cusick, J., "*In Memoriam: John Musa*", **IEEE Computing Now**, 7/15/2009.

[15] Musa, J. D., "*Operational Profiles in Software-Reliability Engineering* ", **IEEE Software**, March 1993.

[16] Musa, J. D., Iannino, A., and Okumoto, K., **Software Reliability: Measurement, Prediction, Application**, McGraw-Hill, 1987.

[17] ibid.

[18] Boisvert, J., *OO Testing in the Ericson Pilot Project*, **Object Magazine**, 7(5):27-33, July 1997.

[19] Jones, C., **Applied Software Measurement: Assuring Productivity and Quality**, McGraw Hill, New York, 1991.

[20] ibid.

[21] Perry, William E., **Quality Assurance for Information Systems**, QED Technical Publishing Group, Boston, 1991.

Send Orders of Reprints at bspsaif@emirates.net.ae
Durable Ideas in Software Engineering, 2013, 233-254

CHAPTER 8

Support

Abstract: Discussion of a topic not often covered in software engineering books. Based on real world experience running a large enterprise support organization responsible for a portfolio of web applications managing hundreds of millions of dollars of revenue. The scope, methods, and techniques of organizing and managing support engineering organization are presented and explained. This includes software delivery, software maintenance, software evolution, and more. Discussion of concepts of system drift introduced for the first time.

Keywords: Software support, software support engineering, proactive monitoring, ITIL, incident response, problem management, change management, system drift, support framework.

8.1. INTRODUCTION

In virtually every Computer Science course student assignments begin with a clean sheet of paper (or an empty file). They begin solving a problem by beginning to code from scratch. In industry this is almost never the case. Instead problems are often described in terms of existing systems. For example, one might hear a request like "it should be just like the ARDVARK system except that it should get its input in real time and it should support 3 new client types and it has to handle all the new data formats from purchasing". This type of request is common and calls on the developer to change the interface architecture, expand the platform support, and expand the database.

Modifying and supporting "new" systems that are often based on existing ones or maintaining legacy systems brings us back to the 80:20 rule of development where 80% of development is modifying and extending existing systems.

In today's world there are few domains that have not already been automated. This led to the rise of packaged ERP (Enterprise Resource Planning) software like Peoplesoft, Saleseforce.com, SAP, and others. If there is a domain that has previously been automated that will serve as the reference architecture for reimplementation and provides a base set of requirements to grow from. In some companies, legacy support is greater than 50% of the IT budget. Naturally, there

James J. Cusick

are always some areas that allow for green field innovation (we can think of thousands of examples today from the apps of the iTunes world) but for core business applications where I have experience and where the significant development and maintenance dollars are spent, gradual evolution of existing systems is a core competency.

In this chapter we will discuss the general pattern of a maintenance program along with some of its core challenges. We will also build on the ideas of the Object Topology introduced earlier to explore a phenomenon we called "topological drift" which happens when technology evolves around a given implementation. Finally we will explore a framework for support and maintenance which I have developed over the last several years and which is being published here for the first time. These topics will display a fairly unusual topic for conversation in software engineering, the practical and real world deployment, maintenance, and support of applications.

8.2. SOFTWARE DELIVERY

After specifying, building, and testing the software, it still has to get into the hands of a customer. This is what people refer to as "production", that is the use of the software not its manufacture. To get the software from development environments to production environments is often a simple copy and configuration, a flip of some bits as it were. However, there is a lot of work associated with this in order to control the process, do it repeatedly, manage configurations, and generally do it right (that is, ensure that customers get what they asked for and paid for). There are several very common software delivery methods which include:

- Packaged software: manufacture & ship.
- Custom: on-site install.
- Turn-key: ready to roll systems.
- Electronic: web based delivery.

In the old days we would cut a version of the software to tape or disk and drive or fly to a customer facility to install it. This seems almost laughable today but we did this only a relatively few short years ago. Even today with large data files the US mail is sometimes the best way to transfer data quickly. However, by and large installation over network infrastructure has taken precedence. For each Operating System and language packaging tools may vary. Tasks for delivery also go beyond simple packaging and bit by bit transfer. They also include client or distributor prep, user training, service and cutover, and support. The extent of tools and their parameters are beyond the scope of this discussion. Instead we will focus on what happens once you accomplish your delivery. Essentially, any system in production is a legacy system. It needs to be maintained and users need to be supported. This will be the focus of the remaining parts of this chapter.

8.3. SOFTWARE SUPPORT

For any large scale development release support needs come to dominate as soon as the release is accomplished. There is usually great fanfare upon a release and people are happy to move on to their next projects. Unfortunately the software that has been released will need care and feeding. In some cases this will be minimal and in other cases it can be a gargantuan task. It has been my experience of late to work in an organization that prefers to hand off from a development team to a support team. This means that knowledge transfer is required between teams. The pattern of support can be seen in Fig. **1** [1]. In this pattern support is highest after the initial release and then undulates with each successive release. What is not shown here is the urgent business calls for help on occasion if something ends up not working.

8.4. SOFTWARE MAINTENANCE

The essence of software support is software maintenance which can be summed up as *"Keeping old systems going and adding to them"* [2]. Once any successful system is in production users and engineers will think of new ways to use it (enhancements). Also, the inherent defects we missed in our test phases (see Chapter 7) will start popping up. These will need to be removed. Thus, the cause of software changes are:

- Correction of errors
- Postponed development
- System enhancements
- Regulatory mandates

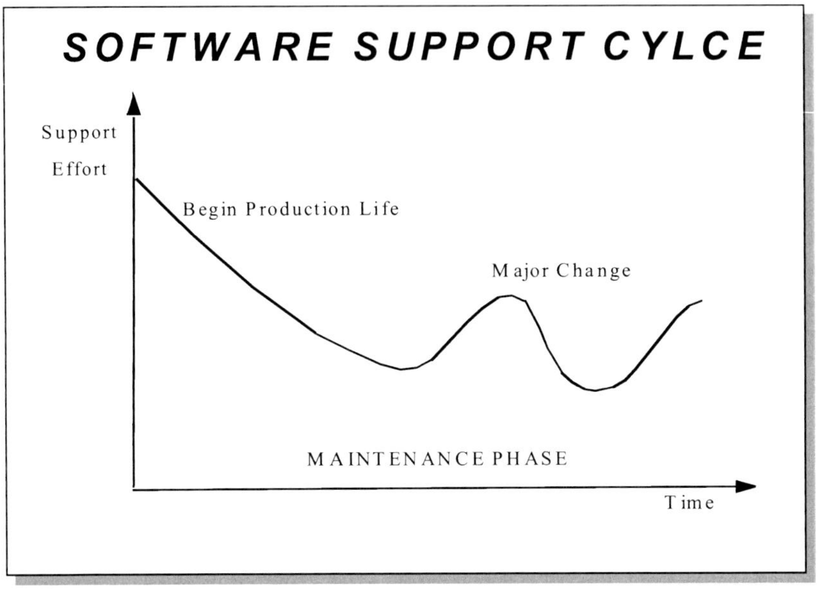

Figure 1: The Support Cycle.

In general, the distribution of software maintenance is more on enhancements. Some studies say as much as 80% of maintenance is enhancement related. Interestingly, for each change there is between a 20-50% chance of introducing a new problem or defect. Thus, in many cases, avoiding change is a stabilizing strategy. A notional maintenance process is provided in Fig. **2** below [3]. This model is similar to the familiar software lifecycles we introduced in Chapter 2 but once again, here we are not assuming a green field environment. In this scenario everything is a change against the existing platform.

The process above can be stated more briefly as:

1. Understand the software

2. Define objectives & approach

3. Implement modification

4. Revalidate Software

5. Repeat or Quit

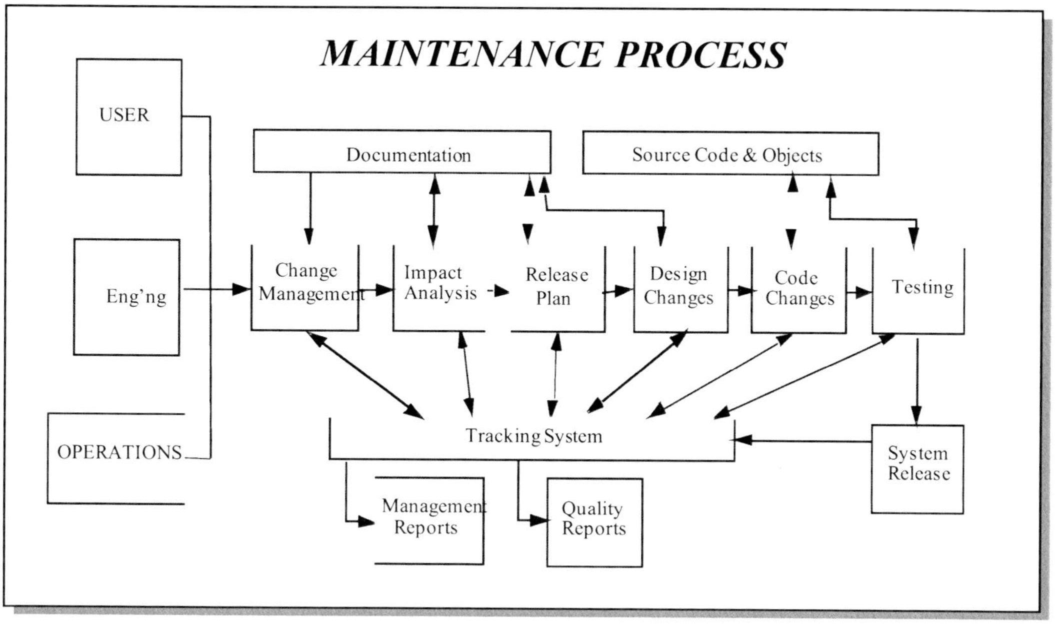

Figure 2: The Maintenance Process.

Within this process one risk is the drop in knowledge over time and the increase in poor design quality as a result (Fig. **3**). One method to fight this is to focus on documentation, knowledge transfer, and retaining some of the original developers as long as possible during the application support cycle.

8.4.1. Inconsistencies from Topological Drift

In considering software maintenance it is critical to keep in mind that technology does not stand still. Platforms, tools, languages, techniques, and human skill are constantly in motion. For RAD projects, Agile projects, or one-off applications this is seldom a major issue. However, for long duration applications this can pose many problems. Consider the Voyager 1 spacecraft now more than 17 billion

Kilometers from Earth and destined to continue downloading information for decades at a fraction of today's common transfer rates [4]. Consider the difficulty in finding expertise on early 70s vintage equipment. This extreme example stresses the fact that while an operational system might still be meeting its mission responsibilities the world of technology will have long since moved on.

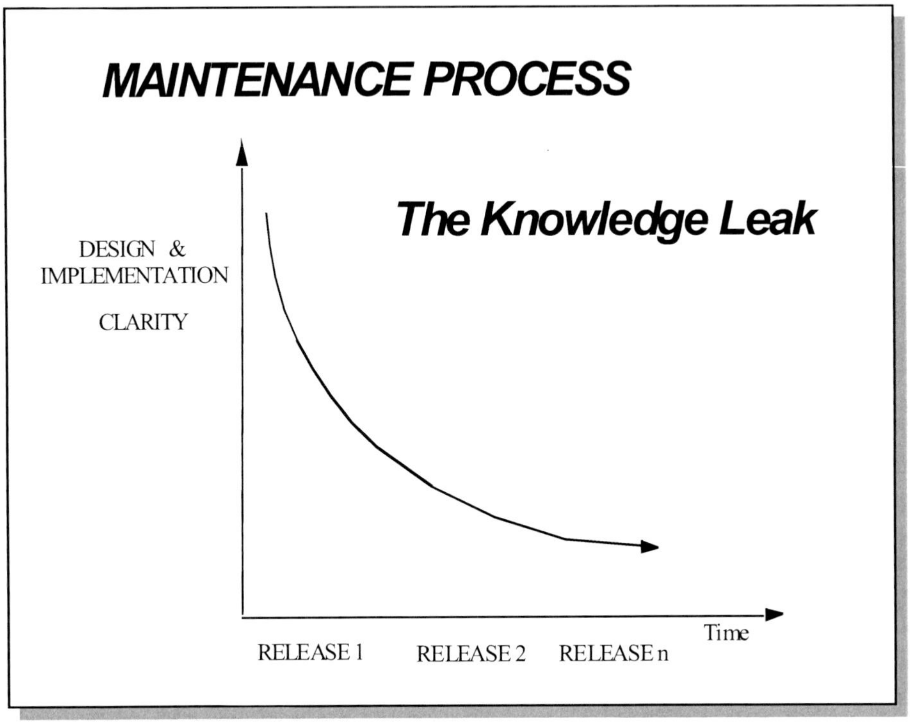

Figure 3: Knowledge Leaks in the Maintenance Phase.

This brings us to an introduction to the concept of Topological Drift. It can flow in many directions. Either technology can flow ahead of you and your system cannot keep up or you are forced to maintain aging technology due to contractual, operational, or other constraints. In this case the manicured playing field has become full of weeds or may have turned to concrete while you were still in the middle of the game. When this occurs, Topological Drift has set in, and inconsistencies pop up like dandelions. The concept of Topological Drift is based on work done with Professor W. Tepfenhart while we were both at AT&T Bell Laboratories. We had developed a model for understanding Object Topologies [5] and continued by looking at maintenance issues among other things.

Fig. **4** demonstrates the nature of Topological Drift. In the first figure a theoretical state of harmony exists between the underlying topological elements in the solution and the crafted artifacts of a development process. The topology elements have a position but also a direction of evolution. For example, languages such as C++ start out and then become standardized after widespread use. The semantics of language are now in motion towards the standard language specification. In the process, systems built with language variants must either maintain their code with aging tools or they must migrate their code to keep up with the language. The second topology of Fig. **4** represents such a scenario. Here a "natural" state is depicted where system artifacts have been left isolated from the underlying topological elements over the course of time. Naturally, it is possible to remain in synchronization with the topology of interest. Indeed this is where the topology can play a critical role. Understanding the technological environment and its evolutionary path allows one to perform a gap analysis and develop plans to prevent the inconsistencies described below.

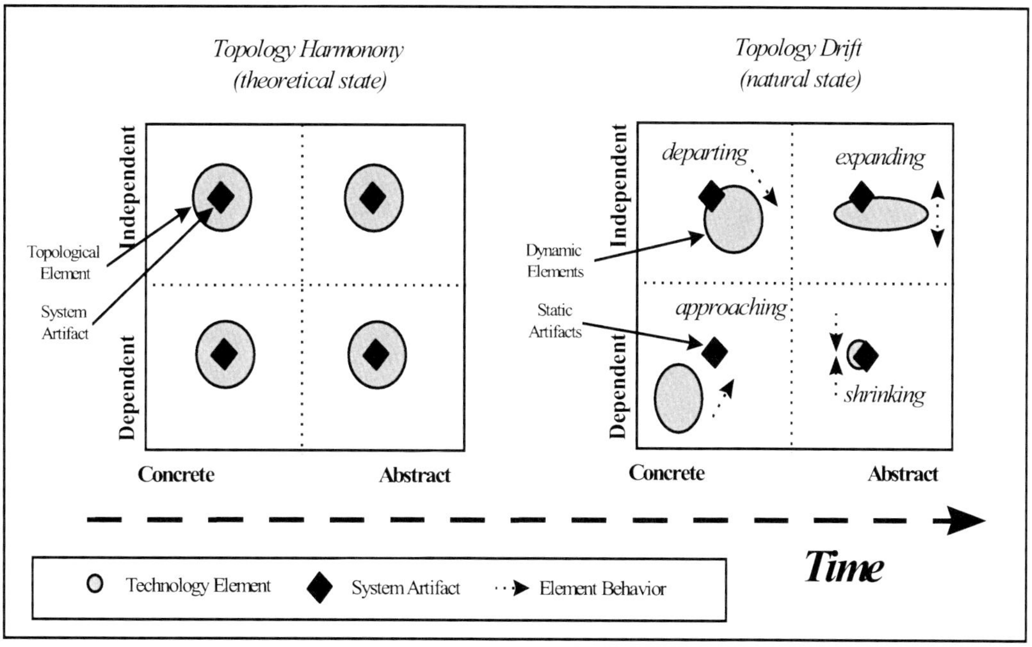

Figure 4: Topology Drift. Technologies evolve over time. Systems may or may not evolve with the underlying technologies. In a perfect world (above left) systems are in harmony with the technology topology they are built on top of. In reality (above right) this is seldom the case. Instead, technologies are as dynamic as the artifacts dependent upon them and are often more dynamic.

8.4.2. Instances of Inconsistencies (Topological Drift Class)

8.4.2.1. Deciding to Embrace

Topology Drift forces one to decide between two undesirable outcomes. The first choice is to abandon any hope of achieving "state-of-the-art". Few businesses can consciously take this route. Thus most of the industrialized world has already decided to embrace the never ending race to the next version of software. Making this decision is very rarely debated seriously but causes many inconsistencies. Users often complain about the pace of change. We recall data entry personnel years ago begging for their old keyboards back following a hardware migration which they could not see as necessary to do their jobs. This scenario is repeated countless times by forced and unwelcome upgrades of software to users, developers, and managers. Often these changes bring major productivity enhancements. Other times they do not. The authors have suffered through three major e-mail transitions recently and have not noticed a marked improvement in either the email service or the end user experience with the software. This same phenomenon occurs frantically today with beta software distributed *via* the Internet. We are, it seems, moving "forward" in our strange embrace with technology regardless of cost or benefits. Fortunately we enjoy the ride.

8.4.2.2. Remaining Embraced

Once embraced you must always race forward to stay in reasonable synchronization with vendor technology. Often this is a game of leapfrog, out-datedness, and frustration. A major inconsistency arises when the developer must synchronize products A, B, and C. To remove a glitch in product A requires an upgrade which triggers an upgrade in B as the current B will not work with the new A. Unfortunately, product C is incompatible with the new product B but there is no conflict with the product A upgrade. This race to remain embraced with the latest working technology and the integration, design, and testing required by developers can be extraordinary in its complexity, mysterious incompatibilities, and high staff cost for resolution.

8.4.2.3. API Evolution

Sometimes APIs shift underfoot just at the height of their usefulness. A common tactic by vendors is to replace an older library with a newer one which has many new capabilities but a completely different API. Developers must choose between rewriting their software or not taking advantage of all the new features. Such changes affect the delivery schedule but are seldom the things funding organizations care about. This is simply a forced re-architecting of the software imposed by the vendor. The resultant inconsistency can be of many forms including a gap between customer feature delivery and porting code to keep up with vendor libraries.

8.4.2.4. Revolutionary Change

In the most dramatic case of Topological Drift (Topological Morphing) the entire field mutates into something else. During the early 1990's many corporate developers struggled to rebuild legacy applications as Client/Server systems only to find out upon delivery that the technical landscape (Topology) had changed (Morphed) into the World Wide Web based application delivery environment. This is the most dramatic instance of topological drift. Today countless developers have been sent forth to recreate what they have just perfected on an inadequate platform. This is ironic since early Client/Server systems were raw, under-powered, and full of glitches which aptly describes early Internet platforms.

8.5. INCONSISTENCIES FROM SYSTEM DRIFT

Section 4 identified a large number of inherent topological factors that can lead directly to inconsistencies in software during the initial development of a system. This was only the beginning. Section 5 described how even if these inherent factors are avoided that technological drift can introduce different kinds of inconsistencies. In this section, another mechanism that can introduce inconsistencies is identified. In particular, inconsistencies can arise when a successful (and consistent) system evolves to meet new needs. The gradual (or often not so gradual) change in an existing system to meet new requirements is termed system drift. The key theme here is one in which the points ideal for an existing system on the topology drift from their original placement to new locations appropriate for the next release of the system.

The topology above (Fig. **5**) illustrates the issues associated with systems that drift. In particular, the next release of a system has to expand from the current system to include the parts of the topology which capture the new features. The development geodesic is jagged in the sense that it goes from what is already there to what must be added in each quadrant in addition to connecting elements in different quadrants.

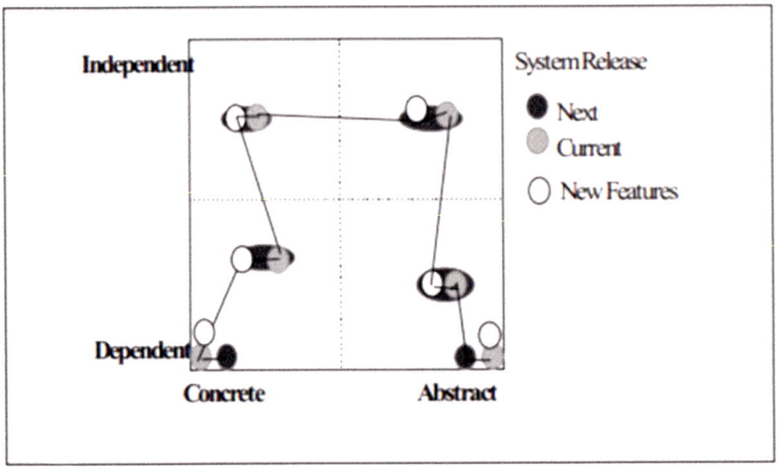

Figure 5: System Drift.

8.5.1. Instances of Inconsistencies (System Drift)

8.5.1.1. Changes in Classification

There are cases in which a system is originally one class of system and as a result of changes in the business it has to evolve into another class of system altogether. The structure and interaction styles appropriate for the original class of system remain throughout the lifetime of the system even after they are no longer appropriate. Inconsistencies in classification manifest themselves as disjoint interaction styles with the program. An example was the Windows NT Server which had as a root the principle of one user - one computer and has never really made the transition to the principle of one computer - many users as was the basis for UNIX.

Another example is a checkbook program that provides the ability to print checks, record expenditures and deposits, and reconcile balances can evolve into a personal financial management system with budgets, investment tracking, and planning capabilities in addition to the original set of capabilities.

8.5.1.2. Contextual Requirement Assumptions

It is common practice for new feature requirements to be written as a delta from pre-existing requirements. The problem is that new feature requirements are often written taking only the new features into account and failing to consider the full implications of their effect on existing features. As a result, existing functionality can degrade as new features are added.

8.5.1.3. Dangling Artifacts

It is often the case when a system evolves that pre-existing functionality is effectively removed from it. However, artifacts of that functionality (code, processes, and conditionals) may remain. While these artifacts should never be executed other inconsistencies in the program can cause their execution. Even if they are never executed, these artifacts can severely inhibit understanding of what the system is actually doing.

8.5.1.4. Missed Modifications

It is often the case when an individual modifies existing code to meet new requirements that a relevant part of the existing system is overlooked. This might be a missed conditional or some obscure subroutine that is invoked well outside the parts of the system within which the individual believes the current feature is bounded. A potential result of a missed modification is that values changed in one part of the system can be undone (or changed further) in another part of the system for an incorrect reason.

8.5.1.5. Fixed Topological Elements

Many parts of a large system exists in a state that cannot be modified. An example is the basic implementation of the architecture represented in the upper left quadrant of the topology. The effort to modify these parts is basically equivalent to re-implementing the entire system. Parts of the program that are capable of supporting a particular style of computing are often incapable of supporting a radically different style of computing. New features which are best implemented using styles of computing which are incompatible with the existing structure must be warped in some fashion to fit the existing structure or it may not be possible to implement the feature no matter what.

8.5.1.6. Inconsistencies Between Optimal And Evolved Systems

As an existing system drifts because new features are added, the pre-existing designs, architectures, and code drift as well. The problem is that the drift originates from the pre-existing location on the topology and is in a direction dictated by the set of reasonable modifications that will provide the new feature. Over time, the location of the topological elements for a system may drift far from where they would be if the system had been implemented from scratch for exactly the same desired functionality. As a result, the evolved system may have poorer performance, inefficient resource utilization, and lower user satisfaction. The optimal system (using the same technologies) might have a very different design, architecture, and performance.

8.5.1.7. Unknown Dependencies

Often a program will have one part that depends on flags set by another part of the program. The only connection between the two parts is the flag. When the part which sets the flag is modified (or left dangling) the flag (which locally may serve no real purpose) can be overlooked and never set as needed. The result is that the program may stop functioning correctly in certain situations that have nothing to do with the new feature under development. This case differs from missed modifications in the sense that missed modifications affect new features while unknown dependencies affect existing capabilities. This source of inconsistency is easily identified when developers state that they fixed one thing only to have another thing break.

8.5.1.8. Spaghetti

When a feature is implemented it may rely heavily on functions and flags that already existed. The feature is extended by adding a new bit of code to the system where possible. This is usually accomplished by introducing if conditions throughout the existing code which force calls to feature specific routines. The problem is that the logical flow through the system for that feature can become distributed across multiple parts and, in fact, unfathomable. The classical example of this is the spaghetti code that almost always resulted from use of computed *goto's* in FORTRAN and Basic.

8.6. A MODEL FOR MANAGING SUPPORT

The system drift phenomenon and maintenance challenges described above need to be placed within a managed process. The Production Support team I have led since 2008 is responsible for the maintenance and operations of a suite of web applications and their environments. The primary goal of the team is to provide 99.9% uptime for all systems and to deliver software, systems, and database updates as required. The support model described here is very close to the one used internally to meet these goals and also covers two other business groups. Thus, this model has been proven out daily for several years by several independent groups and can be recommended for use by others.

To meet the support goals of the team a simple model was developed through a strategic planning and tactical management approach that found its represented in a simple Action Framework. This framework consists of three primary areas:

1. Support Focus.
2. Sustaining Activities.
3. Strategic Investments.

This chapter defines these groups and the sub-elements comprising them. Together these work streams deliver on the goals of the team.

Support Focus

Daily, continuous actions to assure Tier 3 application availability. This includes proactive steps and reactive problem resolution.

Sustaining Activities

Ongoing work to add capabilities to the infrastructure and application base. This includes enhancements, expansions, defect repair, and forward engineering.

Strategic Investments

Both short and long term efforts meant to fundamentally improve the state of system availability. Includes creation of new roles, introduction of new technology, and creation or modification of processes.

8.6.1. Support Focus

Support covers the daily, continuous actions to assure Tier 3 application availability. This includes proactive steps and reactive problem resolution. These actions are the top priority of the support team and all other actions can be delayed or postponed to handle these items.

8.6.1.1. Proactive Monitoring (Automatic and Manual)

The first line of defense in supporting applications and systems is monitoring. This includes both automatic and manual monitoring of the devices, equipment, and applications. Many monitoring techniques are already in place including vendor monitors and alerts as well as custom monitoring tools. These automated tools are monitored regularly and some manual monitoring is also done on a daily basis. The goal of the monitoring is to be alerted to problems early and then to respond to those problems or prevent them from expanding.

8.6.1.2. Incident Response Team

Once a problem is detected it must be responded to. The Incident Response Team (IRT) is an approach to handling any unplanned production event known as Incident Management. The IRT consists of a rotating team structure, a process, and a web site for logging incidents. The IRT team is available 24 hours a day and 7 days a week throughout the year. The mission of the IRT is to respond to incidents and rapidly restore service. The IRT currently covers all web applications as well as all Enterprise applications and is used by other business units also. The team consists of domain experts able to handle any issue or reach out to additional experts as required [6].

8.6.1.3. Production Readiness Exploration & Production Readiness Review

In order to help prepare for new releases coming into production two checkpoints with the development teams are established. The first is the "Production Readiness Exploration" which happens during the Design Phase coincident with the standard architecture review. The second is the "Production Readiness Review" which happens during the test phase.

During the PRE a presentation from the development team is provided of the system's architecture, its capacity impact, an understanding of the deployment footprint, and an identification of required interdependencies with existing systems. The goal of the PRE is to alert the support team of any major upcoming releases and their ramifications and to allow the support team to ask questions around support requirements that development team may need to consider.

The PRR focuses on the immediate release requirements of the application. This involves detailed review of the application as is currently done in transition planning. It would also include final checks for preparedness of both the support team and the development team in making the release ready for production. For both reviews a list of questions can be published to the development teams in advance so they can prepare. These two reviews are required and Production Support does not accept any project into production that has not successfully completed both reviews in addition to the standard transition planning.

8.6.1.4. Web Production Release Review Board

The Web Production Migration Review Board was established to review all production migration requests. The purpose of this board is to approve any and all migrations to production and coordinate their release to insure stability in the environment. Within ITIL this is known as Release Management. The team consists of representatives from the PMO (Project Management Office), QA (Quality Assurance), infrastructure teams, and SE (Software Engineering) which meets daily to review all requests and slot them for the next available release window. Since instituting this approach we have streamlined the release request process, provided consistent planning, established predictable migration windows, and checked requests for technical and quality readiness and potential impacts. As this is a technical readiness review the Board does not make business priority decisions but instead only technical risk and production readiness decisions. The questions we ask have to do with the coding impact, QA scope, and interdependencies that might impact platform stability. Once a request is approved we discuss resource availability and scheduling in order to finally decide on a migration slot. This planning is guided by business priorities which are already communicated to the Board *via* the Triage process. The Review Board's planning horizon is 2 weeks and all decisions are published on an internal Sharepoint site.

8.6.1.5. Production Migration Services

Both database and application code must be moved into the production environment routinely to provide for maintenance and new releases. This work requires careful preparation and coordination. The migrations are provided under the authorization of the Release Board and executed by the support teams and often verified by the business. Most migrations are conducted during off hours and require roll back plans. For large or complex releases or upgrades detailed go-live schedules are needed.

8.6.1.6. Database and Systems Support

The production support team also provides support for both systems and databases in production. This may include emergency troubleshooting of systems, environments, tools, or software. In some cases this requires emergency modifications to configurations, installations, setup, or even replacement of hardware by the vendor. These support services differ from the migration services, application support services, or standard support activities. These support services focus on the hardware, environment, operations, and interactions of the system and database components.

8.6.1.7. Emergency Fixes

In some cases an incident requires an emergency fix. There may be a code issue or a system configuration problem or the database may require an updated query or other technical change. These changes must be conducted rapidly to restore or improve service and cannot wait for planned maintenance bundles or project releases. Often on the fly, corrections must be developed and decisions on deployment must be made often times with short notice or during off hours. In these cases, the Review Board mechanism must be triggered on demand and the change must be certified and risks understood.

8.6.1.8. Ongoing Performance Analysis

The main focus of this area is to respond to performance incidents and monitor instrumentation log data, IIS logs and process info logs to identify and document slow performing pages for each application or other system components such as the database and network and help the application production support teams analyze and resolve performance bottlenecks.

8.6.1.9. Reporting on Applications and Support

The systems and applications being supported can be tracked with many parameters and data points. These elements include throughput of orders, processing levels of CPUs, data transfer rates, *etc.* This information needs to be pulled and organized regularly. The resultant reports should be analyzed for trending and for outlier incidents and system behavior insights.

8.6.1.10. Availability Tracking System

The Availability Tracking System is a key support tool for problem management which captures those IRT incidents that result in outages and performance impacts. The related IRT incidents are reviewed twice a month and relevant tickets are entered into ATS for Root Cause Analysis. The classic formula for Availability is:

$$A = MTBF / MTBF + MTTR \qquad \textbf{(11)}$$

Where

A = Availability

MTBF = Mean time to between failure

MTTR = Mean time to repair

Another way to calculate availability is as a percent of uptime *versus* planned uptime. There are a number of practical challenges in capturing failure data accurately, automatically, and in a reliable manner. There is also an overhead associated with conducting these calculations. However, this type of data is often required by business stakeholders and customers let alone needed from an engineering perspective.

8.6.2. Sustaining Activities

Ongoing work to add capabilities to the infrastructure and application base. This includes enhancements, expansions, defect repair, and forward engineering. This work represents the bulk of the effort of the Production Support team.

8.6.2.1. Production Support Bundle Development

Application Production Support focuses on work item realization and deployment. These work items are about 50% defects and 50% enhancements but this ratio varies. There are application teams dedicated to each major product that is supported in production including all applications and tools. A Triage process prioritizes the work items and the development teams analyze, fix, or create the solution. This work represents a large portion of the work done in Production Support on an effort basis as these development teams are much larger than the other teams.

Each product application development support queue must have a defined target throughput and this should be actively monitored. These queue lengths, if beyond target, must be managed downward.

Production Support teams have started following an agile process based on SCRUM methodology. Existing production support work items form the initial set of "Product Backlog" items. Each application support team work together and identify work items to be included in each "sprint". Teams are using the process for work item management only.

8.6.2.2. Application & Database Build Services

The systems team carries out build services for projects and production support for all web applications. These build services include environment preparation, build execution, build script debugging and corrections, and related technical advisement. The Database Team also carries out build activities for both projects and production support.

8.6.2.3. QA Migration Services

Both the Database and systems administration teams conduct migrations into the QA environments for both projects and production support. Often such migrations follow from a build that may be done first. In some cases, depending upon the change only a migration might be done. The teams also carry out restores upon request.

8.6.2.4. Peer Technical Synch

In order to keep information sharing up between project teams and the application production support teams the Peer Technical Synch activity was created. This activity allows the team leads from all teams working on a product to share plans and look for design impacts. By keeping in close touch these team leads prevent surprises or cases where they might duplicate work, undo each other's work, or otherwise end up in an inefficient path. The Production Support leads have been initiating these synch ups about once a week.

8.6.2.5. Database and System Design Services

The systems and database teams provide a variety of design services for the project teams as well as the application production support teams. In the case of the database team they might be called on to review a schema design, tune a SQL, or develop a script of numerous types. They also might be consulted with for optimal design approaches or for testing methods. The systems team is often requested to provide infrastructure advice such as machine specifications, capabilities, capacity, or related information. They might also provide input to deployment strategies, virtual machine configuration, or other configuration particulars.

8.6.2.6. Ad Hoc Technical Requests

A wide variety of requests are made of the support teams. These might include looking at a new technology, deploying a development tool, collecting data, or making quick modification to an environment or to an application.

8.6.2.7. Special Projects

The support teams often are requested to handle special projects typically of the infrastructure type. Examples of the projects include migrating the network domains in all environments, refreshing servers, evolving storage arrays, and supporting major database migrations in other business units. These projects are typically organized and managed by one of the managers in the group and implemented by one or more of the staff. These projects do not always follow the typical development lifecycle formally as they tend to be shorter duration infrastructure related projects.

8.6.3. Strategic Investments

This category of the Action Framework is meant to list the major effort areas which are longer term in nature, aimed at having significant positive impact on overall capabilities, and are typically staffed by a fractional assignment level by managers. In most cases this work is done on a best-effort basis as the Support and Sustaining categories described above take overall priority.

Both short and long term efforts are included here each of which are meant to fundamentally improve the state of system availability. This category includes creation of new roles, introduction of new technology, and creation or modification of processes to meet the macro goals. In the past this work has focused on a broad set of initiatives identified collectively by the team members in annual strategic planning offsite meetings. The types of strategic efforts need to remain proprietary but have covered such areas as fault tolerant architectures, process definition, training, and more.

8.6.4. Support Framework Conclusions

The Support, Sustaining, and Strategic focus areas cover the immediate, middle term, and long term tasks and activities required to meet the overall goals of Production Support. In addition to the above details an adjunct but integral focus on team issues is being developed. This will attempt to help evolve the support team to better meet these defined challenges and to strive to meet new ones.

8.7. SOFTWARE REENGINEERING

Sometimes, it is necessary to reengineer a piece of software despite all attempts at maintenance. This might be due to a lack of knowledge or a drift in the code base (discussed later). Software Reengineering is the refit of software for new role and/or machines and is a combination of reverse engineering and restructuring. Reverse Engineering is a process of developing a set of specifications by an orderly examination of a type of system without benefit of the original designs and with the purpose of cloning the system [7]. Restructuring is transforming from one representation to another while preserving the subject system's external behavior or functionality. Reengineering motivations and applications include:

Re-hosting, Reuse, Translation, Replacement, Enhancement, Endurance, and Salvage.

Steps of Reengineering Cycle are summarized here and in Fig. **6**:

1. Capture.
2. Reverse Engineer.
3. Enhancement.
4. Forward Engineer.
5. Optimization.
6. Generation.

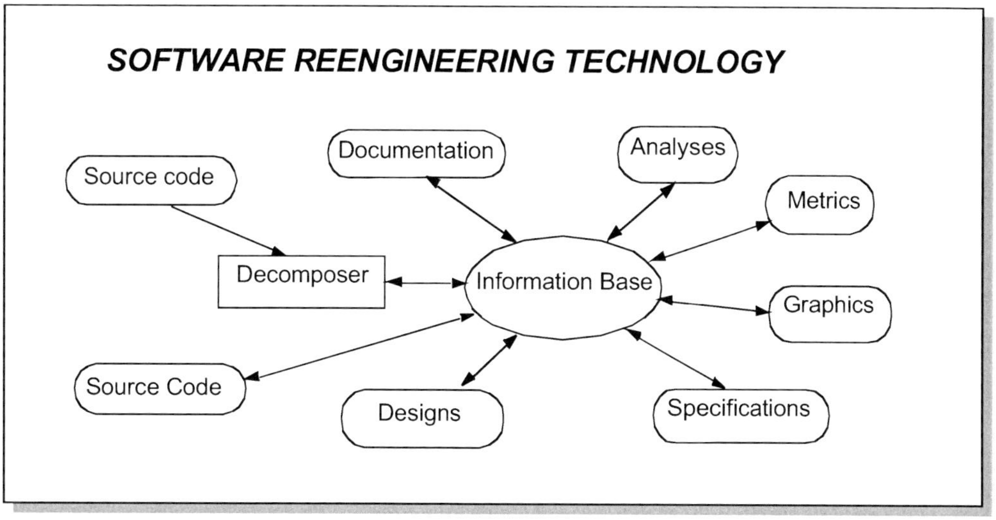

Figure 6: Reengineering Model.

CONCLUSIONS

Support is one of the unloved and usually un-described areas of software engineering yet in many cases large budgets are assigned to these activities even proportional to new work. In this chapter we have reviewed the meaning of support and maintenance, introduced a novel way of looking at system evolution through the use of the Technology Topology, and introduced a specific support model. From these elements an approach to support can be developed. Of particular use in my own work in recent years has been the support model described above. This model has proven to be a useful tool in organizing support work, communicating the value of support work to others, and planning for new initiatives to improve support undertakings.

REFERENCES

[1] McClure, C., **Managing Software Development and Maintenance**, VanNorstrand Reinhold Co., 1981.

[2] Cross, & Chikofsky, "*Reengineering Software*", **IEEE Software**, Jan 1990.

[3] McClure, C., **Managing Software Development and Maintenance**, VanNorstrand Reinhold Co., 1981.

[4] Voyager Mission Home Page NASA, http://www.nasa.gov/mission_pages/voyager/index.html, viewed 11/12/2011.

[5] Tepfenhart, W., & Cusick, J., *Using Technology Topologies to Identify and Manage Inconsistencies in Software*, September, 1997, www.mendeley.com/profiles/james-cusick

[6] Cusick, J., & Ma, G., *"Creating an ITIL Inspired Incident Management Approach: Roots, Responses, and Results",* IFIP/IEEE BDIM International Workshop on Business Driven IT Management, Osaka, Japan, April 19, 2010.

[7] Cross, & Chikofsky, "*Reengineering Software*", **IEEE Software**, Jan 1990.

Send Orders of Reprints at bspsaif@emirates.net.ae
Durable Ideas in Software Engineering, 2013, 255-278

CHAPTER 9

Tools

A poor workman blames his tools.

Anonymous

Abstract: Review of industry tool framework models including Software Engineering Environments, CASE tools, IDEs, and more. Special focus on tool evaluation processes, tool research, environment configuration, and tool assessment practices.

Keywords: SEE, CASE, IDE, CAST, software tools, metrics, project planning, requirements traceability, compliers, test management, workflow.

9.1. INTRODUCTION

Tools to support software engineering have evolved rapidly during the last two decades. From terminal environments with line editors to powerful workstations with integrated development environments (IDEs), sophisticated modeling tools, Computer Aided Software Engineering (CASE) tools, and more. Today's tools resemble platforms more than traditional tools like compilers and debuggers. Many tools today come with communications packages, database interfaces, GUI components and require skill and experience to learn and use properly. In this chapter we will explore some models for organizing tools and also for evaluating tools as the tools themselves change all the time but the need for them will keep reappearing. The tools in my toolbox of importance here are the understanding of what tools are in the scope of the software engineering's reach, how to conceptually organize them and integrate them, and how to evaluate any tool or type of tool in an effective way.

Interestingly, software engineers are the most extensive users of software. We use more tools and more types of tools than any other type of job requiring software. Not only do we use office automation products and mail but we use specialized editors, debuggers, design tools, logic analyzers, code browsers, and other tools both standalone and integrated.

James J. Cusick

9.2. SOFTWARE TOOL ENVIRONMENTS

We can dive software tools into Hi-Case and Low-Case. Consider the life-cycle phases again: requirements, analysis, design, coding, testing. We move from abstract to concrete incrementally. Some tools support the up-front abstract efforts and some support the low level tasks of the concrete implementation phases. We need both kinds. The high level tools enable drawing of models such as Process Flow diagrams, object models, Information Engineering models. Within the lifecycle some tools are horizontal in nature - they support all aspects of the lifecycle, such as documentation. There are also supporting tools for configuration management and documentation (see Fig. **1**).

Vendors will tell you that their tool is the right approach or solution. The critical issue is to know what are the underlying problems that you are facing and not to focus on the current (transient) technical solutions. Tools can be immature so research into the products that may be rushed to market is warranted. Sometimes unstable vendors may disappear quickly. Other times early releases are buggy. However, some tools can also increase productivity so the leap may be worth it.

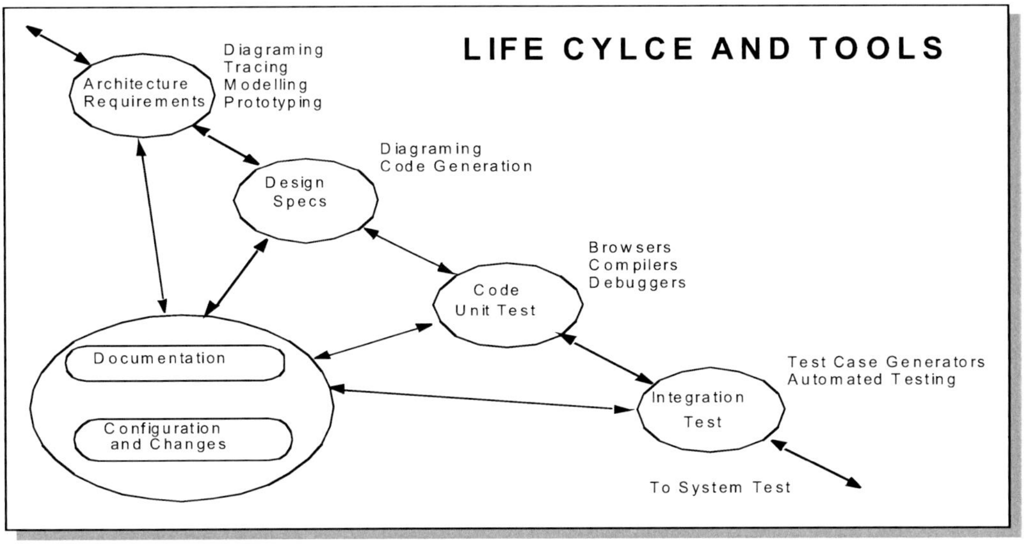

Figure 1: Tool Layers Insipired by Bell Labs Tools Environment.

Several significant starting points can be found in the literature when attempting to derive a suite of standard software development tools to fill out a development environment framework. At the highest level we find the Integrated Project Support Environment (IPSE) model [1]. The IPSE model envelops the following functional areas:

- Process Management.
- Project Management.
- Requirements Management.
- Configuration Management.
- Documentation Management.
- Repositories.
- Project Verification/Validation.

Each specific functional area above describes the detailed tasks in the context of a given development process. For example, *Process Management* may cover modeling, tool coordination, enactment, and process compliance. Using this functional view as the top level of the model allows us to define which tools are needed in support a development team.

CASE (Computer Aided Software Engineering) tools showed great promise but have largely lost their luster as they were somewhat oversold in terms of capability. Instead integrated development environments have survived and thrived. CASE tools tend to provide limited life-cycle support. Normally, CASE tools and Integrated Development Environments (IDEs) focus on specific slices of the IPSE model discussed above. That is, particular CASE tools tend to completely support design modeling and code generation but have limited or no configuration management capability. Furthermore, today's IDEs provide editors, compilers, and debuggers, but rarely offer design modeling capabilities or requirements traceability. They also now support multi language development modeling and such approaches as SCRUM.

Finally, at the lowest level, Brown (1992) provides a detailed explanation of National Institute of Standards and Technology's (NIST) Software Engineering Environment (SEE). SEEs cover issues of common integration services such as

Interface Integration, Process Integration, and Data Integration (see Fig. **2**). SEEs normally provide common services and a set of tools unifying these services. Such services can include:

- Data repository services: storage, relationships, transactions, process support archive, backup).
- Data integration services (version, configuration, query, metadata, states, data interchange).
- Task management services (definition, execution, transaction, history, audit).
- Message services (message delivery and tool registration).
- Administration services (installation, security, *etc.*).

Traditionally, SEEs are actually implemented as proprietary development environments produced under the guidance of a single vendor. Most of these early SEE frameworks have disappeared in the face of more successful IDEs. However, here is an example of what one of these frameworks might provide.

- Configuration and Versioning.
- Incremental & Automated Build.
- C++ Complier/Debugger.
- GUI Builder.
- Class Browsers/Editors.

Today most services as defined in the SEE model are provided by commercial operating systems or operating environments. If your environments of interest has been predetermined, for example, UNIX and Microsoft Windows that will restrict the choice of tools to some degree. I never ruled out a single vendor approach, but due to the typical heterogeneous environments I faced, early research pointed to a hybrid set of tools unified by Operating System or Operating Environment services on each specific platform.

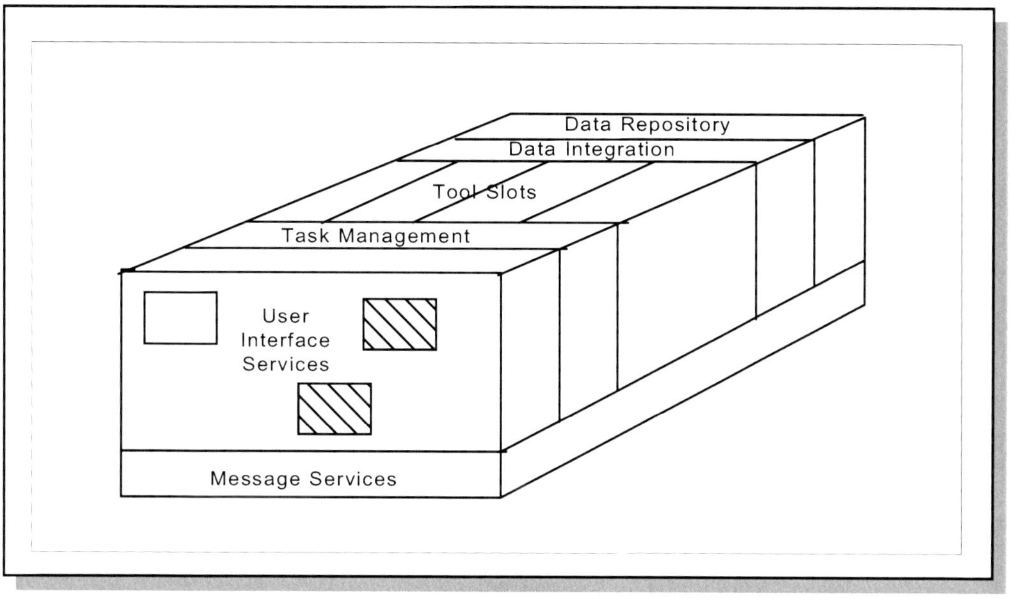

Figure 2: Software Engineering Environment Reference Model (Brown, 1992): The NIST SEE Model is widely recognized as the standard model for discussing tool environments. Thus, within any specific environment or on any computing platform, we expect common services as described here to support process steps *via* any given tool instance.

As reviewed in Chapter 7, there are many types of test tools to consider also. These include:

- Static analyzers.
- Test management tools.
- Test design tools.
- Test execution tools.
- Test quality evaluation tools.

More tool types include: code auditors, test case generators, test data generators, test comparators, test harnesses, coverage analyzer, record & playback.

9.3. SOFTWARE EVALUATION

With these tool environments and frameworks introduced, the next step is populating them. To do this technology evaluation is called for. Evaluating today's software tools can remind one of the old parable of the elephant and the blind men. One man touches its tusk and pronounces it smooth. Another touches its skin and pronounces it rough. Software Development Environments and their composite technologies can produce the same effect on the ill prepared or poorly coordinated evaluation team.

The underlying reason for this, much as in the case of the elephant, is the complexity of the beast under observation and its range of habitat. While the elephant represents a highly adapted biological organism ultimately suited to the variances of its environment, software tools have yet to evolve quite so far. To understand why this is so we must first consider the full scope of development activity which a tool attempts to cover and those which they avoid.

A cursory glance at a few trade journals will indicate that hundreds if not thousands of development tools are available on the market. Today, with the boom in Internet technologies, dozens of new tools enter the market place regularly. Many can be downloaded without much effort but how do you know if they are worth using or recommending? Faced with this situation we were asked to define how to choose the best tools for use in the development of hundreds of business applications. We began a revitalization of the software tool assessment practices of AT&T. These efforts were discussed in a paper on evaluation [2] which was delivered at NASA 's Software Engineering Laboratory conference.

An evaluation methodology was developed based on the concept of fitness-for-use as measured by the construction of architecturally representative applications within a laboratory environment. This method was used to evaluate dozens of commercial software development tools in order to select specific tools as corporate-wide standards.

This chapter focuses on presenting the specifics of our software technology evaluation methodology, including our research efforts, tool taxonomy, and evaluation procedures (especially our use of software architecture-style-derived certifying test suites). This discussion does not present the specific tools selected through the application of this methodology as those will change over time.

9.3.1. Methods of Software Evaluation

Many evaluation techniques are known and meet with varying levels of success. Weighted averaging, benchmarking, figures of merit, *etc.*, each have certain advantages and disadvantages [3]. Our approach is instead centered on the concept of demonstrated fitness for use in the environment of choice as measured by the applicability of any given tool to the dominant software architectures found within the target business environment. This approach reflects the "habitat models" suggested by [4].

This approach stems from viewing evaluation of software from the question: How well does the provided functionality of a product span the needs associated with tasks to be performed using it? Evaluation is highly dependent on the use for which the product is intended and the results are subject to greater ambiguity than evaluations of other classes of products. Many manufacturers of software products will be more than happy to provide metrics for common performance criteria. Other questions are more subtle - does the tool provide the right abstractions, is it easy to use, does it take one hour to do something or ten days. It is these subtle metrics that we intended our evaluation environment to measure and for this we turned to Architecture Styles.

9.3.2. Software Architecture Styles Reviewed

As mentioned early in discussing patterns and architecture styles (at least) four basic architectural styles present in our business applications were identified [5]. These styles are: transaction, data streaming, real time, and decision support. These styles consistently appeared, in part and in full, in a wide variety of systems including those for Financial, Maintenance, Provisioning, and Asset Management domains. We say, in part, because a majority of our systems are actually hybrids of these different architectural styles.

We eventually derived several certification applications from these styles in order to drive our evaluation process. Our core reasoning being that the development of small scale applications modeled after our target development tasks would prove the suitability of the product under evaluation. This turned out to be true for virtually all the products we evaluated. The entire process of which the architecture styles play a key role is now presented in detail.

9.3.3. The Evaluation Process

Our approach to evaluating software technology is to appraise technology as "fit-for-use" if we can succeed in developing a sample application which has a reasonable similarity to our production applications. In other words, we use the product under evaluation in an environment modeled after the target development environment. The process can be summarized in the following manner:

1. Survey the available products.
2. Classify according to a technical framework.
3. Filter the list using screening criteria.
4. Construct evaluation criteria templates.
5. Use the target tools to build an Architecturally Representative Application.
6. Record findings against the templates.
7. Judge the best scores and select the recommended product.

9.3.3.1. Survey the Available Products

The overall evaluation process begins with surveying the tool market for candidate products and classifying them according to a technical framework sometimes called a taxonomy. Consider the survey effort first.

Initial research into software tool availability, capabilities, and trends, can be both rewarding and daunting. The goal of tool research is to identify all or most of the tools currently available for the support of a particular stage of the software development process. This research is technical in that one must understand the technological capabilities of each tool. At the same time, this research is market oriented in that one must also understand trends and supplier positioning. Some of the techniques used in this activity include:

1. **Literature Reviews:** Books, journals, trade press publications. Key information on technical capabilities, product announcements, corporate changes, tool assessments and recommendations are readily available.

2. **Trade Shows and Technical Conferences:** We have found trade shows to be *decreasingly* helpful in identifying technologies of interest. This is due to the generally poor level of technical information available at such venues. Technical conferences on the other hand *remain* helpful in putting the available products into a theoretical or practical context.

3. **Direct Mail:** Believe it or not this is an effective means for collecting information once you are on enough mailing lists. (This may not be ecological but it is economical in terms of time; it only takes a few seconds to sort incoming product information.)

4. **Automated Topic Searches:** We receive weekly or monthly summaries extracted from current publications on software technologies and trends *via* email.

5. **Web Browsing:** This has become a significant source of information and freeware tools. We maintain a list of vendor web sites and this has often provided up to the minute information on particular products.

6. **Vendor Demonstrations:** Slicing through the sales pitch to the technical meat is often difficult but this remains an effective means of collecting detailed product knowledge for selected tools.

7. **Evaluation Copies**: A time or event determined interval of hands-on experience, execution, and utilization of the tools is invaluable in understanding actual tool capabilities (this is discussed in detail below).

8. **Professional Information Services**: Several organizations are under contract to us providing strategic information on the software industry. This information is often helpful but can also be factually incorrect or misleading. These sources are useful more as sounding boards than anything else.

9. **Private Contact Network:** Having a wide network of software professionals to draw upon for knowledge of the industry and technology cannot be overlooked in research efforts. For example, teaching a continuing education course at a local university has brought several new tools to our attention through conversations with students.

10. **Experience:** Having been around the development community for a number of years directly impacts your ability to scan and decipher information on tools. Oftentimes "new" tools end up being familiar tools refaced.

11. **Project Reference**: Having access to the real life trials of hundreds of development projects we know early on what is needed, what works, and what provides less than advertised.

The output of this research includes summary information on current product availability, industry trends, software standards and standards activities, computing techniques and methods, and development resources both internal and external. The specific products or technologies identified during our research efforts are given an initial classification in the tool and technology taxonomy discussed next.

9.3.3.2. Classify According to a Technical Framework

A Software Development Environment (SDE) can be viewed as an integrated set of tools and processes enabling analysts, designers, programmers, and testers to collaborate on the production of high quality software solutions. Traditional Software Engineering Environment (SEE) frameworks support the concept of creating an SDE by creating a view of the computing infrastructure as a unified and sensible environment with specified functional interrelationships instead of just a random assortment of tools [6].

Unfortunately, SEEs are not well suited to the task of tool classification since they are operational in nature. We required a classification scheme to build our SDE recommendations that could be used to organize toolsets of an eclectic nature resulting from our market research. Existing tool taxonomies [7, 8, 9] typically focused on particular application domains, limited platforms, or were designed to cover only CASE tools. Since these taxonomies did not meet the needs of our scope (multi-platform, process driven tool standards), we derived our own classification for software tools.

To begin with our classification scheme inherited some structure from our corporate context. Domains typical of most software engineering environments sometimes fall outside of our mission charter. Our mission was limited to a constrained view of Application Development technologies.

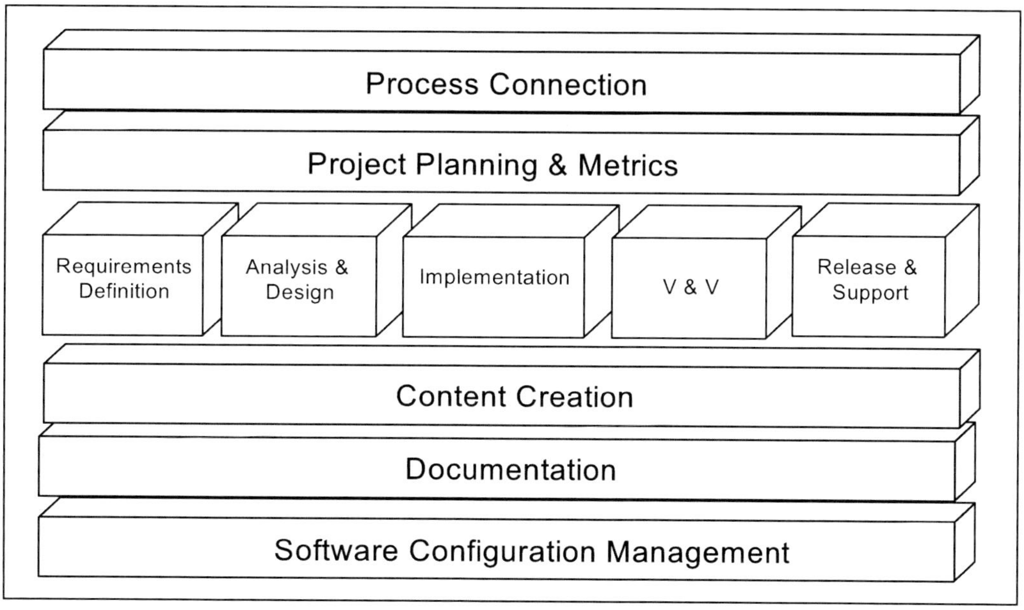

Figure 3: Software Engineering Environment Framework as Tool Taxonomy.

We decided to base our tool classification on an existing software engineering framework provided by Utz [10] and then modify it as needed (**see** Fig. **3**). The major categories provided by Utz are re-defined by us below. Each of these major categories are further detailed into sub-categories. Representative sub-categories are shown below. As our market research efforts turn up tools, we categorize them in the taxonomy. When actively adding to the repository we had approximately 1,000 tools in a database organized by these categories. This database allows us to perform ad hoc queries on tool use within the company and to quickly produce candidate lists when evaluation efforts are begun.

9.3.3.3. The Framework Categories Defined

1. **Process Management**: Tools supporting the specification, implementation, and compliance management of development processes.
2. **Management & Metrics**: Tools supporting the planning, tracking, and measuring of software development projects.
3. **Requirements Definition:** Tools supporting the specification and enumeration of requirements.
4. **Analysis & Design:** Tools supporting high level design and modeling of software system solutions following specific formal methodologies and often including code generation and reverse engineering capabilities.
5. **Implementation (Code/Debug):** These tools allow both low level code implementation to support the edit-compile-debug cycle of development in 3GLs and visual based programming targeted at rapid application development by use of screen painters/generators with graphical pallets of reusable GUI components with 4GLs.
6. **V&V**: Tools providing software verification and validation, quality assurance, and quantification of reliability. These include test case management, test selection, and automated test support.
7. **Release & Support:** Tools targeted at supporting enhancements and corrections to existing code as well as browsers, source code analyzers and software distribution.

8. **Content Creation**: Tools used for developing Internet materials such as electronically published documents, graphics and multimedia components of Internet sites.

9. **Documentation:** Tools supporting creation and distribution of system documentation, specifications, and user information. These tools include documentation storage, retrieval, and distribution.

10. **Software Configuration & Manufacturing:** A broad class of tools related to the control of software components and development artifacts including documentation for the purpose of team based programming, versioning, defect tracking, and software manufacturing and distribution.

9.3.3.4. Selected Tool Taxonomy Sub-Categories

Process

- Process Definition & Compliance.

Project Planning & Metrics

- Project Planning.
- Function Points.
- General Metrics.

Requirements & Definition

- Requirements Trace.

Analysis & Design

- Object Oriented Analysis & Design.
- Structured or Other Design Methods.
- RDBMS Modeling.

Implementation

- Languages.
- Editors.
- Compilers & Debuggers.
- IDEs.
- GUI/Visual Development.
- Cross Platform Development.
- Database Development.
- Components.

Verification & Validation

- Test Management & Design.
- Record & Playback.
- Stress, Load & Performance.
- Coverage.

Release & Support

- Distribution.
- Reverse Engineering.
- Emulation.
- Utilities.

Content Creation

- Web Document Authoring,

- Graphics Authoring,
- Multimedia Authoring.

Documentation & Workflow

- System Documentation,
- Help Authoring,
- Workflow.

Software Configuration Management

- Source Code Control,
- Defect Tracking,
- Configuration or Manufacturing,
- Integrated SCM,
- Automated build and deployment.

9.3.3.5. Filter the List Using Screening Criteria

With a thousand tools in the taxonomy we have to start trimming the list whenever a particular technology sub-category must be evaluated. Using basic technical requirements many candidate tools can be eliminated. Platform support, negative reviews in the trade press, vendor instability or financial losses by a vendor can all be used to quickly eliminate certain products from the evaluation list. If negative criteria do not work we use positive criteria: is the tool "Editor's Choice" or does our development community already use it as a de facto standard? These types of tools need to be on the evaluation list while others should be dropped.

9.3.3.6. Construct Evaluation Criteria Templates

Each of the tool categories in the taxonomy needs specific evaluation criteria to measure the relevant attributes of each tool type in our taxonomy. Towards that end a set of templates must be developed for each type of technology evaluated. These templates resemble the ones found in many trade journals and benchmarking reports. The following must be created or reused:

First, one overall template for generic tool and vendor measurement is provided. This generic template covers such items as documentation, support, pricing, and platform availability. A standard set of issues regarding tools such as iconic design, menu features, ergonomics, printing, and so on, is included.

Each analyst must then define a specific template which covers the technical aspects of the particular class of tool under investigation, if it does not already exist in our repository of templates. This must be created for each category.

9.3.3.7. Use Target Tools to Build Representative Applications

Recall that we are interested in demonstrating "fitness-for-use". To do this we now build a representative application with the product(s) selected for evaluated from the taxonomy. Before evaluating any software technology we must first consider what capabilities it has and how to construct a suitable test suite or if our current set of application specifications will need expansion.

9.3.3.8. Technologies and Their Tasks

Each type of software product dictates certain kinds of tasks that will be the subject of evaluation. For example, word processors might be evaluated in terms of developing on-line (in program) documentation, help files, man pages, hard copy user manuals, and HTML documents. On the other hand, one would not evaluate a compiler in terms of its support of those same tasks. In some cases, products span more than one functional category. For example a C++ IDE might provide a visual programming environment, a class system, and a general purpose compiler. Since each of these is a separate endeavor, an evaluation of a C++ IDE will concentrate, independently, on the visual programming environment, class system completeness, and compiler performance. These are individual and discrete evaluations. Each will need specific resources to carry out the evaluation.

9.3.3.9. Software Resources for Evaluation

The software resources required to complete the data collection demanded by the evaluation template fall into three categories: 1) the software under evaluation; 2) supporting software (*i.e.*, the operating system); and 3) software in the form of test cases (*e.g.*, a sample design to implement). As we have shown, common architectures run through many applications. Our concept was to derive the required test cases from these architecture types or patterns.

Software patterns [11, 12] formalize some of the concepts on recurring underlying software construction themes. We devised evaluation test cases to demonstrate that any tool recommended supported specific computing problem domains but which can be extrapolated to many other domains. Thus we developed and specified a set of representative applications modeled after architectural styles or patterns observed in the field, to serve as certifying test suites for any tool slated for review (see **Table 1**).

Table 1: Representative Applications and their Architecture Styles

		ARCH	STYLE			GUI	STYLE		
Arch/UI Style *vs.* Sample Apps	**OLTP**	**Data Stream**	**Decision Support**	**WWW**	**Forms**	**Active Graphic**	**Alert Panel**	**Map Based**	**Hypertext Browser**
Contact	X		X		X				
COD		X					X		
GEM		X				X			
NetAnalyst			X			X		X	
ToolBase	X		X	X	X				X

The representative applications and their relationship to the generic architecture styles of **Table 2** are briefly described below:

1. **Contact Data Base:** The Contact Data Base is a very simple system for managing contacts on a project-by-project basis. Contacts are managed at the level of tracking individuals associated with a project, individual meetings, and tracking tools employed on the project. This application demonstrates a forms based interface for data entry and reporting.

2. **Co-Operative Document System (CODS):** The Co-Operative Document System allows multiple people to work on the same

document. The basic capability of checking a document into and out of a document control system is augmented with a message broadcasting feature alerting users of a subscribed document's state. This represents a client server system with data streaming and on-line transaction architectural components.

3. **Graphic Enterprise Modeler (GEM):** The graphic organization display provides the ability to model graphically the structure of a corporate organization. It visually illustrates relationships among people, projects, and teams. To find answers to specific questions regarding an organization, the user follows semantically meaningful links and uses active graphics controls. This application demonstrates the user interaction style of the active graphics variety.

4. **NetAnalyst**: This application is a map based data visualization tool. It takes a set of real telecommunications data (the 1994 L.A. earthquake phone traffic) and plots it geographically. This is a common type of application profiling decision support and mapping.

5. **ToolBase**: This is an Intranet based front end to a product tracking database. This application provides for the evaluation of many types of Internet technologies and the extent to which they can support the architectural styles of OLTP and decision support on the Intranet.

Returning to our evaluation process, an appropriate application is selected to test the tool class and development against a set of specifications describing the sample application is begun. Often, the specifications need modification or additional software design efforts need to be conducted to fully stress the products under evaluation (*e.g.*, our Internet application did not test multimedia features as initially designed). Inferior products fail during implementation of the specifications and quickly drop out.

9.3.3.10. Record Findings Against the Templates

Throughout the work of building the sample application, feature performance data must be captured on the custom template constructed for this technical category.

This includes objective and subjective measures. Subjective data includes how intuitive the product was or how friendly the help desk was when called. Objective data includes if the promised features worked and if you could accomplish the task of building the sample application.

Weighted Scoring Method (WSM) is normally used to provide a simple rating mechanism for each product under evaluation. In this method each item in the criteria matrix is assigned a score or weight score. Usually a score of 1 to 5 is given to the product for each criterion. Then an overall score can be derived using the formula below [13]:

$$\text{Score}_a = \sum_{j=1}^{n} (\text{weight}_j * \text{score}_{aj}) \quad \textbf{(12)}$$

9.3.3.10. Judge the Best Scores and Select the Recommended Product

The final step is recommending a product. Out of the short list all products are evaluated. Using the sample application as a test suite the superior product normally emerges. With a WSM technique there is very small opportunity for any ties. The analyst must, however, still exercise their best judgment in selecting a product for recommendation.

9.3.3.11. Evaluation Process Results

Within a laboratory environment we developed these representative applications repeatedly using different software technologies. We also carried out other tasks in support of this simulated development work, such as configuration management, using still more products under evaluation. This approach provided clear evidence of the suitability of one product over another and was much easier to derive than by only looking at a feature capability matrix. We had a high degree of confidence that the product would work on a real development project using this method.

Dozens of tools have been evaluated using this method and still others are currently under examination. From this work many standard products were chosen to become part of the overall body of internal technical standards. Through controlled introduction using pilot projects and consultative jump-starts many of these products have also proven to be successful on large-scale software projects.

9.3.3.12. Porting the Process

Deployment of this technique to a different environment requires minimal modifications. We have reused this process from the evaluation of Windows based tools to the evaluation of Internet based tools seamlessly. To transfer this process to a different development base or user community we recommend making the following changes:

1. The tool taxonomy must be recalibrated to fit your environment and goals. Our taxonomy does not address databases, office automation, or operating systems. You need to add the appropriate technologies to fit you computing framework.

2. Your architectural styles may vary from ours. There may be other significant architectural styles you will need to identify.

3. After adjusting the framework and architectural styles you now need to document your screening criteria and create your detailed evaluation criteria templates. A good template typically requires a couple of days for an analyst to create. They are reusable and typically only one is necessary per technical category.

4. *Execute.* This is the crucial step where the watch-word is "emulation". That is, emulation of your actual development process and tasks.

We are confident that by following these simple steps the process we have been using for the last two years can be re-deployed in any software development technology evaluation laboratory.

9.4. ASSESSMENT AND TECHNOLOGY TOPOLOGIES

Building on this method and using the ideas from our Technology Topology work we also developed further methods for technology evaluation. Determining the extent to which a given product supports the capabilities described above is the essence of technology assessment within the context of our Relational Topology. To illustrate how product analysis using the Relational Topology can be conducted consider two popular database technologies: Sybase's SQL Server™ database product and Microsoft Access™. Each of these technologies offer similar capabilities for the organization, storage, and retrieval of information. However, the underlying technology of each is significantly different. Using our Relational Technology Topology we can demonstrate how.

Consider the range of relevant technology elements for our selected tools. All of the technology elements are in theory valid for both Access and Sybase. We shall soon see that upon most elements in the Topology the two products score quite differently. Such variance is what we term 'degree-of-freedom'. Specifically, this is a measure of the extent to which the implementation of a particular Topological element allows flexibility. Or, stated another way, it represents the range or use around an ideal Topological element. For each element the implementation can be judged for "degree-of-freedom" using a descriptive matrix.

For example, the *Conceptual Analysis Model* element matrix might contain the characteristics "supports IDEFX1" or "supports DFD". The answers to these questions determine the degree-of-freedom for that element ranging from 0 to 100% of the maximum score for the weighted sum of the element's attribute matrix. Table **1** below is an abridged evaluation criteria template for just such a tool. Normally we would find if the feature is supported, rate it, and total the scores *versus* the maximum possible score. In this case a score of 160 translates to a 'degree-of-freedom' of 91% (the percent of possible points). Thus we suggest that a traditional evaluation methodology should be followed by an additional step of aggregating the results into a metric tied to the core capabilities of the technology domain as depicted on the appropriate topology. We do not rule out the possibility that a superior means of calculating this measure can be derived. However, the merits of a weighted averaging technique such as this are well known [14] and support our overall purpose adequately.

In our example, we can see that the two technologies provide a good contrast (Table **2**). Note that the scores are approximations and do not reflect a value judgment on our part. It should be pointed out that both products can be enhanced by the use of auxiliary products. So for example, while the Sybase product offers no integrated modeling capability it is a relatively simple matter to purchase the vendor's modeling tool and insert it into the development environment. However, some things are easier to add in than others. In the case of Access it would be difficult or even impossible to make a quick adjustment (either by vendor or user) in order to make up for the inherent limitations of its Architecture Style. Selecting a tool from this table we may look for the technology that provides us with the appropriate range of application implementation support or the one that provides the best modeling capabilities based on our requirements.

Table 2: An abridged evaluation criteria template for Conceptual Modeling.

FEATURE	WEIGHT	SCORE	TOTAL	POSSIBLE
Data modeling, ER Diagrams:	5	5	25	25
IDEF1X	5	5	25	25
Chen	5	5	25	25
Other	0	0	0	0
Normalization validation:	5	4	20	20
1st Normal Form	5	5	25	25
2nd Normal Form	5	5	25	25
3rd Normal Form	5	3	15	15
Boyce-Codd Normal Form	3	0	0	15
TOTAL			160	175

We can also plot these findings on the Relational Technology Topology to see visually how the two technologies line up both against the abstractions of the Topology and against each other (Table **3**). In terms of architecture and database engine Sybase overpowers Access while in terms of design support (through integrated modeling and Wizard technology) Access offers much more to the developer. A more significant impact of these findings is that the types of activities a designer is expected to carry out will be more constrained by one tool than the other (for example trying to conduct E-R Diagramming in Sybase). Finally, and perhaps most significantly, the 'degree-of-freedom' on such critical Topology elements like Architecture Style, will be carried directly into the application implementation a designer is attempting to build. A distributed multi-user system in Access will be limited in terms of performance and the number of simultaneous users as predicted by the limited 'degree-of-freedom' in its Architecture Styles scoring.

Table 3: Two Databases Compared on the Topology's Elements.

	Sybase		**Access**	
Topology Element	**Description**	**Degree-of-Freedom**	**Description**	**Degree-of-Freedom**
Specifications	None	0%	None	0%
Modeling	None	0%	Limited	50%
Design Patterns	None	0%	Many templates with Wizard support	80%
Architecture Styles	Distributed, true-relational, robust multi-user	90%	File implementation, pseudo-relational, primarily single user	25%
Database Engine	High performance	90%	Low performance	40%
Canned Queries	Yes	75%	No	0%
Applications	Range (low-high)	90%	Range (low-med)	30%

9.5. EVALUATIONS AND TOOLS CONCLUDED

Using applications derived from clearly relevant architectures keeps the evaluation process honest. Analysts with development backgrounds typically feel more comfortable building an application than acting as a software critic. Simulating the development tasks in this way does not solve all the problems with technology evaluation. Politics and compromise are inescapable factors when making decisions that will commit a corporation to spending or not spending large sums with any given vendor. Also, some variability remains in the scoring technique. Each analyst tends to have peculiar habits in working through a 200 item feature matrix. One may score "high" or "low" while another may include "medium". Nevertheless, we feel confident that architecture styles add a healthy modicum of extra validity to the otherwise typical process we have described.

CONCLUSIONS

Without the appropriate set of tools a software engineer cannot build a suitable application to meet requirements. For the software engineer tooling is very critical. Sometimes it is determined by the technology choice, other times there are many choices that need to be worked through. While a formal tool architecture may not be required in all cases a reference model as described here can be helpful. In filling in that reference model with practical tools that fit the problem space an evaluation process as defined here has proven highly useful.

REFERENCES

[1] Sharon and Bell, "Tools That Bind: Creating Integrated Environments", **IEEE Software**, March 1995.

[2] Cusick, J., & Tepfenhart, M., "Software Technology Evaluation: Proving Fitness-for-Use with Architectural Styles", **Proceedings of the 21st NASA Software Engineering Laboratory Workshop**, NASA Goddard Space Flight Center, MD, December, 1996.

[3] Konti, J. and Tesoriero, R, "A COTS Selection Method and Experiences in its Use", **Proceedings of 20th NASA Software Engineering Workshop**, Greenbelt, MD, November, 1995.

[4] Brown, *et al.*, "A Framework for Evaluating Software Technology", **IEEE Software**, September 1996, pp39-49.

[5] Belanger, D., *et al.*, "Architecture Styles and Services: An Experiment on SOP-P", **AT&T Technical Journal**, Jan/Feb, 1996, pp54-63.

[6] Brown, *et al.*, **Software Engineering Environments: Automated Support for Software Engineering**, McGraw-Hill, 1992.

[7] Kara, D., "Client/Server Development Toolsets: A Framework for Evaluation and Understanding", **Application Development Expo**, New York, NY, April 4, 1995.

[8] Fuggetta, A., "A Classification of CASE Technology", **Computer**, Dec. 1993.

[9] Sharon, D., "A Reverse and Re-Engineering Tool Classification Scheme", **IEEE Software Eng. Tech. Committee Newsletter,** Jan. 1993.

[10] Utz, W., **Software Technology Transitions: Making the Transition to Software Engineering,** Prentice Hall, Englewood Cliffs, NJ, 1992.

[11] Gamma, *et al.* **Design Patterns: Elements of Reusable Design**, Addison-Wesley, 1995

[12] Coplien, J., & Schmidt, D., eds., **Pattern Languages of Program Design,** Addison-Wesley, 1995

[13] Konti, J., "A Case Study in Applying a Systematic Method for COTS Selection", **Proceedings of 18th International Conference on Software Engineering,** Berlin, Germany, March 25-26, 1996.

[14] ibid.

Send Orders of Reprints at bspsaif@emirates.net.ae
Durable Ideas in Software Engineering, 2013, 279-291

CHAPTER 10

The Profession and the Future

Abstract: A look at the history and potential of the software engineering field. Starting from the days of Babbage a model for software work is presented and an argument is made around the impact of software developers in the world at large now and in the future.

Keywords: Software engineering, professionalism, knowing, making, doing.

10. INTRODUCTION

I have written several times in the past about the software profession, its meaning, and its future prospects [1, 2]. Naturally, predicting the future is a fool's errand so I have tried to focus my comments on trends and their likelihood of lasting not stating with certainty what the future will look like. Nevertheless, I think it is valuable after covering so much territory in the earlier chapters of this eBook to dip into the discussion once more.

As I write this chapter the summer of 2011 is drawing to a close. Global economic conditions are unstable at best. Within the US there is a high level of unemployment and major sectors of the economy like real estate remain battered from the downturn of 2008. Following the dot.com crash of 2000 I wrote that if one wanted a career that could help change the world (for the better) then software had excellent prospects for doing so. I still believe so. Even with the difficulties in the economy recruiting talented developers remains challenging as there are many options available. Prospects for engineers remain positive despite the challenges.

10.1. THE PAST

In thinking about the future it is sometime useful to start with looking at the past. Fig. **1** depicts the rough generations of software developers we have seen. Babbage and Ada Pascal are seen as the 19th century forerunners to modern computing engineers and programmers. While there are some earlier technologies that can be considered computational in nature in concept Babbage begins the march towards modern computing. In the 1930s and 40s the first electronic programmable computers become available so we stand here today only 3 to 4

James J. Cusick

generations apart from those who started us on the path of modern computing. Today the span and scope of computing has nearly no limits in industry and society. From booming social media, robotics, informatics, and even gaming, software technology plays a central role.

In a way this eBook with its set of tools laid out is meant to capture in a compact format the techniques that I have seen that work in most software projects. The discussions here have been largely technology agnostic. These tools can be applied equally well to one platform as to another. The question becomes where are these tools headed. I would venture to say that some of them will be with us as engineers for a very long time. Just as concrete, invented by the ancient Romans, is still with the civil engineer, I do think methods such as Cyclomatic Complexity and Operational Profiles will be tools available to future generations of software developers and they will be relevant.

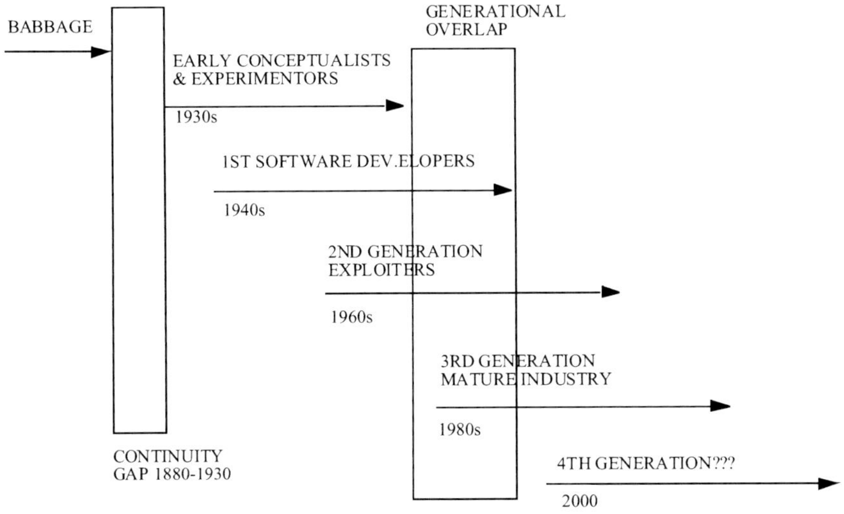

Figure 1: Generations.

Building on this concept of programming generations we can look at the scope of applications. From the earliest military and government applications businesses then began looking to computing for solutions to problems and productivity gains. Today the application scope we witness, as mentioned, is nearly without limit (see Fig. **2**). The future will surely bring additional scope to the application of software. There has historically been a long list of things which it was assumed computers could not do such as walk or see or talk. But these limits have all fallen by the wayside. It is safe to say without a crystal ball that other limits will also fall given time.

10.2. SOFTWARE ONE MORE TIME

In the past [3] I have also written that for software and software engineering to be successful the software produced must:

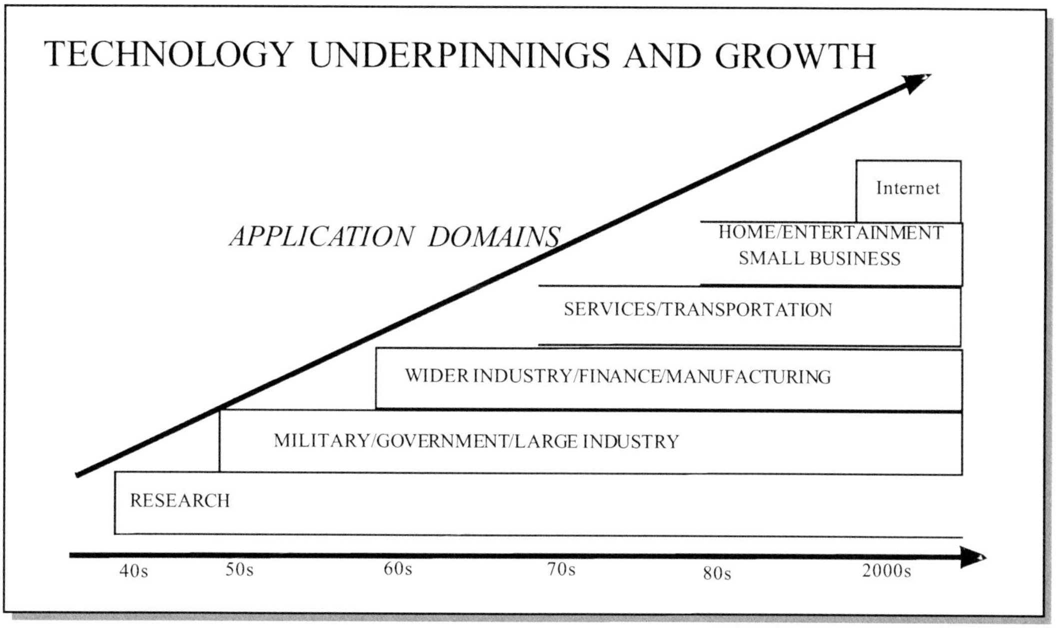

Figure 2: Software Application Growth.

1. Fulfill customer requirements.
2. Be of known reliability.
3. Provide an acceptable user experience (fun, useful).
4. Be delivered on time and on budget.
5. Derive its design from requirements methodically.
6. Support code and documents that are maintainable.

I still see these characteristics of software as vital. In recapping the tools presented in this eBook we can see that we have covered all of these areas from requirements to reliability to scheduling to the incremental development of code from requirements and finally to support.

Put another way, According to van Vliet [4], software engineering must handle the following tasks:

- Support the development of large-scale systems.
- Help master complexity.
- Facilitate organization and communication.
- Manage the evolution of software.
- Help engineers and teams to achieve results efficiently.
- Help engineers and teams to achieve effective solutions.

If software engineering cannot meet future needs, then what else can be done? There are many ways to develop software. A subset of these approaches might include [5]:

- Hobbyists.
- Hacker (as artisan) or hacker (as unskilled or pirate).
- Informal teams.
- Process-oriented teams.
- Open source.
- Experimental/educational/research.
- Technology (natural language, code generation).

- Global software development.

Consider these approaches one at a time. It should be noted that many significant software products were developed by hobbyists or amateurs. A good example is the first spreadsheet developed by two business school graduate students. This source of software will continue to be a hothouse both for products and for talent because of the ubiquity and low entry cost of computers since the advent of the PC. This approach, however, does not scale well and cannot solve the future requirements outlined previously.

A "hacker", according to Eric Raymond [6], is an artisan, problem solver, and enthusiast. This term also stems from the much earlier times (circa 1620) and refers to an inexperienced and unskilled person. Within the software community hackers might be very skilled programmers or programmers attempting to use computers for criminal activities. It is also common to hear reference to "hacking up some code", which might mean programming skillfully or throwing something together inelegantly. As a whole, this approach relies on some degree of heroism and individual effort of some distinction. As an alternate to software engineering none of these interpretations leaves much confidence that this model is anything more than a professional version of the hobbyist. This approach also falls short of our needs.

Informal teams and process teams can both play a role in solving the needs outlined previously. For smaller efforts and less-critical operational environments, a loosely structured team might work well. Developing elaborate process-driven teams has also proven to fulfill the needs at hand. By defining the phases of work, inputs, outputs, roles, and responsibilities, and then managing this process carefully, it has been possible to build many of today's largest and most successful systems.

Of significant interest recently have been open-source projects such as Linux, Apache, and others. The approach centers on loosely coordinated teams working on problems of interest and relying on extensive peer review. While this approach has produced laudable results, there are weaknesses in projecting that it will meet future technical and managerial needs. The open-source community is largely a "by programmers, for programmers" culture. Today's open-source solutions include compilers, editors, browsers, and assorted system-level software. Doing interesting projects is the goal. This is often the opposite of society's needs. It is generally not very interesting to the independent code artisan to solve yet another financial analysis or retail application problem. Further, open source requires as a prerequisite the ability and availability of volunteer hacking. By most accounts funding must be derived from activities in addition to the hacking of open-source code. By definition this precludes open source as a broad solution for software solutions development that must be predictable in budget, scope, and schedule. Linux was developed over a 10-year period by thousands of individuals. An important question for software engineering is whether this could be repeated and if so, how long would it take. Open source has played a role in software from at least the early days of UNIX, if not earlier. It will continue to play a role in the future, but it is not likely to be the future for all software problems.

Aside from various academic environments and experimental approaches to software development, the only other significant alternate will stem from technology. Natural language interfaces may, in the future, allow engineers to create software in radically different ways. Biocomputers may be genetically engineered to replicate in self-adaptive ways to the information processing and storage needs of future application demands [7]. The promise of achieving a world like the one described by Kurt Vonnegut in "Player Piano" [8] where machines would build still more machines seemed fanciful 60 years ago. Today, all one needs to do is walk into an automobile factory to see this vision as reality. The software world of the future may mimic this reality sooner rather than later. Until then, process and engineering methods will continue to evolve to bring us to our near-term future of more efficient and effective systems realization.

Finally, I have written extensively about Global Software Development [9, 10]. This is a model which in my view started with the beginnings of the computer age and has accelerated in the last 20 years. Today we have passed the point of no return with this model. For scale and wage advantages global development approaches will remain with us. The only question is to what extent they will be used and what flavor will be used, *i.e.*, captive, leveraged, or fully outsourced. The important point around this model is that the tools used by a global team will not be any differnet than the ones discussed here. Unfortunately, in my experience, often times global teams are less experienced and are not aware of these tools and do not use them to full advantage.

10.3. AN INTELLECTUAL EFFORT MODEL

In this eBook we have covered many aspects of software engineering from a tools perspective. In trying to put the whole picture together we can think of an intellectual effort model I first introduced in 2003 [11]. The concept was based on a model developed by Etienne Borne and Francois Henry [12] who described three broad categories of human activity derived from classical Greek thought:

1. Theorization (knowing).

2. Poetics or artisanship (making).

3. Practical attainment (doing).

All three forms of activity exist in software work in an enriching blend. Within software, you must inquire about the real world and learn a domain to specify a desired solution— this is equivalent to knowing. You must also model, design, and build the solution—this is equivalent to making. Finally, you must deploy and operate the solution—this is equivalent to doing. Fig. **3** shows the traditional lifecycle steps in software and how they relate to these classical forms of human activity.

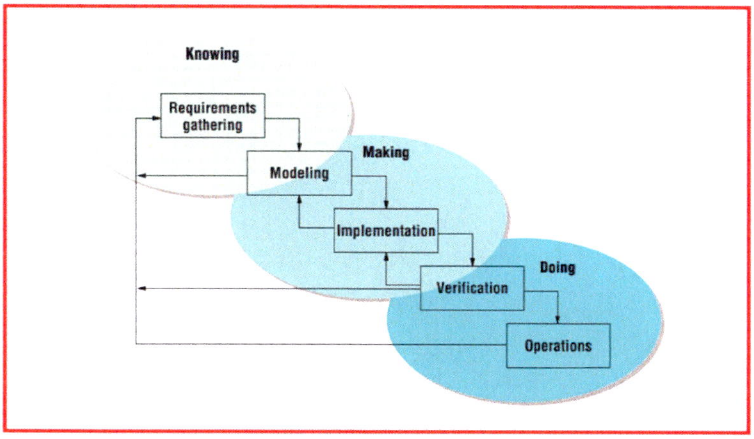

Figure 3: Understanding Software Development in an Intellectual Model.

The relevance of this model is that, once again, in a technology agnostic way, we must still reason about a problem, develop solutions for it, and operate the solution. This model matches very well to the layout of this eBook and provides guidance for the future. In whichever technology one chooses to work these elements must be provided for. So in the future we might see new tools developed for each of the lifecycle components overlaid on the knowing, making, doing triade.

10.4. THE TECHNOLOGY

While we have generally been focused on software, hardware engineers have provided us with generation after generation of advances in electronics and miniaturization, transistors, silicon chips, data storage, memory, and all the rest. Today, the computer market place only 50 years after it was hatched has surpassed all of its own expectations. In today's market we enjoy a choice of vendors in nearly every type of technology. Operating system choices are scalable in price and configuration. Computers today are also highly interoperable. This was not the case even 15 or 20 years ago. Computers available were basically mainframes and minicomputers, PCs were just being born. Today the situation provides a plethora of technical platforms from generic PCs to custom digital devices of ever dimension especially mobile devices. The range and versatility has been a bonanza for the software engineer. Consider that the mechanical engineer is still tied to steel and asphalt from most bridge structures just as was the case 100 years ago. But the software engineer quite literally can build an inventory system on top of a technological infrastructure with barely any common part to the last such system built only 5 years ago. This places an extraordinary burden on the software engineer in terms of knowledge acquisition and integration capabilities. This also places a premium on software portability, comptonization, and flexibility.

Again, from the hardware point of view you have a whole range of computers. You can even go to one vendor now and get your PDAs all the way up to massively parallel computers for highly advanced computational needs. You can buy it all from one vendor or buy devices at every level in an architecture from different vendors due to operating systems that work across different architectures and common protocols. This was not the case 20 years ago. If you bought a DEC computer then you would be using a DEC operating system. Today you can mix and match especially due to protocols like TCP/IP, HTTP, and Web Services. This insures that in most situations a heterogeneous environment will be the only one that satisfies the computing needs. Again the software engineer is placed in the position of having to understand multiple platforms, rely on vendor interfaces and protocols for integration, and deal with more complex architectures than in the past. Once again software engineering practices are hard pressed to keep up with the variety of scenarios including mixed language designs and distributed development methods. From a future standpoint this pace of change will not slow down.

As far as development itself, in the early days the equipment manufacturers were the only vendors for applications. If you wanted a piece of software to run on your IBM mainframe you had to buy it from IBM. This is no longer the case. You can get software that runs on any computer from virtually any vendor. Vendors today provide a list of computers and operating systems they run on which can hardly fit on their brochure. Think about that as an engineer. Students today try to learn how to program in C on PCs, maybe a little Windows or UNIX, and eventually C++, Java, or Ruby (as we discussed in Chapter 1). Instead imagine what it would take to allow your next program to run on any midrange computer. That means anything from a single chip Pentium up to a multiprocessor Tandem computer. This is a very complex task. Some people wonder why Windows operating systems typically were late to market, for example. Think about all the device drivers that Windows must support. It is quite a chore to handle all the varieties of equipment in the field. If you ever buy audio electronics you may know that if you go to a retail electronics store the component you purchase may no longer be in manufacture. Often the model is discontinued by the time it reaches the retail shelf. Computers are not like that yet but they are getting very close. Now developers must provide backward compatibility for hundreds or even thousands of devices. Luckily, now the OS vendors are providing most of that support so if you go with those standard routines you will not have a problem keeping up. Nevertheless, the downside to the power, choice, and scale of today's computing equipment is a burden placed on the software engineer to buffer the complexities of these technologies. In the future the life of the programmer will continue to be challenged in this direction.

10.5. THE WEB & MOBILE

There is little one can write about the web to indicate the extent to which it has changed so many people and industries in just the few years from 1994 when its full scope was beginning to emerge. For software development there have been several significant changes worth noting. First of all it is the speed at which software distribution now occurs. There are generally two methods of taking advantage of the Web's distribution speed: 1) many systems themselves appear as web pages and thus new versions can be made available immediately following testing; and 2) software packages can be posted on a web site for download and remote installation at any time and can be accessed at any time. This speed of distribution fundamentally alters the software development life-cycle which we discussed. The life-cycle has been compressed further and feedback from customers can be instantaneous.

Other relevant impacts of the web on development include the rapid-fire sharing of information within and between development teams. In large development shops today each project maintains an Intranet web page containing background information, contacts, schedules, designs, and specifications. This content is available to virtually anyone in the corporation who might need it. Within the team this enhances communication and external to the team this promotes technical cooperation on allied projects.

Furthermore, the very nature of Internet and Web technologies have created all new architectures and implementation strategies. Just a few years ago the issue of what type of client needed support in an application architecture (X Windows or Microsoft Windows) could produce a major rift in a development plan. Today such discussions are rare. Using the Web as the great equalizer, development projects are rapidly bypassing this issue in favor of a "universal" client. While there may be some difficulties in pursuing this path nearly all corporate development today is attempting to find a win-win situation by utilizing the Web. For software engineers this has several major impacts. First of all the universal client restricts the freedom of the software engineer since the Web client interface remains mostly a slave to HTML or Java applets and some proprietary solutions. Not all applications can be shoehorned into such constraints. Also, not every application is a hypermedia application (*e.g.*, command and control). Thus the whirlwind of the Web has forced software engineering into the corner of scripting, hypermedia, and reduced performance architectures in order to gain universal portability.

10.6. THE FUTURE

With the history of software engineering summarized in this way and the current trends in technology buffeting our direction we may wonder what will be next in software engineering. The "*software crisis* " is defined as a chronic condition where we have constant cost overruns, late schedules, poor quality, and unmet user expectations. I can attest that this crisis still plays out in some areas of the industry. This paints a fairly grim picture of software engineering and software development. Normally a crisis is something that peaks and passes. But the software industry has been in this situation for 40 years and is constantly called on for more [13]. What can we do to keep ourselves straight in this world of heterogeneous, interoperable, systems and what can we expect?

What we can do today is to stay focused on the job of software development. Regardless of the platform one develops for there are certain fundamentals that are going to contribute the most to a project's goals. Engineering is based on managed progress towards results. The methods and technology that succeed in this will create the future of software engineering. Today's brilliant stars of Object-Oriented methods, Java, and the Internet will yield to tomorrow's advances. But notice the perseverance of such methods as GANT, PERT, COCOMO, modularity, white box and black box testing. These methods provide lasting resources and tools to software engineers. Building on them will be techniques in architecture, system integration and generation, visual programming, and more.

One trend that may strengthen is the need for certified software engineers. As society realizes is utter helplessness without software products, suddenly the people who build software will come under more scrutiny. This has already begun to happen (for example, some US states have considered legislation requiring government administered certification for programmers). It will not be enough for someone to be self-taught. Technology and familiarity with technology does not automatically result in working software systems. It is the discipline, training, and experience that makes a software engineer. New generations of software users will demand more features, better software, and overall will have increased expectations from the products they purchase.

10.7. WHY IT MATTERS

For most of the several million programmers working today what matters is getting the job done. That is, fulfilling requirements with solid code on schedule. For me what matters is the excitement of where this young field is going and how it will change the way in which those millions of programmers meet their future requirements. It has been exciting to watch the field develop and each year offer more and better methods to the working engineer. It also matters because it is from the experiences of the working programmer that codified approaches often arise in software engineering. The identification, refinement, and packaging of new methods is a process which all of us can contribute to, not just researchers or academics. I believe that in exploring the detailed and varied concepts of software engineering in the preceding chapters the manner in which they develop has been shown of importance. The techniques we present have gone through elaborate processes to become accepted as part of the body of software engineering capabilities, yet each one remains open for improvement in this youthful science.

CONCLUSION

We have come to the end of this discussion of the tools, concepts, ideas, and methods in my virtual toolbox of software engineering. There is always more to say in such a broad area. I will leave it to the chronicles of text books and the software engineering body of knowledge project to provide the definitive and encyclopedic versions of what matters in software engineering. Here I have simply tried to accumulate the list of approaches, ideas, concepts, and tools that have worked for me and most importantly will work in the future.

REFERENCES

[1] Cusick, J., "*Software Engineering: Future or Oxymoron?*", **Software Quality Professional**, American Society for Quality, June, 2001.

[2] Cusick, J., "*How the Work of Software Professionals Changes Everything*", **IEEE Software**, Vol. 20, No 3., pp. 92-97, May/June, 2003.

[3] Cusick, 2001.

[4] van Vliet, H., **Software engineering: Principles and practice**. New York: John Wiley & Sons. 1996.

[5] Cusick, 2001.

[6] Raymond, E., **The cathedral & the bazaar**. Sebastopol, Calif.: O'Rielly, 1999.

[7] Akula, B., & Cusick, J., "*Effects of Overtime on Stress and Software Quality*", **The 4th International Symposium on Management, Engineering, and Informatics: MEI 2008**, June 29th - July 2nd, 2008, Orlando, USA.

[8] Vonnegut, K., **Player piano**. New York: Charles Scribner & Sons, 1952.

[9] Cusick, J., & Prasad, A., "*A Practical Management & Engineering Approach to Offshore Collaboration*", **IEEE Software**, Vol. 23, No. 5, pp 20-29, Sept/Oct, 2006.

[10] Cusick, J., *et al.*, "*Global Software Development: Origins, Practices, and Directions*", **Advances in Computers**, vol. 74, Elsevier's Academic Press, July, 2008.

[11] Cusick, 2004.

[12] Borne, Etienne, & Henry, Francois, **A Philosophy of Work**, Sheed and Ward, New York, NY, 1938.

[13] Pressman, R., **Software Engineering: A Practitioners Approach**, 4th ed., McGraw Hill, New York, 1996.

Appendix 1: List of Tools, Concepts and Methods

CHAPTER 1 - INTRODUCTION

- The Scientific Method
- Reading and Writing
- Quantification
- Problem Solving Skills
- Abstraction
- Process
- Planning and Project Management
- Modeling
- Programming
- Tools and Language Selection
- Innovation
- Training and Education
- Architecture

CHAPTER 2 – PROCESS

- Process as a Transform
- Cybernetics
- Process Frameworks
- CMMI (Capability Maturity Model Integrated)

James J. Cusick

- ITIL (Information Technology Infrastructure Library)
- Agile Methods
- Quality Improvement and Process Evolution
- Reusable Object Processes with Domain Modeling
- Flow Charts
- Design Cycle
- Metrics for Process Improvement
- GQM (Goal-Question-Metric)
- Function Points
- Function Point Backfiring
- CoCoMo (Constructive Cost Model)
- Complexity Metrics
- Reliability, Availability, Performance Measurements

CHAPTER 3 - PLANNING

- Planning
- Risk Management
- Management
- Triple Constraint
- Deliverables
- Work Break Down Structure (WBS)

- Estimation and Estimation Models
- Resourcing
- Scheduling
- Gannt Chart
- PERT Analysis
- CoCoMo
- Function Point Pocket Planner
- Communication, Inclusiveness, and Teamness

CHAPTER 4 - REQUIREMENTS

- Evolution of Systems
- Modeling
- Prototyping
- Early/Often Feedback
- Context Diagrams
- Analysis Models
- Design Models
- Data flow Models
- Data Dictionaries
- State Transition Diagram
- Entity Relationship Diagram

- Defining the Problem (Analysis)
- Soutioning (Design)
- Conflict Resolution
- Active Listening
- Information Gathering, Synthesis, Presentation
- Classes and Objects
- Generalization
- Instantiation
- Attributes, Operations, use Cases

CHAPTER 5 - ARCHITECTURE

- Architecture as map from Requirements to Implementation
- Elements, Form, Rationale
- Components, Connectors, Constraints
- SOA (Service Oriented Architecture)
- Architecture Styles
- Architecture Patterns
- Tiered Architectures

CHAPTER 6 - IMPLEMENTATION

- Author's triangle
- Templates

- Experience reports
- Language selection
- Incremental development
- Design conversion to code
- Modularity
- Span of control
- Data structures
- Information hiding
- Cohesion
- Coupling
- Algorithms
- Tool environments (IDEs, SCM)
- Process assessments
- Process analysis
- Process design
- Deployment and education
- Process charting
- CMMI, ITIL, Agile
- Questionnaires and Interviews
- Recruitment

- Role Definition
- Team member selection
- Task assignment and tracking
- Appraisals
- Mentoring
- Recognition
- Conflict resolution
- Budgeting and adminstration

CHAPTER 7 - TESTING

- Testing lifecycles
- Definition of testing
- Phases of testing
- Test architecture
- Test management
- Test scenarios
- Test design
- Test cases
- Test factors
- Test execution
- Test measurement

- Glass box testing
- Black box testing
- Flowgraph testing
- Boundary value analysis
- Operational Profiles
- Reliability engineering
- Defect Removal Efficiency
- Reviews

CHAPTER 8 - SUPPORT

- Delivery
- Support
- Maintenance
- Topological drift
- Inconsistencies
- Monitoring
- Incident response
- Problem management
- Root cause analysis
- Release management
- Change management

- Migration execution
- Performance analysis
- Availability tracking and reporting

CHAPTER 9 - TOOLS

- Tools and the lifecycle
- CASE (Computer Aided Software Engineering)
- IDE (Integrated Development Environment)
- SEE (Software Engineering Environment)
- Configuration and versioning
- Incremental & automated build
- Complier/Debugger
- GUI Builder
- Class Browsers/Editors
- Static analyzers
- Test management tools
- Test design tools
- Test execution tools
- Test quality evaluation tools
- Evaluation practices
- Tool classification schemes

Appendix 2: List of Acronyms

- 4GL – Fourth Generation Programming Language
- API – Application Programming Interface
- ASP – Active Server Pages
- AUT – Application Under Test
- C/S – Client/Server
- CASE – Computer Aided Software Engineering
- CGI – Common Gateway Interface
- CMM – Capability Maturity Model
- CMMI – Capability Maturity Model Integrated
- COCOMO – Constructive Cost Model
- COCOMO II – Constructive Cost Model II
- CPU – Central Processing Unit
- CRC – Class, Responsibilities, Collaborators Card
- DBA – Data Base Administrator
- DEC – Digital Equipment Company
- DFD – Data Flow Diagram
- DRE – Defect Removal Efficiency
- DSS – Decision Support System
- DTMF – Dual Tone Multi Frequency
- EDI – Electronic Data Interchange
- ERD – Entity Relationship Diagram
- ERP – Enterprise Resource Planning
- FP – Function Point

James J. Cusick

- GFCI – Ground Fault Circuit Interrupter
- GQM – Goal, Question, Metric
- GUI – Graphical User Interface
- HTML – Hyper Text Markup Language
- HTTP – Hyper Text Transmission Protocol
- IBM – International Business Machines
- IDE – Integrated Development Environment
- IDEFX1 – Integration Definition for Information Modeling
- IE – Information Engineering
- IEEE – Institute of Electrical and Electronics Engineers
- IIOP – Inter-ORB (Object Request Broker) Protocol
- IPSE – Integrated Project Support Environment
- IRT – Incident Response Team
- IT – Information Technology
- ITIL – Information Technology Infrastructure Library
- JDBC – Java Database Connector
- KLOC – Thousand Lines of Code
- LAN – Local Area Network
- LOC – Line of Code
- MAC – Macintosh Computer
- MS – Microsoft Corporation
- MTBF – Mean Time Before Failure
- MTTR – Mean Time to Repair
- NASA – National Aeronautics and Space Administration
- NATO – North Atlantic Treaty Organization

- NIST – National Institute of Standards and Technology
- NT – New Technology (Microsoft NT)
- OCX – OLE Custom Control File Extension
- OLE – Object Linking and Embedding
- OLTP – On Line Transaction Processing
- OO – Object Oriented
- OOA – Object Oriented Analysis
- OOD – Object Oriented Design
- OOP – Object Oriented Programming
- OP – Operational Profile
- OS – Operating System
- OT – Object Technology
- PC – Personal Computer
- PDF – Portable Document Format
- PERT – Program Evaluation and Review Technique
- PMO- Project Management Office
- PMP – Project Management Professional
- PRE – Production Readiness Exploration
- PRR – Production Readiness Review
- QA – Quality Assurance
- R&D – Research & Development
- RAD – Rapid Application Development
- RDBMS – Relational Database Management System
- RF – Radio Frequency
- ROI – Return on Investment

- RPC – Remote Procedure Call
- SaaS – Software as a Service
- SAPI – Server Application Programming Interface
- SASD – Structure Analysis and Structure Design
- SCAMPI – Standard CMMI Appraisal Method for Process Improvement
- SCM – Software Configuration Management
- SDE – Software Development Environment
- SE – Software Engineering
- SEE – Software Engineering Environment
- SEI – Software Engineering Institute
- SEO – Search Engine Optimization
- SOA – Service Oriented Architecture
- SOAP – Simple Object Access Protocol
- SQL – Structured Query Language
- STD – State Transition Diagram
- STE – Software Test Environment
- SVN – Subversion Source Code Control Tool
- SWOT – Strength, Weakness, Opportunity, Threat analysis technique
- TCP/IP – Transmission Control Protocol/Internet Protocol
- TDD – Test Driven Development
- U.S. – United States
- UML – Unified Modeling Language
- URL – Universal Resource Locator
- V&V – Verification and Validation

- VM – Virtual Machine
- VRML – Virtual Reality Markup Language
- WAN – Wide Area Network
- WWW – World Wide Web
- XML – Extensible Markup Language

Index

James J. Cusick

B

C

D

E

F

G

H

I

M

N

O

P

Q

R

S

U

V

W

X

Made in United States
Orlando, FL
04 November 2026

90205813R00205